24.95
Edu Tech
8-13-90

W9-AHZ-796

OSCAR WILDE'S
LONDON

OSCAR WILDE'S
LONDON

A Scrapbook of Vices and Virtues

1880–1900

**WOLF VON ECKARDT,
SANDER L. GILMAN
AND
J. EDWARD CHAMBERLIN**

*Anchor Press
Doubleday & Company, Inc.
Garden City, New York*
1987

Designed by Wilma Robin

Library of Congress Cataloging-in-Publication Data
Von Eckardt, Wolf.
Oscar Wilde's London.
Includes index.
1. Wilde, Oscar, 1854–1900—Homes and haunts—England—
London.   2. London (England)—Social life and customs—
19th century.   3. London (England)—Intellectual life—
19th century.   4. Authors, English—19th century—
Biography.   I. Gilman, Sander L.   II. Chamberlin, J.
Edward, 19453–   .   III. Title.
PR5823.V6   1987   306'.09421'1   87-987
ISBN: 0-385-09703-4

ACKNOWLEDGMENTS

We wish to thank the following for their help:

Our editor Loretta Barrett and copy editor Glenn Rounds, at Doubleday; John Bidwell and Thomas Wright of the William Andrews Clark Memorial Library, Los Angeles; Jane Marsh Dieckmann, who prepared the index; Kate Bloodgood and Howard Grier at Cornell University, who helped edit and retype segments of the manuscript; the librarians and curators of the Kodak Museum; The Royal Photographic Society; The Victoria and Albert Museum; The Guildhall Library; The Olin Library and The Mann Library, Cornell University; The London Transport Executive; The Barnardo Photo Library; The Library of Congress; The London Museum; The National Portrait Gallery; The William Morris Gallery; The Borough of Greenwich; The Sutcliffe Gallery, Whitby; The Salvation Army Archives; The Tate Gallery; The Detroit Institute of Art; as well as Kathleen Wahl, who aided us with retyping the manuscript. A special thanks goes to David Paisey of the British Library for his friendship.

CONTENTS

Introduction   ix

1   *Art and Life*   1

2   *Lilies and Sunflowers*   28

3   *The Call of the Stage*   54

4   *Readers and Writers*   80

5   *London's Growth*   97

6   *. . . and London's Shame*   126

7   *The Lower Classes*   146

8   *Religion, Spirits, and Hosanna*   167

9   *The Sounds of London*   178

10   *Virtues of Sport*   200

11   *Jumbo and Sundry Diversions*   219

12   *Juliets of a Night*   238

Epilogue   262

Notes   265

Selected Readings   272

Index   279

INTRODUCTION

This book is not about Oscar Wilde. It is about the city that made Oscar Wilde Oscar Wilde.

It is about London from the fall of 1879, when Oscar Wilde, having graduated from Oxford, took rooms with Frank Miles at 13 Salisbury Street, until the spring of 1897, when Wilde was released from Pentonville Prison and took the night boat to Dieppe, never to return to England.

Wilde's London was a meteoric moment in history, one of those convergences of time and place when the flow of events suddenly seems to speed up, to become more intense, to sparkle with exceptional brilliance, and to accelerate change.

It was the end of the Victorian Age. The Queen's Golden and Diamond jubilees, celebrating the fiftieth and sixtieth anniversaries of her reign, in 1887 and 1897, were, in fact, the most dominant festive events of the period. Everyone cheered, absolutely everyone. Some officials, to be sure, worried that Socialists and Irish radicals might cause embarrassment. A Labour newspaper grumbled that some of the common people sent out on the streets to cheer the Queen might actually curse her. But if there was any cursing, it was well stifled. The truth at both jubilees was that the common people, "the other nation," as Disraeli had called the poor and the dispossessed, loved the old lady as much as the rich and the noble.

Her presence, her rule, her Pax Britannica held a proud and protective mantle over the seething intellectual ferment that was to make the twentieth-century world so totally different from her nineteenth-century world. The changes were not only social, economic, and technological. The Arts and Crafts movement in Oscar Wilde's day gave us entirely new expectations of art in an age of industrialized mass production. Darwin, Havelock Ellis, and others opened new vistas on the position of humans in nature and human nature itself.

The year Wilde arrived, the first electric street lighting was installed. By the time he left, not only main thoroughfares, but also private homes, offices, shops, the new department and chain stores, the old pubs and inns, and the new "monster hotels," were electrically lit. The distinction between day and night was all but eliminated from city life. There was metropolitan bustle from dawn to dawn.

The Greater London metropolis was tempestuously growing. When Wilde arrived, it had roughly 4.7 million inhabitants. When he left, there were about half as many more. Many of them—perhaps the world's most polyglot lot—were toiling in the docks and warehouses of a great world harbor that made London the hub of international trade. Shipping made the Empire proud and rich but kept most of its workers squalid and poor. Thirteen railroad terminals, impressive people's palaces of steel and glass, kept overland trade and travel in restless motion. Within London, more and more people traveled in the ever-expanding "tube," or underground railways, far below the muck of congested streets. Fast, efficient public transportation made it possible for the growing mass of Londoners to escape crowded slums into neat if monotonous suburbs of interminable rows of small homes and tiny gardens.

The suburbs, in turn, saved the charm, appeal, and unpredictable arrogance of "this old English gentleman," as urban historian E. A. Gutkind calls London.[1] The exodus of workers and lower-middle-class families to the new suburban communities relieved the pressure for dense, massive, and ugly tenements in the center city. The streets of the East End, to be sure, were mostly mean and the people who crowded them—often a large family in one room—were miserable. But the Western part of the center city, with its royal palaces, government offices, public buildings, and elegant shopping streets, was left to the wealthier classes. Until after World War II, when a few unfortunate skyscrapers were built, London's buildings remained low and varied and its cityscape human. It was and remains a big cluster of neighborhoods, villages, and townships held together by well-kept garden squares and large, beautiful parks.

London was a city of extremes. The upper crust, or "society," enjoyed a genteel ostentation, particularly during the Season, which Henry James called "the British carnival." The "lower orders," most of them impoverished farm workers who kept flocking to the city in search of work, often endured degrading hardships. Far from freeing workers from staggering toil, the machine enslaved people. But in London, the rumblings of an awakening proletariat, which elsewhere threatened the existing order, came not so much from those who suffered, as from those who cared. Karl Marx sought to abolish the injustices of capitalist industrialization by abolishing the social system which produced it. The Fellowship of the New Life, founded in 1883, and soon called the Fabian Society, sought to reform the system. George Bernard Shaw, Sidney Webb, Beatrice Potter (later Mrs. Sidney Webb), and their friends would permeate and gradually change existing political institutions to avoid violent class struggle and bring about social justice by democratic means. The Fabian aim was not to assert proletarian supremacy but human dignity. This small group of intellectuals had a decisive influence on what was at the time the most industrialized nation of the world.

If socialist thought, whether revolutionary or evolutionary, changed what was believed to be the immutable social order, Darwinism changed what was believed to be the immutable natural order. Marxists and Fabians shook up the belief that by some divine law a few people were born to rule over others while the majority was more or less stuck with their station in life. Naturalist Charles Robert Darwin's book *On the Origin of Species by Means of Natural Selection* shook up the belief that the Creation was a six-day wonder. Darwin's first study appeared in 1859, but its inestimable influence on scientific thought and the "infallibility" of conventional religious teaching was only beginning to be fully felt in Oscar Wilde's time. The appearance of the first volume of psychologist Havelock Ellis's seven-volume *Studies in the Psychology of Sex* (1897–1928) further added to the enormity of intellectual upheaval at the end of the nineteenth century. The upheaval was, as always, reflected in the *Zeitgeist*. It was echoed in—among many other things—the seething emotions of Richard Wagner's music and the disturbing psychological insights of Henrik Ibsen's plays, which became suddenly popular in Wilde's London.

John Ruskin and William Morris's Arts and Crafts movement made a big splash that echoed throughout the Western world and changed the relationship of art and life. Inadvertently, it also produced Aestheticism, the predominant and certainly the flashiest *Weltanschauung* of the period.

Ruskin and Morris were deeply disturbed that ever more of the tools and furnishings of human life—from buildings we need for shelter, to spoons we need to eat, or pens we need to write—were being fabricated by machine. Their fear was not so much that quality would suffer. Machine work can be more precise than handicraft. It was that industrialization would lead to commercialization and materialism, that without the human touch and dedication to creating the object, beauty would be lost. They saw in the Gothic style of the Middle Ages the apogee of a spiritual craftsmanship and beauty. Art historian Ruskin prolifically proclaimed this belief. Poet, artist, and printer Morris assiduously practiced it. In 1859, Morris had his friend, architect Philip Webb, build for him the famous Red House at Bexley-heath, Kent, in which Webb not only copied Gothic architecture, but also seriously attempted to adapt the old style to new, late-nineteenth-century needs. Morris and his friends followed up with countless and unfailingly original carvings, stained glass, carpets, wallpaper, chintzes, and furniture, which led to the formation of their own firm. In 1874, the firm was reorganized and run solely by Morris as Morris & Company. He produced beautiful books and book bindings at the Kelmscott Press, which he founded in 1891.

Morris attached himself to the most fashionable painters and poets of the day, the brotherhood of Pre-Raphaelites, including Dante Gabriel Rossetti and Sir Edward Burne-Jones. The group adapted Ruskin's innocent artistic admiration for the medieval simplicity which prevailed before Raphael. In adding their enthusiasm to that of Morris, certain styles of painting and interior decoration became dogma. "Only Beauty brings Salvation." Oscar Wilde became the foremost proponent of this doctrine.

As Max Beerbohm observed, Wilde did not invent Beauty; but he was the first to trot her around, peacock feathers and all, first in London society, soon all over England and America. He usually advertised his Aestheticism, as the dogma was soon called, by pinning a sunflower or a lily to his lapel, donning velvet breeches and silk stockings, and muttering such super-aesthetic words as intense, utter, consummate, precious, and sublime. It seemed to give him pleasure to pose as the butt of countless cartoons and to inspire the public to associate him with Gilbert and Sullivan's satirical comic opera *Patience.*

But there was a more serious side to the Arts and Crafts movement, as there was a serious side to Oscar Wilde, who deeply felt the horrors of blight that were also London. As a style, Morris's handsome designs passed on, as have other styles in the relentless change of human taste. But Morris's recognition that, while machines can make goods and make them well, they cannot make them lovable, let alone beautiful, remains as valid as ever. In a human world, technology cannot do without art to shape it. Technology and commerce alone do not make a human civilization.

Wilde understood this, too, just as he was aware of the revolutionary changes in thought that took place in his time, which he reflected in his writing. He was thus not only a product of this meteoric moment in history, but took part in shaping it and adding to its brilliance. "One can only write in cities," he once said, "the country hanging on one's walls."

Here is his city.

OSCAR WILDE'S
LONDON

1

ART AND LIFE

Oscar Wilde was not sure what he wanted to do when he left Oxford for London in 1878. "God knows," he told his friend David Hunter Blair, "I won't be a dried-up Oxford don, anyhow. I'll be a poet, a writer, a dramatist. Somehow or other I'll be famous, and if not famous, I'll be notorious."[1]

Wilde was sure, however, that whatever he would do, he would do it in London. Dublin, where he had grown up, held no appeal, and not much in the way of family ties. His older brother Willie was in London, working as a journalist. Their mother had followed him there, trying to establish the kind of salon she had presided over in Dublin. Florence Balcombe, the Dublin girl he fancied himself in love with, had announced that she would marry another. Above all, London was discovering Beauty, and Beauty was Oscar Wilde's consuming passion. At Oxford he had admired the gospels of John Ruskin and Walter Pater. Ruskin taught the history of art and architecture and proclaimed the ugliness of machinery, the dignity of manual labor, and the imperatives of earnest and deeply moralistic beauty. Pater, a man of letters and not so inclined to moral instruction, turned the worship of Beauty and of the Aesthetic Life into a cult. Wilde became its foremost apostle.

The apostle and his faith arrived in London at a propitious moment. The Prince of Wales was resting from the revels of his youth. Queen Victoria was in continued seclusion. Balls and entertainments, both at court and in the houses of the nobles, were notably fewer than they had been in previous years. The vogue of the opera was passing. In sum, noted Max Beerbohm, "society was becoming dull." But politics were not; and society changed with the times.

"St. Pancras Hotel and Station from Pentonville Road at Sunset" by John O'Connor, 1884. Designed by Sir Gilbert Scott, this huge Gothic Revival castle displays the romantic spirit of the Victorians in its most effusive manner. The damp and smoky street, with its horse-drawn trams, is typical of Oscar Wilde's London. (London Museum)

Left, Queen Victoria. Official photographic portraits like these were sold throughout her realm to grace lower- and middle-class homes. The upper classes decorated their drawing rooms with painted portraits of Her Majesty. (Kodak Museum)

Right, His Royal Highness, Albert Edward. His reputation as a sensuous rake was the opposite of that of his prudish mother, whose name designates not only an age but also an attitude. (Kodak Museum)

"The Royal Family at Windsor Castle," 1887, by L. Tuxen. The antipathy between the Queen and her heir, who was never granted official duties during his mother's lifetime, seems apparent in the way Prince Edward is shown turning his back to his mother, whose eyes are focused on one of her grandchildren. (Guildhall Library)

Above, Queen Victoria in a garden tent at her castle at Balmoral, Scotland. She is attended by an Indian servant since, thanks to her Prime Minister, Benjamin Disraeli, she was also (since 1876) Empress of India. She is signing documents brought to her in separate boxes for each of the government departments. (National Portrait Gallery, London)

Above, Edward, Prince of Wales, with umbrella and binoculars, about to depart by rail from London's Stockwell Station for a trip to the country. Prince Edward traveled extensively throughout his future realm as well as the rest of the world. (Guildhall Library)

His Royal Highness, the Prince of Wales's visit to the Prime Minister. Of all the stately homes in England, none was more humane in its atmosphere and "Victorian" in its style than Hughenden Manor, the home Disraeli had built for himself. (From The Graphic, *Olin Library, Cornell University)*

"In 1880 . . . came the Dissolution and the tragic fall of Disraeli, and the sudden triumph of the Whigs. How great was the change that came upon Westminster thenceforward must be known to anyone who has studied the annals of the incomparable Parliament of 1880 and the succeeding years. Gladstone, with a monstrous majority behind him and revelling in the old splendour of speech that neither the burden of age nor six years' sulking had made less; Parnell, pale, deadly, mysterious, with his crew of wordy peasants that were to set at naught all that had been held sacred by the Saxon—the activity of these two men alone would have sufficed to raise this Parliament above all others. What of young Randolph Churchill, who, despite his halting speech, foppish mien, and rather coarse fibre of mind, was yet the most brilliant parliamentarian of the century? What pranks he and his little band played upon the House! How they frightened poor Sir Stafford and infuriated the Premier. What of the eloquent atheist, Charles Bradlaugh, pleading at the Bar, striding forward to the very mace, while the Tories yelled and mocked at him, hustled down the stone steps with the broadcloth torn to tatters from his back? Imagine the existence of God being made a party question! I wonder if such scenes can ever be witnessed again at St. Stephen's as were witnessed then. Whilst these curious elements were making themselves felt in politics, so too in Society were the primordia of a great change. The aristocracy could not live by good breeding alone. The old delights seemed vapid, waxen. Something new was wanted. And thus came it that the spheres of fashion and of art met, thus began the great social renascence of 1880."[2]

London was growing, relentlessly growing. Driven by "the snorting steam and piston stroke" of the Industrial Revolution, as William Morris put it, bustling with the commerce of an expanding empire, London had changed from an important but unspectacular capital into the largest and richest city in the Western world. It had the largest population, the biggest port, the most advanced sewage system, the most bridges. It was, furthermore, building a new kind of railway system which, through a series of tunnels and underground stations, held this far-flung accretion of towns, villages, neighborhoods, and new housing developments together. The "Underground," built between 1863 and 1914, brought the new suburbs within reach of the center and people at the center within reach of the cricket and football fields on the perimeter. The city Oscar Wilde made his realm was mind-boggling in its size and complexity—and yet still somehow unspectacular.

The ideas of Ruskin and Pater had preceded Wilde to London. The hotbed of the new artistic enthusiasm was the center of Chelsea. As Max Beerbohm recalled, "Swinburne, Morris, Rossetti, Whistler, Burne-Jones, were of this little community—all of them men of great industry and caring for little but their craft. Quietly and unbeknown they produced their poems

"The Beaconsfield Cabinet," by C. Mercier. In 1876, Disraeli, the son of a Jewish bookseller and literary critic, was made Earl of Beaconsfield by his admiring Queen. This was the last official portrait of him with his cabinet. William Ewart Gladstone succeeded him as Prime Minister. (National Portrait Gallery, London)

or their pictures or their essays, read them or showed them to one another and worked on."

But if Beauty had existed before, continued Beerbohm, "It was Mr. Oscar Wilde who first trotted her round. This remarkable youth . . . began to show himself everywhere, and even published a volume of poems in several editions as a kind of decoy to the shy artificers of Chelsea. The lampoons that at this period were written against him are still extant, and from them, and from the references to him in the contemporary journals, it would appear that it was to him that Art owed the great social vogue she enjoyed at this time. Peacock feathers and sunflowers glittered in every room, the curio shops were ransacked for the furniture of Annish days, men and women, fired by the fervid words of the young Oscar, threw their mahogany into the streets. A few smart women even dressed themselves in suave draperies and unheard-of greens. Into whatever ballroom you went, you would surely find, among the women in tiaras and the fops and the distinguished foreigners, half a score of comely ragamuffins in velveteen, murmuring sonnets, posturing, waving their hands. 'Nincompoopiana,' the craze was called at first, and later 'Aestheticism.' "[3]

The trotter-round of Beauty first shared rooms with Oxford friend and painter Frank Miles at 13 Salisbury Street, off the Strand, a fashionable dis-

"The Fourth Party," as depicted by Vanity Fair. *During the final decades of the nineteenth century, politics became complicated as younger politicians within the established Liberal and Conservative parties began to challenge the grand old men of their grandfathers' generation. Outstanding was Randolph Churchill (left) with his political allies, including the future foreign minister Arthur Balfour (third from left). (National Portrait Gallery, London)*

trict at the time. Miles was doing sketches of society ladies, and of such beauties as Lillie Langtry. Wilde was meeting them all, and falling in love with London. He had little money—selling some poems now and then—but an increasing determination to make of life—his life, London life—a work of art. Life was painting and poetry and theater; art was tea parties, picnics, balls, or just an elegant gesture or an exquisite decoration. He dressed extravagantly, declaring that reformation of dress was of far more importance than a reformation of religion. On occasional evenings he could be seen "in a velvet coat edged with braid, knee-breeches, black silk stockings, a soft loose silk shirt with a wide turn-down collar and a large flowing green tie."[4] "A really well-made buttonhole," said Oscar Wilde, "is the only link between Art and Nature."[5] "For what is Nature?" he asked. "Nature is no great mother who has borne us. She is our creation. It is in our brain that she quickens to life. Things are because we see them, and what we see, and how we see it, depends on the Arts that have influenced us. To look at a thing is very different from seeing a thing. One does not see anything until one sees its beauty. Then, and then only, does it come into existence. At present, people see fogs, not because there are fogs, but because poets and painters have taught them the mysterious loveliness of such effects. There may have been fogs for centuries in London. I dare say there were. But no one saw them, and so we do not know anything about them. They did not exist till

Art had invented them. Now, it must be admitted, fogs are carried to excess. They have become the mere mannerism of a clique, and the exaggerated realism of their method gives dull people bronchitis. Where the cultured catch an effect, the uncultured catch cold."[6]

The remedy for life's ills and nature's shortcomings, then, was, in the slang of today, a permanent "high" on Art and Beauty and Truth. Some of Wilde's mentors were already well up there, in fine aesthetic form. Walter Pater wanted art to be a habit of "exquisite passions." Success in life was to him "to burn always with this hard, gemlike flame, to maintain this ecstasy." He demanded "art for art's sake," art that "comes to you professing frankly to give nothing but the highest quality to your moments as they pass, and simply for those moments' sake."[7] Mortality and utility were not welcome in Pater's mansion of art, and propriety was only a teatime visitor.

Wilde accepted London as it was:

> *The Thames nocturne of blue and gold*
> *Changed to a Harmony in gray;*
> *A barge with ochre-colored hay*
> *Dropt from the wharf: and chill and cold*
> *The yellow fog came creeping down*
> *The bridges, till the houses' walls*
> *Seemed changed to shadows and St. Paul's*
> *Loomed like a bubble o'er the town.*
> *Then suddenly arose the clang*
> *Of waking life; the streets were stirred*
> *With country wagons; and a bird*
> *Flew to the glistening roofs and sang.*
> *But one pale woman all alone,*
> *The daylight kissing her wan hair,*
> *Loitered beneath the gas lamps' flare,*
> *With lips of flame and heart of stone.*[8]

The poem is at once precious in its romanticism and precise in its realism. Others were less able to combine the two ways of seeing. William Morris, for example, saw no art in the real nature of London that he wrote about several years earlier; and he invoked Beauty only in the service of his own pastoral dream:

> *Forget six counties overhung with smoke,*
> *Forget the snorting steam and piston stroke,*
> *Forget the spreading of the hideous town;*
> *Think rather of the packhorse on the down,*
> *And dream of London, small, and white, and clean,*
> *The clear Thames bordered by its gardens green.*[9]

Lady Randolph Churchill, the mother of Winston Churchill. Born Jennie Jerome in Brooklyn, New York, she was one of the American beauties whose accents Oscar Wilde noted on the London streets during the Season. (Kodak Museum)

William Gladstone, photographed by A. J. Melhuish in 1886. Disraeli's political archrival, Gladstone was one of the most influential moral gadflies. He brought London prostitutes home with him to lecture them about the sinful errors of their ways while feeding them cakes and hot chocolate. (Victoria and Albert Museum)

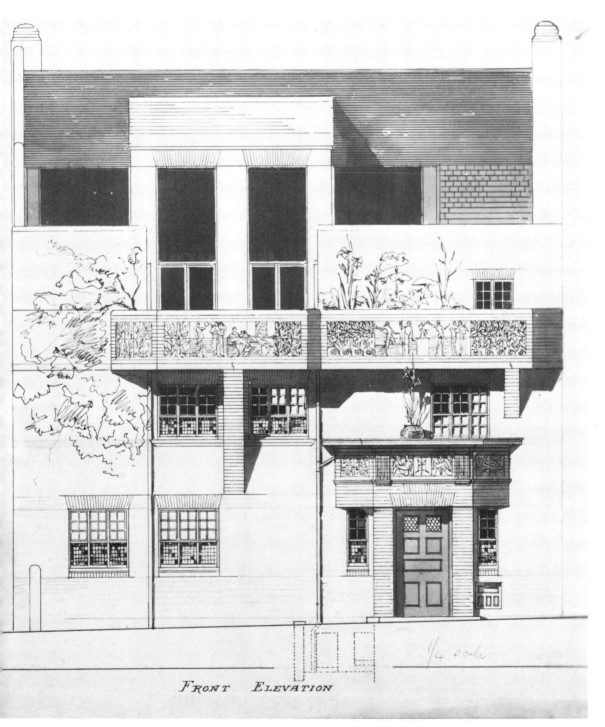

FRONT ELEVATION

1/4 scale

Design for the house of painter Frank Miles at 1 Tite Street, with its Aesthetic "vegetable" façade. Wilde lived with Miles from 1879 to 1880 and was introduced by him to London society, including Lillie Langtry, whose portrait Miles painted. (Victoria and Albert Museum)

But this dream had its own power. In due course it led to Ebenezer Howard's Garden City movement, which, with modifications, practical idealists all over the world still consider a most promising "peaceful path to real reform," as Howard called it.

Aestheticism, the cult of "faddling hedonism," as someone remarked, was instructively satirized by Sir William Schwenck Gilbert and Sir Arthur Sullivan in their comic opera *Patience.* It opened in 1881 and became one of the most popular musicals on the Anglo-American stage. It shaped the middle-class image of Aestheticism, a slightly envious image. By placing Art above everything, the Aesthetes seemingly managed to live without working. Art was an escape from the drudgery of the world, not a means of remedying its sad and desperate side.

One of the songs begins:

> *If you're anxious for to shine in the high*
>   *aesthetic line as a man of culture rare,*
> *You must get up all the germs of the*
>   *transcendental terms, and plant them*
>   *everywhere.*
> *You must lie upon the daisies and discourse*
>   *in novel phrases of your complicated state*
>   *of mind,*
> *The meaning doesn't matter if it's only idle*
>   *chatter of a transcendent kind.*
> *And every one will say,*
> *As you walk your mystic way,*
> *If this young man expresses himself in terms*
>   *too deep for me,*
> *Why what a very singularly deep young man*
>   *this deep young man must be!*

As Oscar Wilde noted: "Art never harms itself by keeping aloof from the social problems of the day: rather, by so doing, it more completely realises for us that which we desire. For to most of us the real life is the life we do not lead."[10]

To many Londoners Oscar Wilde was the butt of Gilbert and Sullivan's satire. And D'Oyly Carte, who produced the opera, and was a marketing genius, recognized the publicity value of this.

Despite growing fame and social success, money was scarce for Wilde in 1882. He therefore consented to go to America to help publicize Gilbert and Sullivan's parody. "Of course, if one had enough money to go to America, one would not go," said Oscar Wilde.

An "ass-thete" and clown, some American newspapers called him. But his first American lecture tour was, on the whole, a success. On his return he

16 Tite Street in Chelsea, where Oscar Wilde and his wife, Constance, lived from May 1884 until Wilde's conviction in 1895. It was designed by E. W. Godwin, with the assistance of the painter James McNeill Whistler. Whistler and the American painter had their studios on the same street. Justice Wills, who sentenced Wilde to prison in 1895 also lived on the same street. Across the street from these comfortable houses were the slums of Chelsea. The drawing is taken from the autobiography of Wilde's friend and lover Lord Alfred Douglas, Oscar Wilde and Myself. *(Olin Library, Cornell University)*

reported that really Americans have everything in common with the English people except, of course, the language. He also observed that when good Americans die, they go to Paris; when bad Americans die, they stay in America. By January of 1883 Wilde, too, was in Paris, doing some writing, meeting Victor Hugo, Verlaine, Zola, Mallarmé, and other literary celebrities, and dreaming of fame and fortune.

When Wilde married Constance Mary Lloyd in May 1884, he took a house at 16 Tite Street in Chelsea, where he lived until his trial in 1895. The street is near the Chelsea Embankment and its lovely esplanade, just west of the Chelsea Hospital Gardens, where the colorful Chelsea Flower Show is still held every May.

A pleasantly undistinguished residential street, Tite Street was, at the time, greatly favored by artists. Others who lived there were the American painters James McNeill Whistler and John Singer Sargent. Wilde had earlier lived with Frank Miles on the southern end of Tite at No. 1.

The Wildes' new house, built ten years before they moved in, is a narrow, brick row house in the "Queen Anne" style that was the rage in the 1870s and '80s. The style, of course, had nothing to do with Queen Anne. It is, rather, an eclectic concoction of Elizabethan and Tudor Gothic domestic architecture, with a helping of English Renaissance and a dash of Tuscan. The exterior of Wilde's house is appropriately ornate without being the least bit ostentatious.

Walter Horatio Pater, Wilde's tutor at Oxford. He was the theorist of the Aesthetic movement whose motto, "Art for Art's Sake," summarized the new art of Oscar Wilde's time. Pater's Studies in the History of the Renaissance *provided the theoretical basis for the Pre-Raphaelite Movement. (Private Collection, Gilman)*

Constance Wilde had a fairly generous allowance from her Lloyd grandfather and this enabled the young couple to have the house decorated and furnished to Wilde's particular taste. Their decorator was the architect Edward William Godwin, who designed the town halls at Northampton and at Congleton, Cheshire, but was known mostly for the almost revolutionary simplicity and elegance he brought to the small London houses of some of his artist friends. One of them was Frank Miles's Tite Street house where Wilde had lived a few years before he married. Another decorator was Whistler, who helped with the interior design of the Wilde house (and who married Godwin's second wife Beatrix after the architect's death).

Like most middle-class row houses at the time, the Wildes' house had four floors with two rooms on each floor. On the ground floor was a spacious hall, with Oscar Wilde's study in front and the dining room with a view out

"A Promising Young Aesthetic," as caricatured by Punch *in 1879. The caption reads:*

Old Boy: *Ullo! What's* your *name?*
New Boy: *Dante Michael Angelo Salvator Rosa Nupkins!*
Old Boy: *Is* that *all? What's your father?*
New Boy: *Poet, painter, sculptor, architect, and musician.*
Old Boy: *Crimini! Is he great?*
New Boy: *The greatest that ever lived.*
Old Boy: *I never! And what are* you *going to be?*
New Boy: *The same as my father, only greater.*
Old Boy: *Oh my!*

(Kicks Young Nupkins, and exit)
(Olin Library, Cornell University)

over a small garden in the back. On the first floor, in front, was the drawing room, and at the back was a smoking room that was also used as a guest room and dressing room. The rest of the house was taken up with bedrooms and nurseries.

Vyvyan Holland, Wilde's younger son, recalls that: "The colour scheme of Oscar Wilde's study on the ground floor was red and yellow, the walls being painted pale primrose and the woodwork red. A cast of the Hermes of

Cartoon from Punch, *1881, shows "O.W." saying, "O, I feel just as happy as a bright sunflower!" The caption reads:*

> *Aesthete of Aesthetes!*
> *What's in a name?*
> *The poet is* Wilde,
> *But his poetry's tame.*

(Olin Library, Cornell University)

Praxiteles stood on a red column in a corner by the window. A few small pictures adorned the walls: a Simeon Solomon, a Monticelli, and a delicate drawing of Mrs. Patrick Campbell, the famous actress, by Aubrey Beardsley. Apart from these, and a large writing-desk which had once belonged to Thomas Carlyle, the room was furnished entirely with books; Greek and Latin Classics, French literature and presentation copies of contemporary European authors predominated. It was here . . . that most of Wilde's serious work was done."[11]

And it was here that a bankruptcy auctioneer sold paintings and presentation copies, personal letters and children's toys, in a mockery of a public auction, conducted—if that is the word—while Wilde lay in prison awaiting his trial. The vindictiveness of his creditors was matched only by the indifference of the brokers, and by the greed of the souvenir hunters who stole everything they could lay their hands on.

Wilde was intensely involved in the decoration of what was by all accounts a lovely house. He wrote to architect W. A. S. Benson: "I have seen far more rooms spoiled by wallpapers than by anything else: when everything is covered with a design, the room is restless and the eye disturbed. A good picture is always improved by being hung on a coloured surface that suits it, or by being placed in surroundings that are harmonious to it, but the delicacy of line in an etching is often spoiled by the necessarily broad, if not coarse, pattern on a block-printed wallpaper.

"My eye requires in a room a resting-place of pure colour, and I prefer to keep design for more delicate materials than papers, for embroidery for instance. Paper in itself is not a lovely material, and the only papers which I ever use now are the Japanese gold ones: they are exceedingly decorative, and no English paper can compete with them either for beauty or for practical wear. With these and with colour in oil and distemper a lovely house can be made . . . I hope, and in my lectures always try to bring it about, that people will study the value of pure colour more than they do."[12]

At 16 Tite Street the Wildes entertained politicians such as the radical John Bright and the intellectual Arthur Balfour; writers of all sorts, including Robert Browning, Algernon Charles Swinburne, Mark Twain, and John Ruskin (who was asked, but declined because of failing health, to be godfather to one of the Wildes' children); and a wide range of theater and society people, with pride of place given to such bright lights as Ellen Terry, Sarah Bernhardt, and Lillie Langtry.

While Dandy Aestheticism set the tone for the upper registers of Oscar Wilde's London, church workers, social reformers, nostalgic romantics, and utopian dreamers saw Truth and Beauty elsewhere: in sober good citizenship or in visions of marching off to war against the enemies of God and the Empire.

Even those who stayed at home fervently believed in improving their surroundings. Everyone shared the credo of the arts and crafts crowd—an environmental determinism which firmly believed that beautiful surroundings produce beautiful people and that, conversely, slums generate diseases of the mind as well as of the body. The faith of the beneficial influence of a good environment carried over into the twentieth century and motivated the original modern revolution in architecture and urban planning. The recognition of the infectiously ill effects of urban deterioration led to important reforms and public health measures.

Some, not content with environmental determinism, advocated hereditary determinism, a romantic foreboding of genetic manipulation. Wilde called it "Nemesis without her mask . . . the last of the Fates and the most terrible."[13] Thomas Robert Malthus, a century earlier, offered "moral restraint" as a means of checking overpopulation, poverty, and distress. Under the influence of Darwin's theories, the thought led to Darwin's cousin Fran-

Bunthorne in Patience

A. SEER'S PRINT, N.Y.—COPYRIGHTED.

Above, poster for the New York performance of Gilbert and Sullivan's Patience, *a musical parody of the Aesthetic Movement, which Wilde publicized on a lecture tour through the United States. The tour had been initiated by Colonel F. W. Morse, a New York entrepreneur, who produced the show. (Library of Congress)*

Right, Oscar Wilde in June 1882, photographed in an Alabama photo studio during his lecture tour of the United States. His pictures were sold to the Patience *audience as a souvenir of an "archetypal" aesthete. (Library of Congress)*

Al fresco tea party at Earl's Court pavilion in 1885, photographed by Paul Martin, one of the first noted candid camera photographers who set out to capture daily life. (Victoria and Albert Museum)

cis Galton's new word, "eugenics," and the notion (opposed by Galton) that selective breeding, as well as a more beautiful living environment, would "improve" the human race. Wilde's interest was in breeding a prettier human profile: "if the poor only had profiles there would be no difficulty in solving the problem of poverty."[14]

But most people were content to advocate civic rather than genetic improvement as the most promising way to achieve Beauty and make London a better place to live, worthy of its destiny as a great imperial city.

The architect William Richard Lethaby, who founded London's Central School of Arts and Crafts, wrote in 1896: "Unless there is a ground of beauty, vain it is to expect the fruit of beauty. Failing the spirit of Art, it is futile to attempt to leaven this huge mass of 'man styles' by erecting specimens of architects' architecture, and dumping down statues of people in cocked hats.

Three little girls in Victoria Park; another Paul Martin photograph. (Victoria and Albert Museum)

"The Proposal," photographed in 1888. While photographers like Paul Martin captured real life, others staged romantic scenes which they sold as home decorations. (Victoria and Albert Museum)

"We should begin at the humblest plane by sweeping streets better, washing and whitewashing the houses, and taking care that such railings and lamp-posts as are required are good lamp-posts and railings, the work of the best artists attainable . . . At present, London is as structureless as one of its own fogs."15

What Oscar Wilde's London was debating was really a simple question: Art for art's sake or art for people's sake?

William Morris preached that "beauty, which is what is meant by art . . . is no mere accident to human life . . . but a positive necessity." Morris kept scolding "the rich and influential among us . . ." and wanted to stop "this sluttish habit" of cutting down trees, littering, vandalism, and "increasing hideousness" of advertising posters. He feared that because of people's indifference "modern civilization is on the road to trample out all the beauty of life, and to make us less than men."16

Wilde, on the other hand, was not a scold. He offered London elegance. It was an elegance of nonchalant intensity, of serious triviality; it was a precious confusion of life and art, with a flair for combining the serious and the not-so-serious. "Art is the only serious thing in the world," he insisted, adding that "the artist is the only person who is never serious." Wilde's subtitle of *The Importance of Being Earnest* is *A Trivial Comedy for Serious People.*

For thoughtful people today, Wilde may in the end have gotten the better of the argument. In "The Soul of Man Under Socialism," he pondered prophetically: "The State is to make what is useful. The individual is to make what is beautiful. And as I have mentioned the word labour, I cannot help saying that a great deal of nonsense is being written and talked nowadays about the dignity of manual labour. There is nothing necessarily dignified about manual labour at all, and most of it is absolutely degrading. It is mentally and morally injurious to man to do anything in which he does not find pleasure, and many forms of labour are quite pleasureless activities, and should be regarded as such. To sweep a slushy crossing for eight hours on a day when the east wind is blowing is a disgusting occupation. To sweep it with mental, moral, or physical dignity seems to me impossible. To sweep it with joy would be appalling. Man is made for something better than disturbing dirt. All work of that kind should be done by a machine . . .

"For what man has sought for is, indeed, neither pain nor pleasure, but simply Life. Man has sought to live intensely, fully, perfectly. When he can do so without exercising restraint on others, or suffering it ever, and his activities are all pleasurable to him, he will be saner, healthier, more civilised, more himself. Pleasure is Nature's test, her sign of approval. When man is happy, he is in harmony with himself and his environment. The new Individualism, for whose service Socialism, whether it wills it or not, is working, will be perfect harmony. It will be what the Greeks sought for, but could not, except in Thought, realise completely, because they had slaves, and fed them; it will be what the Renaissance sought for, but could not realise completely except in Art, because they had slaves, and starved them.

A lady out for a "push" in her chair along the new Thames Embankment, parasol and fluffy dog in tow. The picture was taken with one of London's first hand-held Brownie cameras, using roll film. It was invented by the American George Eastman and became the rage after its introduction at the turn of the century. (Kodak Museum)

It will be complete, and through it each man will attain to his perfection. The new Individualism is the new Hellenism.''

Morris and Ruskin argued that machine production, commerce, and the industrial city were antithetical to the priceless individualism and true social value of art. Wilde put it more bluntly: "A work of art is the unique result of a unique temperament. Its beauty comes from the fact that the author is what he is. It has nothing to do with the fact that other people want what they want. Indeed, the moment that an artist takes notice of what other people want, and tries to supply the demand, he ceases to be an artist, and becomes a dull or an amusing craftsman, an honest or a dishonest tradesman. He has no further claim to be considered as an artist. Art is the most intense mode of individualism that the world has known. I am inclined to say that it is the only real mode of individualism that the world has known."[17]

Great art, said Pater, "has something of the soul of humanity in it."[18] "Soul" was a term that Oscar Wilde and his circle used often.

His London had it.

Her grandchild has her own pram . . .
(Kodak Museum)

. . . while daddy has a "Brownie."
(Kodak Museum)

And when she grows up, she will have a pram for her
dolly. (Kodak Museum)

"The Street Doctor," photographed by J. W. Thompson. For working-class families, medicines were expensive, and few of them could afford to travel to Harley Street, where most of the good doctors practiced, let alone be treated there. They bought their remedies from peddlers of patent medicines, and often attempted to cure tuberculosis with "cough preventatives." Thompson's photographs of lower-class London life are clearly staged, but give an accurate if sanitized picture. (Olin Library, Cornell University)

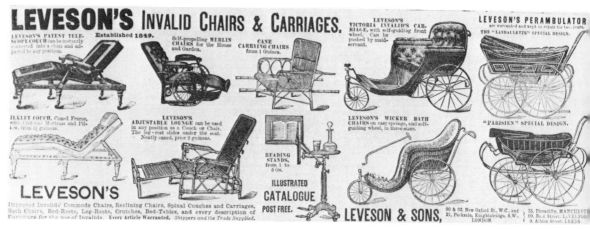

Pushchairs, carriages, prams, and such were one of London's growing specialized industries. (The Graphic, *Olin Library, Cornell University)*

"The Queen's Jubilee Thanksgiving Festival" in 1887, celebrating the fiftieth year of Victoria's reign, as depicted in the conservative Illustrated London News. *The crowds almost vanish beneath the overpowering image of Westminster Abbey, representing the enduring and unchangeable monarchy. The Queen was both Head of State and Head of the Church. (Olin Library, Cornell University)*

Here the Jubilee parade reaches Trafalgar Square. The monumental aspect of London still dominates; the crowds seem to serve as decoration. (Illustrated London News, *Olin Library, Cornell University*)

*The Queen's Golden Jubilee Garden Party at Buckingham Palace, June 29, 1887. (*The Graphic, *Olin Library, Cornell University)*

The Queen arriving at Westminster Abbey at her Diamond Jubilee, ten years later. (Kodak Museum)

Oscar Wilde in 1891, the year the poet Lionel Johnson introduced him to Lord Alfred Douglas, the third son of the eighth Marquess of Queensberry. It was the beginning of a passionate and fateful friendship. (National Portrait Gallery, London)

Sketch of Oscar Wilde as the aging Aesthete by William Rothenstein, member of the circle of artists and writers who frequented the Café Royal in London. Wilde died on November 30, 1900, exiled in Paris. (William Andrews Clark Library, University of California at Los Angeles)

2

LILIES
AND SUNFLOWERS

London was in the grip of a "sentimental passion for a vegetable fashion," as the song in Gilbert and Sullivan's *Patience* had it. Sinuous botanical forms in manifold twists and curls decorated just about everything from ladies' gowns to wrought-iron fences, from Tiffany lamps to building façades. When Oscar Wilde's Lord Arthur, the hero of the story "Lord Arthur Savile's Crime," wanders into Covent Garden market, he sees it—as a good aesthete should— as a work of art in vegetables: "and the great piles of vegetables looked like masses of jade against the morning sky, like masses of green jade against the pink petals of some marvelous rose."[1]

The fashion had its beginnings in the small store which Arthur Lasenby Liberty opened in 1875 on Regent Street. It flourished into a style and a movement generally known as Art Nouveau. Artists like the Dutch Vincent van Gogh, who experienced London firsthand, and the Viennese Gustav Klimt, who created his own Central European version, architects like the American Frank Lloyd Wright, who merged it with an American sense of the pragmatic, and the Catalán Antonio Gaudí, who added to it the arabesques of Moorish style, carried it forward into the art and architecture of our time.

In London, Liberty's store, or "art warehouse," specialized in oriental silks and simple fabrics described as "Persian pink, Venetian red, terracotta, ocher-yellow, sapphire and peacock blue, sage, olive, willow green, soft brown and drab." Favorite motifs included lilies and sunflowers. Among the steady customers were William Morris, Dante Gabriel Rossetti, Edward Burne-Jones, James McNeill Whistler, Norman Shaw, and Edward Godwin, as well as the costume designers for popular satires of aestheticism such as *Patience*. The fashion spread to Paris, where Liberty opened a shop in 1884; and to New York, where Louis Comfort Tiffany was already in business. Tiffany's designs, commented the New York *Morning Journal,* "belong to no school unless the ultra-aesthetic school of [Oscar] Wilde."[2]

This "ultra-aesthetic school" was centered around a paradox: the fashion for things of delicate artifice was at the same time a fashion for things that

Aubrey Beardsley's design for the binding of Sir Thomas Malory's Le Morte d'Arthur, *1893. Beardsley brought his own idiosyncratic style of ingenious artistry to the Art Nouveau "vegetable fashion." Like Tiffany lamps, and the art of the Vienna Secession, Beardsley represented, as a New York newspaper remarked, the "ultra-aesthetic school of Oscar Wilde." (Victoria and Albert Museum)*

were natural—wild silk woven by hand into designs of ingenious artistry, for example. It was the perfect fusion of art and nature, one of the ideals of aestheticism.

There was also another paradox here: the arts and crafts that were made to raise the popular taste often became the precious artifacts of the elite. When Tiffany began experimenting with blown glass in the 1890s, it was part of an effort to provide practical lamp shades at affordable prices for the average household. What he produced were objects of delicate, rare, and impractical beauty.

Art Nouveau was more than Pre-Raphaelite maidens and faintly decadent vegetables carved in onyx or formed of stained glass. It was as much a new faith as it was a new style. It was a sect, as it were, of the new faith

William Morris, photographed by Frederick Hollyer in 1884. The founder and leader of the Arts and Crafts movement in England and the United States, Morris was a poet, translator, painter, furniture and interior designer, printer, and publisher. To advance his goal of improving both the quality of life and public taste, he founded his own press (the Kelmscott Press), a design store (Morris, Marshall, Faulkner & Company), and helped found the Social Democratic Federation. (Victoria and Albert Museum)

John Ruskin, photographed by Frederick Hollyer. Champion of a return to medieval ideals in art and architecture and critic of industrialization, materialism, and commercialism, Ruskin, like no critic before or after him, made art and design a hot, popular, moral issue. He was idolized by Oscar Wilde. (Victoria and Albert Museum)

whose prophet was John Ruskin and whose apostle was William Morris. Ruskin believed that Art and Architecture—that is, the Art and the Architecture he approved of (which was mostly Gothic)—would bring redemption from the sins of a Victorian world that had fallen from grace and worshiped the machine. Morris carried this faith into the mundane articles of daily life, such as furniture and wallpaper. He believed that the evils of industrialization could be exorcised by the virtues of humble craftsmanship inspired by art.

William Morris was a poet and a political activist. But on his membership card of the socialist Democratic Federation, he described himself as "Designer." Design, he wrote, "is at the root of the whole matter. Everything made by man's hands has a form, which must be either beautiful or ugly; beautiful if it is in accord with Nature, and helps her; ugly if it is discordant with Nature, and thwarts her; it cannot be indifferent . . . [Some forms] do not necessarily imitate Nature, but . . . the hand of the craftsman is guided to work in the way that she does, till the web, the cup, or the knife, look as natural, nay as lovely, as the green field, the river bank, or the mountain flint . . ."[3]

John Ruskin said, in essence, that ornament is the basis of architecture. Morris added that ornament is the basis of civilized society. His decoration combined "clearness of form and firmness of structure with the mystery which comes of abundance and richness of detail . . ."[4] He put his theories into practice by establishing a business enterprise—called "The Firm"—of artists and craftsmen who integrated design, production, and distribution in a socialist spirit. It was very successful; in fact, to Morris's dismay, it was all but taken over by the fashionable and the wealthy. Some years later, Ezra Pound lamented that Beauty was "now decreed in the market place." Morris tried to ensure that this did not happen. He wanted Beauty to be decreed in the workshops of his friends and followers.

If Ruskin and Morris were essentially populist, Wilde and Whistler were elitist. It should have been a nice balance, but it certainly unbalanced Ruskin, whose objections to Whistler's art became the subject of the most curious trial in the annals of the history of art. Only in Oscar Wilde's London would the question of aesthetic and commercial value of a work of art become the reason for a legal confrontation. The real question which the trial addressed was the function of art—was it to edify and educate or was it to be beautiful? Whistler's paintings, wrote art critic Ruskin in the curious periodical publication—really a series of letters to the working classes—that he called *Fors Clavigera,* were works of an "ill-educated conceit" and "wilful imposture" and the artist a "coxcomb" who asks "two hundred guineas for flinging a pot of paint in the public's face."[5]

Whistler sued for libel. The trial was one of the highlights of the London Season in 1878, the year Wilde came down from Oxford. The Victorian virtues of "industry" and "thrift" were on trial. At one point Ruskin's lawyer established that the painting in question, "Nocturne in Black and Gold,"

DAYS WITH CELEBRITIES. (46).

MR. RUSKIN.

John Ruskin's outspoken opinions on art and artists earned him a full-page cartoon in an 1882 issue of Moonshine, *a satirical magazine. Known as a friend of the workingman (he founded a working-class college at Oxford) and a stern teacher of the middle class, Ruskin championed painter J. M. W. Turner but got into a nasty libel suit with Whistler. (William Andrews Clark Library, University of California at Los Angeles)*

took Whistler two days. "For the labour of two days then, you ask two hundred guineas?"

"No," replied Whistler, "I ask it for the knowledge of a lifetime."[6]

Ruskin lost, but Whistler did not win. He was awarded damages of only a farthing and had to declare bankruptcy. "Sympathy in Blue and Gray" was no substitute for an "Arrangement in Gold and Silver," quipped a creditor.

Oscar Wilde at first supported Whistler, noting that he "is indeed one of the very greatest masters of painting, in my opinion. And I may add that in this opinion Mr. Whistler himself entirely concurs."[7] But later they were spitting at each other. First Whistler wrote, in a letter to the *World:* "What has Oscar in common with Art? except that he dines at our tables, and picks from our platters the plums for the pudding he peddles in the provinces. Oscar—the amiable, irresponsible, esurient Oscar—with no more sense of a picture than of the fit of a coat, has the courage of the opinions . . . of others!"

Wilde replied: "This is very sad! With our James, vulgarity begins at home, and should be allowed to stay there."

"A poor thing, Oscar—but for once, I suppose, your own," returned Whistler.[8]

Whistler's most talked-about work, the dining room of Frederick Leyland's house at 49 Prince's Gate in Kensington, was praised by *The Times* on February 15, 1877, as "a single experiment in decoration . . . the ornamentation being entirely derived from the beautiful plumage of the peacock displayed in various forms." The whole interior is "so fanciful and fantastic, and at the same time so ingenious and original in motive as to be completely Japanesque."[9] Whistler himself referred to it as a "Harmony in Blue and Gold."

Japanesque was the rave. From fans and fabrics to "Tokio Tooth Powder"—which purportedly contributed to the pearly white teeth of Japanese ladies—there was a wide market for Japanese artifacts. Architects such as Edward Godwin, who designed Whistler's house on Tite Street, adopted the Japanese style for coffee tables, sideboards, and entire rooms decorated with wallpapers designed around motifs such as "Peacock" or "Sparrow and Bamboo." Japanesque pottery was so popular that in 1879 Wedgwood brought out an entire table service also called "Sparrow and Bamboo." But it was the Worcester Royal Porcelain Works that did the most to popularize the elements of Japanese design. It also did much to popularize Aestheticism. In 1881, it issued a wonderfully zany parody, in the form of a teapot which consisted of a male and a female character from *Patience* standing back to back, one arm raised to form the spout, the other arm drooping to form the handle. The base is inscribed, "Fearful consequences through the laws of Natural Selection and Evolution of living up to one's teapot." It sold briskly.

Aubrey Beardsley was reputed to have owned what one visitor described as "the finest and most explicitly erotic Japanese prints in London." His sensuous drawings were, in his own words, "suggestive of Japan, but not

"Acanthus" on woolen damask produced by Morris & Company. (Victoria and Albert Museum)

"Saville" armchair produced by Morris & Company. (William Morris Gallery)

Façade of the Morris & Company store at 449 Oxford Street, the outlet for Morris's manufactured decorator's items. (William Morris Gallery)

KELMSCOTT PRESS, UPPER MALL, HAMMERSMITH.

March 31st, 1894.

This is the Golden type.

This is the Troy type.

This is the Chaucer type.

Halliday Sparling, 8, Hammersmith Terrace, London, W., to whom should be addressed all inquiries as to books to which no publisher's name is attached.

Prospectus for the Kelmscott Press, March 1894. Although machine type composition was available, Morris designed, cut, and set the type for all his publications by hand. All his books were hand-printed on hand-made paper and hand-bound. (William Morris Gallery)

really Japanesque." Beardsley had originally wanted to be a writer, and tried, as he put it, to "crush out" his instinct to draw, ostensibly because writing paid and drawing did not . . . at least not yet. But his weird figures would not stay crushed and soon did bring him money and fame. "Words fail to describe the quality of the workmanship," he said about his early illustrations. "The subjects were quite mad and a little indecent. Strange hermaphroditic creatures wandering about in Pierrot costumes or modern dress; quite a new world of my own creation."[10]

Beardsley's later work was at once abstract and naturalistic, combining the beauty of pure line and ideal form with grotesque caricature. Among the most haunting were his illustrations for Oscar Wilde's *Salome.* They called attention to the banned play and brought its illustrator notoriety. Even Beardsley himself, who converted to Catholicism in the last year of his life, seemed to share the misgivings some people felt about some of his work. Just before he died in 1898, at the age of twenty-five, he ordered his publisher, Leonard Smithers, to destroy all his erotic drawings. Fortunately, Smithers did not comply, perhaps because he rather liked them. Wilde once called the publisher "the most learned erotomaniac in Europe." He added, "he loves first editions, especially of women; little girls are his passion."[11]

"Not until we have learnt to understand Beardsley or Dostoevski or Manet as we understood Bismarck shall we reach the stage of culture," asserted the German art critic Julius Meier-Graefe at the time. "The point is not whether these men were artists, statesmen, or anything else; they have age at their fingers' ends, each in the art particular to himself."[12]

There were, of course, many fine illustrators in London besides Beardsley; and, thanks to printers such as William Morris, much enthusiasm for making fine books. Foremost among the illustrators were Kate Greenaway, Walter Crane, Randolph Caldecott, and Charles Ricketts, who was also a painter, collector of Japanese prints, distinguished stage designer, and one of the most imaginative—and fashionable—designers of books in London. Among his most notable book designs were those for Thomas Hardy's *Tess of the d'Urbervilles* and for a number of Wilde's books, including *The Sphinx* and *The Picture of Dorian Gray.*

The idea that beautiful objects not only raised the level of taste, but according to Wilde "can speak to the soul in a thousand different ways,"[13] dominated the middle class. They were better, nobler, nicer, because they were surrounded with objects decreed by the Aesthete tastemakers as "beautiful." Nor was Beauty limited to objects. It was everywhere.

Artistic book design and other "improvements" fostered by the Arts and Crafts movement were "rapidly spreading through all classes of society. Good taste is no longer an expensive luxury to indulge in—the commonest articles of domestic use are now fashioned in accordance with its laws, and the poorest may have in their homes at the cost of a few pence cups and saucers and jugs and teapots, more artistic in form and design than were to be found twenty years ago in any homes but those of the cultured rich.

Stained-glass window of St. John the Baptist designed by William Morris. Like Louis Comfort Tiffany in New York, Morris rediscovered the beauty of stained glass and helped make it fashionable for home decoration all over the English-speaking world. (William Morris Gallery)

"And to whom are we indebted for these advantages? Why, to the Aesthetes, the fools and idiots of Philistine phraseology."[14]

The phraseology was rampant in such tastemaking magazines as *The British Architect, Decoration,* and *The Artist: Journal of Home Culture.* There were also a number of popular books propagating the Arts and Crafts cult. The most influential were Charles Locke Eastlake's *Hints on Household Taste in Furniture, Upholstery and Other Details,* the Reverend William John Loftie's *A Plea for Art in the House,* and Mrs. Mary Eliza Haweis's series on *The Art of Beauty* (1878), *The Art of Dress* (1879), and *The Art of Decoration* (1881).

Wilde used these books to provide him with lecture material for his American tour in 1882. Being presented to the United States as the representative of British Aestheticism, as a living character from *Patience,* Wilde chose to speak on the Beautiful as present in the home, not in the art gallery.

Typical William Morris interiors. Morris's ideal to have all furniture hand-made was in conflict with his ideal to furnish the homes of all classes "artistically." He eventually permitted affordable machine-made copies of his designs. They sold well. (Victoria and Albert Museum)

Above, Jane Morris, wife of William Morris. Her features epitomized the Pre-Raphaelite ideal of female beauty—and made red hair and prominent upper lips fashionable. (Kodak Museum) Left, Jane Morris as painted by Dante Gabriel Rossetti. Right, "Winged Thought" by Simeon Solomon. (William Morris Gallery)

It seemed an ambitious mission. But no more so than the attempt to reach the British middle class in their crowded suburban homes.

Yet Beauty entered even humble cottages and tenements—and not only with polemic songs and jokes. She entered personified by Pre-Raphaelite painters such as the Brotherhood—Dante Gabriel Rossetti, William Holman Hunt, John Everett Millais, and others. As Haweis observed: "Those dear and much abused 'prae-Raphaelite' painters whom it is still in some circles the fashion to decry, are the plain girls' best friends. They have taken all the neglected ones by the hand. All the ugly flowers, all the ugly buildings, all the ugly faces, they have shown us have a certain crooked beauty of their own . . .

"Morris, Burne-Jones, and others, have made certain types of face and figure once literally hated, actually the fashion. Red hair—once, to say a woman had red hair was social assassination—is the rage. A pallid face with a protruding upper lip is highly esteemed . . . Only dress after the prae-Raphaelite style, and you will be astonished to find that so far from being an 'ugly duck' you are a full fledged swan!"[15]

In large measure, the extraordinary success of the Arts and Crafts movement was due to the extraordinary variety of its products. It concerned itself with all the tools and implements of life, "from the coffee cup to city planning," as Mies van der Rohe much later described the concerns of one of its offsprings, the Bauhaus in Germany. The "vegetable fashion"—known as *Jugendstil* in Germany, *Le Style Moderne, Style Nouille,* and *Style Métro* in France, *Sezessionsstil* in Austria, and *Modernismo* in Spain—was but the earliest manifestation of a still valid belief that a civilized society can be sustained only if art and good taste achieve control over machine production and commercialism. For all their frothy decadence, Oscar Wilde and the other Aesthetes immeasurably advanced this cause under the banner of the lily, the sunflower, and Beauty.

Wilde told an American audience: "You have heard, I think a few of you, of two flowers connected with the aesthetic movement in England, and said (I assure you, erroneously) to be the food of some aesthetic young men. Well, let me tell you that the reason we love the lily and the sunflower, in spite of what Mr. Gilbert may tell you, is not for any vegetable fashion at all. It is because these two lovely flowers are in England the two most perfect models of design, the most naturally adapted for decorative art—the gaudy leonine beauty of the one and the precious loveliness of the other giving to the artist the most entire and perfect joy. And so with you: let there be no flower in your meadows that does not wreathe its tendrils around your pillows, no little leaf in your Titan forests that does not lend its form to design, no curing spray of wild rose or brier that does not live for ever in carven arch or window or marble, no bird in your air that is not giving the iridescent wonder of its colour, the exquisite curves of its wings in flight, to make more precious the precociousness of simple adornment."[16]

Self-portrait of Dante Gabriel Rossetti. The son of Italian emigrants to England, Rossetti saw himself as an otherworldly outsider destined to re-create an idealized Renaissance of his own invention. (William Morris Gallery)

Sir Edward Coley Burne-Jones photographed by Frederick Hollyer. Burne-Jones was the most popular member of the Pre-Raphaelite Brotherhood. His work was marked by mysticism and exotic ornamentation. (Victoria and Albert Museum)

Sir John Everett Millais. A co-founder, with Holman Hunt and Rossetti, of the Pre-Raphaelite movement, he illustrated Trollope's novels and Tennyson's poems. (Kodak Museum)

"King Cophetua and the Beggar Maid" by Sir Edward Burne-Jones.
*The romantically idealized fantasy of medieval life was depicted with
photographic realism. (The Tate Gallery)*

J. W. Waterhouse's "The Lady of Shallot" (above) and Millais's "Ophelia" (below) show the remarkable uniformity of Pre-Raphaelite painting, which remained popular for some thirty years. (The Tate Gallery)

The greatest influence of the Arts and Crafts movement in general and John Ruskin in particular was on architecture. Ruskin saw true virtue in only the Gothic style. His influence was so strong that many handsome Georgian buildings were destroyed to accommodate Gothic Revival structures. Typical Arts and Crafts buildings are Collingham Gardens, Lincoln, 1884 (above), and the Elephant and Castle pub, rebuilt c. 1899 (below). (Victoria and Albert Museum)

Prince Albert Memorial, designed by Sir G. Gilbert Scott, 1872, at Kensington Gardens, London, seems a gigantic medieval reliquary. The square, pinnacled spire which protects a statue of the Prince, rises one hundred and seventy-five feet into the air. Four groups, representing Engineering, Agriculture, Manufactures, and Commerce, stand at the corners of the pedestal. Four huge marble compositions, personifying Europe, Asia, Africa, and America, mark the corners of the platform. (Library of Congress)

"Nocturne in Black and Gold, the Falling Rocket" c. 1874, by James McNeill Whistler. Ruskin said of this painting that Whistler had been "tossing a paint pot in the face of the public." Ruskin lost the resulting libel suit, but Whistler did not win. The suit bankrupted him. Quipped a creditor: " 'Sympathy in Blue and Gray' was no substitute for an 'Arrangement in Gold and Silver.' " (Detroit Institute of Art)

Above, "The Private View," an illustration from the 1882 Christmas issue of the World. *Actually, the view was not so private, what with the Prince of Wales (center) in attendance. Oscar Wilde is in the lower left corner, leaning on his elbow; above and to the left of his head is James McNeill Whistler. (Olin Library, Cornell University)*

Right, cartoon of Whistler after winning his lawsuit against John Ruskin, from The Entre'acte Almanack, *a satirical annual. (Olin Library, Cornell University)*

Mr. J. WHISTLER.
An Arrangement in Done-Brown.

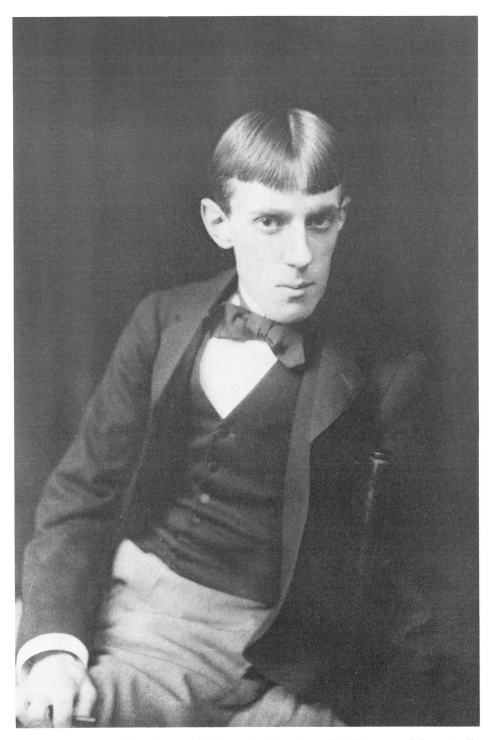

Aubrey Vincent Beardsley photographed by Frederick Hollyer. The illustrator of the erotically infamous Yellow Book, *Beardsley has been described as "the most notorious proponent of the grotesque in the late nineteenth century." Before he died at the age of twenty-six, he insisted that his most erotic drawings be destroyed. They weren't. (Victoria and Albert Museum)*

An illustration by Aubrey Beardsley for Oscar Wilde's Salome, *which was originally written in French. It was translated into English by Alfred Douglas (with "schoolboy faults" which Wilde corrected) and published with Beardsley's illustrations in 1894. Wilde did not like the illustrations, saying they were "too Japanese, while my play is Byzantine." Beardsley, on his part, maliciously caricatured Wilde in several illustrations. The face in the lower-right corner of this one clearly bears Wilde's features. (Olin Library, Cornell University)*

Aubrey Beardsley vignette from Salome *by Oscar Wilde. (Olin Library, Cornell University)*

3

THE CALL
OF THE STAGE

With the opening of D'Oyly Carte's Savoy Theatre on the Strand, in October 1881, London's theatrical life was suddenly cast in a new light. It came from twelve hundred electric arc lamps, fed by six generators. Everything suddenly looked different: stage and foyer, actors and audiences, plays and their messages.

Richard D'Oyly Carte got his start young in life as a lecturer and theatrical agent. In 1875 he produced *Trial by Jury,* the first successful operetta with lyrics by W. S. Gilbert and music by Sir Arthur Sullivan. This launched a partnership which prospered for some twenty years. The first four Gilbert and Sullivan musicals *(The Sorcerer, Pinafore, Penzance,* and *Patience)* were performed at the Opéra Comique. Then the partnership built its own house, the Savoy, which made the company famous in the entire English-speaking world as the "Savoyards."

The Savoy, named after the famous palace built in the thirteenth century by Peter of Savoy, was the first public building lit by electricity—an experiment, D'Oyly Carte admitted, "that may succeed or fail." He assured his audience that built-in gas lamps, the pilot lights aflame, were standing by just in case. But he explained that electric illumination, which was installed in the Paris Opéra that same year, reduced the fire risk, heat, and foul air that gas brought with it. Electric lights could also be used to illuminate the drama far more effectively. The house could go entirely dark, all light focused on the stage.

D'Oyly Carte started the stagecraft of lighting when he tinted one hundred of his first seven hundred and fifteen stage lamps blue to create night

The New Savoy Theatre on the Strand as depicted by the Illustrated Sporting and Dramatic News. *Built by producer Richard D'Oyly Carte for the production of Gilbert and Sullivan operas, it opened in October 1881. The Savoy was the first public building in London to be lit by electricity and gave the "Savoyards" their name. (Olin Library, Cornell University)*

Program pages, including advertising, for the August 5 and 21, 1885, performances of Gilbert and Sullivan's Iolanthe *and* The Mikado, *designed by Alice Havers. (Victoria and Albert Museum)*

effects. As the American novelist Booth Tarkington noted, electricity changed the very art of acting. In the dimness of gaslight, actors had only to play their parts. Now they had to look their parts as well.

The new brightness in the foyer subdued the garish decorations of both the ladies in the audience and the theater itself. The ladies put aside their colored stones and heavy cosmetics and took to wearing diamonds and softer makeup. The decor of the Savoy and of theaters in general became more dignified. "Without adopting either the styles known as 'Queen Anne' and 'Early English,' or entering upon the so-called aesthetic manner," explained D'Oyly Carte, "a result has now been produced which I feel sure will be appreciated by all persons of taste. Paintings of cherubim, muses, angels, and mythological deities have been discarded, and the ornament consists entirely of delicate plaster modelling designed in the manner of the Italian Renaissance. The main colour tones are white, pale yellow and gold—gold used only for backgrounds or large masses and not following what may be called, for want of a better or worse name, the Gingerbread School of Decorative

Art—for gilding relief work or mouldings . . . The stalls are covered with blue plush of an inky hue and the balcony seats are of stamped velvet of the same tint, while the curtains of the boxes are of yellowish silk, brocaded with a pattern of decorative flowers in broken colours."[1]

The audiences of the 1880s delighted in their new surroundings. Theater was quite the fashion, mostly as an escape from the tedium of lives that were debilitating (if one had to work for a living) or boring (if one did not). There was theater for every taste, from high tragedy to burlesque. And the theaters became places where the taste of each class was shaped and directed, where there was even some mixing of classes. The children of the upper middle class went to the Christmas pantomime, for instance, with the children of the "lower orders." This revolutionary atmosphere meant that experimentation, even though within limits set by the state censor, could (and did) take place. Sexual topics, long taboo on the British stage, appear for the first time. For Wilde the theater of his time presented "more vulgarity than vice . . . What we require is more imaginative treatment, greater freedom from theatric language and theatric convention. It may be questioned, also, whether the consistent reward of virtue and punishment of wickedness be really the healthiest ideal for an art that claims to mirror nature."[2]

Thus British theater came of age, whether in the music halls, with songs still sung today, or the great dramatists, homegrown ones such as Oscar Wilde and George Bernard Shaw, or imported ones, such as Henrik Ibsen.

The most fashionable of theaters was the Lyceum, just beyond the Savoy on Wellington Street, now a dance hall. It was at the Lyceum that Sir Henry Irving experienced his greatest triumphs. He began his long connection with that stage in 1871, and took over the management in 1878, with Ellen Terry as his leading lady. The partnership between Irving and Terry lasted until 1902. Irving died in 1905.

Ellen Terry was the prototypical leading lady of the London theater. Her life was itself a melodrama. She started on stage with her sister Kate when both were still children and was soon a great success. At the age of sixteen, she married the painter George Frederick Watts. They separated after a few years when Ellen ran off to live in Hertfordshire with Edward Godwin, the architect who built Whistler's house on Tite Street and helped with the renovations of the Wildes' house. Terry and Godwin never married, but had two children, Edith and Gordon Craig. Terry later described the night of Edith's birth: " 'The Earthly Paradise' [by William Morris] was coming out at the time my children were born. I lived in the sweet country— in the middle of a common—and I forgot my pangs whilst reading *The Watching of the Falcon* on a certain bitter sweet night in December when Edy, my first child, was born. They were playing in the church 'Of rest in the Lord.' I heard them as I passed through the village—alone—feeling frightfully ill and afraid. I could never forget that music and that poem. It was all lovely and awful."[3]

Ellen Terry returned to the stage in 1875, parted from Godwin, got a divorce from Watts, and married an actor named Charles Kelley. The marriage did not shake the earth, but did give her children a certain legal status. She was becoming a great figure once again, acting with such notables as Squire and Marie Bancroft in the Prince of Wales's Theatre. Wilde sent her his first play, *Vera, or the Nihilists,* specially bound with her name stamped in gold on the binding. It was a nice gesture, but did not improve the play, which, along with *The Duchess of Padua,* was produced and failed in New York. These plays were melodramas, drawing on a tradition already understood as dying by the 1880s. Even though *Vera* purports to have a plot which reflects the contemporary fear of anarchism, a fear of the collapse of the present order, it is basically an old-fashioned melodrama with stilted, oratorical language. *The Duchess of Padua* is even worse. Written in a peculiar pseudo-Shakespearean English, it is hardly readable, never mind playable. It will be a decade until Wilde discovers the key to the theater of his day, a social satire that would make people laugh and cry at the same time.

Henry Irving was an extraordinary anomaly, cutting an unlikely figure with his spidery legs and sideway walk. His nasal tone of voice sounded to George Bernard Shaw like "a highly cultivated neigh." Yet, he was an actor of commanding talent and enigmatic charm. His first great success, establishing his reputation in a single night, was as Mathias in Leopold Lewis's *The Bells,* an adaptation of the French play *Le Juif Polonais* or *The Polish Jew.*

A typical Victorian melodrama, this play is about Mathias, the mayor and innkeeper of an Alsatian town, who many years ago, impelled by poverty, murdered a Polish Jew. Although he is above suspicion, his conscience so haunts him in his nightmares, enacted on stage, that it kills him. "It will be obvious," wrote the drama critic of the London *Times,* "that the efficiency of this singular play depends almost wholly upon the actor who represents Mathias . . . It is a marked peculiarity of the moral position of Mathias that he has no confidant, that he is not subjected to the extortions of some mercenary wretch who would profit by his knowledge. He is at once in two worlds, between which there is no link—an outer world that is ever smiling, an inner world which is purgatory. Hence a dreaminess in his manner, which Mr. Irving accurately represents in his frequent transitions from a display of the domestic affections to the fearful work of self-communion . . . with a degree of energy that, fully realizing the horror of the situation, seems to hold the audience in suspense."[4] The London playwright, playgoer, and professional gossip George Sims wrote: "The play left the first-nighters a little dazed. Old-fashioned playgoers did not know what to make of it as a form of entertainment. But when the final curtain fell, the audience, after a gasp or two, realized that they had witnessed the most masterly piece of tragic acting that the British stage had seen for many a long day, and there was a storm of cheers."[5]

Opposite, Dame (Alice) Ellen Terry, the leading lady of the London theater. The daughter of actors, she made her debut at the age of six. She led a dramatic life, much of it as an acting partner of the famous Sir Henry Irving. In 1925, at the age of seventy-eight, she was created a Dame of the Grand Cross of the British Empire. (Kodak Museum)

Irving repeated his triumph in *The Bells* over eight hundred times during the next thirty years, up to two nights before his death. He was equally applauded as Hamlet, as Mephistopheles in Goethe's *Faust,* and as Tennyson's *Becket.*

Wilde was a devoted admirer of Irving. In 1885 Irving and Terry appeared in *Hamlet* at the Lyceum, which Wilde reviewed in detail, describing their impression on the audience: "As regards Mr. Irving's own performance, it has been already so elaborately criticised and described, from his business with the supposed pictures in the closet scene down to his use of 'peacock' for 'paddock,' that little remains to be said; nor, indeed, does a Lyceum audience require the interposition of the dramatic critic in order to understand or to appreciate the Hamlet of this great actor. I call him a great actor because he brings to the interpretation of a work of art the two qualities which we in this century so much desire, the qualities of personality and of perfection. A few years ago it seemed to many, and perhaps rightly, that the personality overshadowed the art. No such criticism would be fair now. The somewhat harsh angularity of movement and faulty pronunciation have been replaced by exquisite grace of gesture and clear precision of word, where such precision is necessary. For delightful as good elocution is, few things are so depressing as to hear a passionate passage recited instead of being acted. The quality of a fine performance is its life more than its learning, and every word in a play has a musical as well as an intellectual value, and must be made expressive of a certain emotion. So it does not seem to me that in all parts of a play perfect pronunciation is necessarily dramatic. When the words are 'wild and whirling,' the expression of them must be wild and whirling also. Mr. Irving, I think, manages his voice with singular art; it was impossible to discern a false note or wrong intonation in his dialogue or his soliloquies, and his strong dramatic power, his realistic power as an actor, is as effective as ever. A great critic at the beginning of this century said that Hamlet is the most difficult part to personate on the stage, that it is like the attempt to 'embody a shadow.' I cannot say that I agree with this idea. Hamlet seems to me essentially a good acting part, and in Mr. Irving's performance of it there is that combination of poetic grace with absolute reality which is so eternally delightful. Indeed, if the words easy and difficult have any meaning at all in matters of art, I would be inclined to say that Ophelia is the more difficult part. She has, I mean, less material by which to produce her effects. She is the occasion of the tragedy, but she is neither its heroine nor its chief victim. She is swept away by circumstances, and gives the opportunity for situation, of which she is not herself the climax, and which she does not herself command. And of all the parts which Miss Terry has acted in her brilliant career, there is none in which her infinite powers of pathos and her imaginative and creative faculty are more shown than in Ophelia. Miss

Opposite, Sir Henry Irving. The actor who first introduced a natural manner of performance to the London stage and drew huge crowds wherever he performed, he and his leading lady, Ellen Terry, toured the United States eight times. He died in 1905, at the age of sixty-seven, and is buried in Westminster Abbey. (Kodak Museum)

Sir Henry Irving and Ellen Terry in Shakespeare's Much Ado About Nothing *at the Lyceum Theatre, October 11, 1882. (Victoria and Albert Museum)*

Terry is one of those rare artists who needs for her dramatic effect no elaborate dialogue and for whom the simplest words are sufficient. 'I love you not,' says Hamlet, and all that Ophelia answers is, 'I was the more deceived.' These are not very grand words to read, but as Miss Terry gave them in acting they seemed to be the highest possible expression of Ophelia's character. Beautiful, too, was the quick remorse she conveyed by her face and gesture the moment she had lied to Hamlet and told him her father was at home."[6]

Ellen Terry's contribution to the London repertoire was no less popular than Irving's, and no less elusive. She had star quality. The novelist and playwright Charles Reade recalled: "Her eyes are pale, her nose rather long, her mouth nothing particular, complexion a delicate brick-dust, her hair rather like tow. Yet somehow she is beautiful. Her expression kills any pretty face you see beside her. Her figure is lean and bony; her hand masculine in size and form. Yet she is a pattern of fawn-like grace. Whether in movement or repose, grace pervades the hussy."[7]

Her first memorable part was as Olivia in an 1878 adaption of Oliver Goldsmith's *The Vicar of Wakefield,* by W. G. Wills. Clement Scott gave the performance its epic significance: *"They* came to see her; *we* saw and applauded; *she* conquered—everybody."[8]

At the Lyceum, she played the wide range of parts that Irving chose for her—from Shakespeare's Lady Macbeth to Comma in Tennyson's *The Cup* (1881). Henry Labouchère, the fairly liberal member of Parliament and rather radical journalist, wrote in his periodical *Truth* that "the age that gave us the Grosvenor Gallery must necessarily adore an Ellen Terry, for she is the embodiment of the aspirations of modern art. With her waving moments and skill at giving life to drapery, she is the actress of all others to harmonize with gold backgrounds and to lounge under blossoming apple trees."[9]

While Ellen Terry was the "embodiment of modern art" in *The Cup,* down the street in the Savoy Theatre, similar audiences were listening to Gilbert and Sullivan's satire of the "greenery yallery, Grosvenor Gallery" boys. Both satire and object of satire, existing side by side, were part of the London theater scene.

Acting became respectable. In 1883, Prime Minister William Gladstone sent a private message to the Lord Chief Justice: "Would it be too audacious to offer Irving a knighthood? Please let this be most secret: for I should have to hold diverse consultations before acting."[10]

The honor was not unheard of for distinguished performing artists. Arthur Sullivan had been knighted. But, then, Irving was an actor. With discreet melodrama, he declined, telling his friend Stephen Coleridge, who was the son of the Lord Chief Justice and a devout admirer of Ellen Terry, "that an actor differed from other artists, musicians and the like, in that he had to appear in person every night appealing directly to the public favor . . . that there was a fellowship among actors of a company that would be impaired by an elevation of one member over another; that his strength as a manager and power as an actor lay far more in the suffrages of the plain folk in the pit than in the patronage, however lofty, of the great people; that he knew instinctively that large numbers of these same plain folk would be offended at their simple Henry Irving accepting decorations of a titular kind."[11]

Twelve years later he did accept. Two of Queen Victoria's knights were actors: Sir Henry Irving and Sir Squire Bancroft.

Bancroft and his wife, Marie Effie Wilton Bancroft, first played and managed the Prince of Wales's Theatre on Coventry Street, east of Piccadilly, and then took over the Haymarket Theatre, two blocks south.

The Haymarket Theatre was renovated for the Bancrofts by the ubiquitous Phipps, who abolished the "pit" under the first balcony to make room for expensive seats below and cheap seats on the upper balcony. But the "pitties," relegated to the "gods," demanded their pit, and delayed the opening night performance for twenty minutes with their protests. In time, however, the pit disappeared.

The Bancrofts worked closely with Thomas William Robertson, the actor and dramatist, who had hoped to reform the English theater with his

"Why not?" asks this cartoon in The Entre'acte Almanack *of 1883 about the proposal of granting knighthood to the actor Henry Irving. The caption says: "In 1783, used to say: 'Mother! mother! Here be the players a commin'! Take in the clothes!' But in 1883?" Actually, Henry Irving refused the unprecedented honor at the time, but became Sir Henry twelve years later. (Olin Library, Cornell University)*

dramas of domestic affairs, his "cup and saucer" plays. While seeming more true to life than the melodramas at the Lyceum, Robertson's plays still seemed wooden, especially in contrast to the new, realistic dramas coming from the Continent.

But "home life ceases to be free and beautiful as soon as it is founded on borrowing and debt," says Henrik Ibsen in *A Doll's House* (1879). And borrowing, debt—and worse—were closer to many a real life than even Robertson would admit on the stage. It would take some time before Londoners would see *A Doll's House* in a proper production and good translation, but Ibsen's often shocking message of sordid social reality finally reached London's stages in the late 1880s.

One of the London playwrights who came under Ibsen's influence was Henry Arthur Jones, who began as a writer of melodramas such as *The Silver King* (with Henry Herman, produced in 1882). Jones wrote some sixty plays of social and moral criticism but never transcended his initial melodramatic roots.

As one contemporary observed:

> *The Stage has got a mission,*
> *The Stage has got a call;*
> *That great is its position,*
> *Must be distinct to all.*
> *It gilds the pill of knowledge,*
> *And sermons finds in stones,*
> *To fling at school and college—*
> *Says Henry Arthur Jones.* [12]

More exciting than his prolific achievements were Jones's ambitions: "We are on the threshold, not merely of an era of magnificent spectacular and archaeological revivals, but of a living, breathing drama," he wrote, "—a drama that shall not fear to lay bold and reverent hands on the deepest things of human life today, and freely expose them, and shall attempt to deal with the everlasting mysteries of human life as they appear to nineteenth-century eyes." [13]

Henry Arthur Jones's name is often mentioned with that of his contemporary, Arthur Wing Pinero, a playwright and actor in Irving's Lyceum company. In his early years as a playwright, Pinero was associated with an important set of stage figures—John Hare, who was a prominent actor with the Bancrofts' company in the plays of Thomas Robertson, and with the Kendals. William Kendal was a romantic actor, and his wife, Madge, was known for her "educated" talent as both a comedienne and a tragic actress. Madge was Tom Robertson's sister. Together, Hare and the Kendals managed the St. James's Theatre on King Street in the heart of the West End, and presented much of Pinero's early work. In 1888, the Kendals went on a successful tour of the United States.

Hare then moved to the Garrick Theatre, which had been built for him near the foot of Charing Cross Road. It opened with Pinero's *The Profligate,* which presented the audience with the radical notion that a woman has a right to expect her husband to be just as chaste as he expects her to be. By dealing directly with the Victorian double standard, the play established Pinero as a serious social dramatist.

Pinero's greatest successes were to come several years later with plays such as *The Second Mrs. Tanqueray,* which is about a woman with a past

seeking acceptance in respectable society, and *Trelawney of the 'Wells,'* which offers an effective account of the way in which the conventions of life and art can interfere with both. The "Wells" of the title is a disguised version of Sadler's Wells.

An early play of Pinero's, *The Squire,* caused one of London's frequent theater scandals. The fuss started in 1881, when suggestions were made that *The Squire* was plagiarized from Thomas Hardy's *Far from the Madding Crowd.* The facts were suspicious. Hare had rejected J. W. Comyns Carr's adaption of Hardy's novel just before he accepted Pinero's play and the plots were similar. Furthermore, Hare claimed to have mislaid the Carr-Hardy manuscript, though he eventually found and returned it. One ominous night, Hardy, Carr, and the noted lawyer George Lewis were seen, stone-faced, in a box of the St. James's, watching *The Squire.* But no writs were served. When the Hardy adaption was finally performed a year later, it was not nearly as successful as Pinero's piece. The International Copyright Convention of 1886 put an end to such "borrowings."

Pinero's greatest hit was *The Second Mrs. Tanqueray,* which surprised those who thought that a play about a serious subject, done in a serious way, could not make money in the London of the time. The première at the St. James's was directed by George Alexander. Paula, the heroine, was played by Mrs. Patrick Campbell, an actress of great beauty and wit, best remembered today for her association with George Bernard Shaw. Paula became one of the great roles of the period, played by Madge Kendal, Eleanora Duse, Ethel Barrymore, and Tallulah Bankhead.

The first rave review came from William Archer, the theater critic of London's *World* as well as a translator and promoter of Ibsen's work. "It is possible," wrote Archer, "that *The Second Mrs. Tanqueray* may bring in only (say) five percent on the time and money invested, whereas a piece of screaming buffoonery or trivial sentimentality might have brought fifteen. But, frankly, isn't the pure joy of effort and triumph cheap at the money? . . . I am no despiser of childish art, so long as there are brains in it, and I am far from urging that the stage should show us nothing but Second Mrs. Tanquerays. I have not, thank goodness, outgrown my taste for lollipops, if only they be delicately flavoured, and not too heavily 'loaded' with plaster-of-Paris; but one cannot eat nothing but candy, year out, year in, and yet preserve one's self-respect and one's digestion . . . The limitations of Mrs. Tanqueray are really the limitations of the dramatic form. To say that Mr. Pinero has not entirely overcome them is merely to say that he has not achieved a miracle reserved for the very greatest artists in their very happiest inspirations. That is a totally different thing from saying, as in the case of *The Profligate,* 'This is false; that is feeble; here is an inconsistency; there an impossibility.' There is no illogical compromise in Mrs. Tanqueray, nothing impossible, nothing flagrantly improbable . . . In brief, the play is modern and masterly . . . It interests and absorbs one; it satisfies the intelligence

---

Opposite, Sir Arthur Wing Pinero, actor and prolific playwright, was among the most successful theater people in Oscar Wilde's London. (Kodak Museum)

more completely than any other modern English play; but it is not in the least moving. Not once during the whole evening were the tears anywhere near my eyes. Yes, once—when Mr. Pinero came before the curtain, and the house rose at him. Then I felt a thrill of genuine emotion to think that here at last, in spite of all the depressing and stunting influences of our English theatrical world, was a man who had the will and talent to emancipate himself and give the artist within him free play—to take care of his soul, and let his pocket, for the nonce, take care of itself."[14]

Pinero's pocket turned out to be well lined. He earned thirty thousand pounds on the play, quite possibly because it is not entirely without melodrama. In the final scene Paula's stepdaughter learns of her sordid past. Paula discusses this discovery with her husband, Aubrey, who knew of it all along, but was determined that it should make no difference:

> *Paula:* I believe the future is only the past again, entered through another gate.
> *Aubrey:* That's an awful belief.
> *Paula:* To-night proves it. You must see now that, do what we will, you'll be continually reminded of—what was. I see it . . . You'll do your best—oh, I know that—you're a good fellow. But circumstances will be too strong for you in the end, mark my word.
> *Aubrey:* Paula—!
> *Paula:* Of course I'm pretty now—I'm pretty still—and a pretty woman, whatever else she may be, is always—well, endurable. But even now I notice that the lines of my face are getting deeper; so are the hollows about my eyes. Yes, my face is covered with little shadows that usen't to be there. Oh, I know I'm "going off." I hate paint and dye and those messes, but, by-and-by, I shall drift the way of the others; I shan't be able to help myself. And then some day—perhaps very suddenly, under a queer, fantastic light at night or in the glare of the morning—that horrid, irresistible truth that physical repulsion forces on men and women will come to you, and you'll sicken at me.
> *Aubrey:* I—!
> *Paula:* You'll see me then, at last, with other people's eyes; you'll see me just as your daughter does now, as all the wholesome folks see women like me. And I shall have no weapons to fight with—not one serviceable little bit of prettiness left me to defend myself with! A worn-out creature—broken up, very likely, sometime before I ought to be—my hair bright, my eyes dull, my body too thin or too stout, my cheeks raddled and ruddled—a ghost, a wreck, a caricature, a candle that gutters, call such an end what you like! Oh, Aubrey, what shall I be able to say to you then? And this is the future you talk about! I know it! *(He is still sitting staring forward; she rocks herself to and fro as if in pain.)* Oh, Aubrey! Oh! Oh!
> *Aubrey:* Paula—! . . .[15]

"The Court in the Highlands—Her Majesty at the Play at Abergeldie Castle," 1881. The first play Queen Victoria attended after twenty years of mourning the death of Prince Albert was The Colonel, *a satire of the Aesthetic movement by F. C. Burnand. The illustration appeared in* The Graphic, *an influential London newspaper. (Olin Library, Cornell University)*

Many novelists of the period were drawn to the stage. One of them was Henry James. His first play to be produced on the London stage, *The American* (1891), was a modest success. It had seventy performances.

His second, *Guy Domville,* was a dismal failure. Toward the end of the last act, Domville proclaims:

"I am the last, my lord, of the Domvilles!"

"It's a bloody good thing you are," a voice from the audience shouted.[16]

George Bernard Shaw was kinder: "The truth about Mr. James' play is no worse than [that] it is out of fashion," he wrote. ". . . As it happens, I am not myself in Mr. James' camp: in all the life that has energy enough to be interesting to me, subjective volition, passion, will, make intellect the merest tool. But there is in the centre of that cyclone a certain calm spot where cultivated ladies and gentlemen live on independent incomes or by pleasant artistic occupations. It is there that Mr. James' art touches life, selecting whatever is graceful, exquisite, or dignified in its serenity. It is not life as imagined by the pit or gallery, or even by the stalls: it is, let us say, the ideal

George Bernard Shaw in 1884 at age twenty-eight. He was already an established music and drama critic in London. (Kodak Museum)

Mrs. Patrick Campbell, née Beatrice Stella Tanner. The actress began her career in 1893 in the title role of Pinero's The Second Mrs. Tanqueray. She had a long, witty, and celebrated correspondence with George Bernard Shaw. (Kodak Museum)

Program for the première performance of Oscar Wilde's The Importance of Being Earnest, *February 14, 1895, at the St. James's Theatre. "In fifty-three years of acting," recalled Allan Aynesworth, who played Algernon Moncrieff, "I never remember a greater triumph." (Olin Library, Cornell University)*

of the balcony; but that is no reason why the pit and gallery should excommunicate it on the ground that it has no blood and entrails in it."[17]

Kate Terry Gielgud—the niece of Ellen Terry and mother of Sir John Gielgud—was less tolerant than Shaw: "It is all very well to talk about literary drama, but for a play to deserve the name of drama at all, it must be in the first place comprehensible and in the second, dramatic. There is one dramatic scene in *Guy Domville* in the second act, but there is only one, and that one springs from nothing. I am curious to hear whether Mr. James himself has any definite idea of what his characters are driving at. He has most certainly not succeeded in conveying one to the audience and the St. James' company seems also uncertain as to the precise frame of mind they have to represent."[18]

James was mortified. As playwrights usually do, he blamed the audience. "How can my piece do anything with a public with whom *that* is a success," he allowed.[19] *"That"* was Oscar Wilde's *An Ideal Husband,* and a success it was.

Wilde's play had opened two nights earlier than James's at the

Haymarket with the Prince of Wales in the royal box. Very different than Wilde's first two attempts at writing for the stage, *An Ideal Husband* is a work which relies on wit and subtlety, playing on the lively artifices of life, rather than on the natural tedium of melodramatic conventions. It is a play about the upper class, written in the distanced language of that class for the amusement of a middle-class audience. It was Wilde's revenge on W. S. Gilbert and it placed Wilde at the forefront of British social satirists.

Prince Edward would not abide Wilde's protestations that the play was very long. "Cut not a single word," was the royal admonition. James's opinion was that *An Ideal Husband* was "helpless, crude, bad, clumsy, feeble and vulgar," but judgment of drama was not his strong point. After a run of only a few weeks, *Guy Domville* closed at the St. James's to be replaced by Wilde's second success of the year and his deservedly best known play, *The Importance of Being Earnest.* "In fifty-three years of acting, I never remember a greater triumph," reminisced Allan Aynesworth, who played the role of Algernon Moncrieff. "The audience rose in their seats and cheered and cheered again."[20]

The première of *The Importance of Being Earnest,* on February 14, 1895, raised Wilde's already impressive stature as a popular playwright. *Lady Windermere's Fan,* in 1892, and *A Woman of No Importance,* in 1893, were well received.

Salome, in 1892, further enhanced Wilde's preeminence. He wrote the play in French, but the world première was to be in English at the Palace Theatre in London with Sarah Bernhardt in the title role. It was already under rehearsal when the Lord Chamberlain banned the play under a rule dating from the Reformation that forbade the representation of biblical figures on the British stage. Its subsequent publication launched another dazzling meteor over the London sky of the period. The volume was one of the first to be illustrated by Aubrey Beardsley's drawings of deliciously macabre decadence. The English translation was done by Wilde's young friend and lover, Lord Alfred Douglas. Married, with two young sons, sometime in the late 1880s Wilde became part of a circle which flaunted its homosexual orientation. For some, this was little more than a public pose; for Wilde it was more.

The first night of *The Importance of Being Earnest* was fateful for Oscar Wilde. The Marquess of Queensberry, the father of Lord Alfred Douglas, had bought a ticket. It was obvious that, obsessed with seeking revenge for Wilde's amorous involvement with his son, Queensberry wanted to make trouble. Wilde arranged with the theater manager to have the ticket returned. Police prevented the Marquess from entering the theater when he arrived anyway with a bouquet of carrots and turnips which he intended to hurl at Wilde's curtain call. A few days later, Queensberry left a card at Wilde's club, the Albemarle, provocatively addressed "To Oscar Wilde posing as a sodemite (sic)." Wilde instantly sued Queensberry for libel, lost the suit, and was himself arrested on criminal charges of homosexual offenses with minors. The first trial ended in a hung jury. A second trial found him guilty and on May 25, 1889, Wilde was sentenced to two years' hard labor. His name was taken off the playbill at the St. James's Theatre as soon as the scandal broke. Even before his conviction, *The Importance of Being Earnest* was replaced by Henry Arthur Jones's *The Triumph of the Philistines*. "Really, the luck is against the poor British drama—the man who has more brains in his little finger than all the rest of them in their whole body, goes and commits worse than suicide in this way," lamented William Archer.[21]

Archer, the drama critic for *The World*, is best remembered today for translating Ibsen and introducing him to English-speaking audiences. Others, too, wanted to revive the British stage by using Continental models. Many writers, such as Henry Arthur Jones and Henry Herman, were still captured by the spirit of the theater in which virtue had to be rewarded and evil punished. It horrified Wilde.

Jones's *The Breaking of a Butterfly* (1884), his version of *A Doll's House*, was a travesty of the original. Jones saw himself as rescuing British drama from the "gruesome kitchen-middens" of Ibsen's Continental world.[22]

Despite appeals for a new kind of drama, the London theater was still unsympathetic to Ibsen's "naturalism." Henry Irving, though the leading actor of the day, never performed Ibsen. Critic Clement Scott said it clearly: "There is no pleasure in revelling in what is unwholesome and disagreeable. The playhouse is not a charnel house; the drama is not a dissecting knife . . . We must enforce the good, without showing the bad."[23]

But in the end, Archer prevailed. He was supported by Shaw, Eleanor Marx (the youngest daughter of Karl Marx), her common-law husband Edward Aveling, May Morris (the daughter of William), and a small group of other friends. In July 1889, Archer's translation of *A Doll's House* was produced at the Novelty Theatre and at last secured for Ibsen a prominent place on the English stage.

Ibsen, in turn, paved the way for Shaw's plays with all their polemical instincts and missionary zeal. His *Widower's House* created a furor in 1893, in part, no doubt, because it was a bad play. Then came *Arms and the Man*, a play delightfully subversive in its easygoing satire of Victorian melodramatic conventions. They also made the stage an important platform for the promotion of women's rights. But Shaw's dramas also reflected a satiric view of the nature of society quite unfamiliar to the viewer of Ibsen's work. This satirical touch is taken from Wilde's world of words in the service of social criticism.

Then as now, however, there was the business side of show business. Theaters constantly changed hands, sometimes in startling ways. Sadler's Wells for instance, London's oldest theater, was transformed into a roller-skating rink in 1876, and within two years, turned into the arena for Profes-

Opposite, Sarah Bernhardt at the peak of her international fame. Wilde wrote his Salome *for her. The play was already in rehearsal at the Palace Theatre when, in June 1892, it was banned because of a medieval law that prohibited the respresentation of biblical figures on stage. Bernhardt never played the role. (Kodak Museum)*

sor Pepper, magician ("late of the Royal Polytechnic, Honorary diploma of Physics and Chemistry of the Lords Committee of Council on Education, Associate of Civil Engineers, etc., etc."), and on to a variety of circus and performing troupes, including illegal boxing and wrestling matches. In 1878, Sadler's Wells was bought by Mrs. Bateman, a theatrical entrepreneur, who had just sold the Lyceum to Henry Irving.

Under Mrs. Bateman's brief management (she died three years later), the Wells provided a variety of entertainment, including what came to be known in America as "Vaudeville." Like television today, it introduced the performing arts to the masses and vice versa to the ultimate benefit of both. Variety shows engraved themselves deeply into our popular cultural consciousness. The acrobat Leotard, for instance, who played the Alhambra in the 1860s, not only gave his name to his snugly fitting garment, he also became the subject of the famous song by George Leybourne:

> *He'd fly through the air with the greatest of ease,*
> *A daring young man on the flying trapeze.*
> *His movements were graceful,*
> *All girls he could please,*
> *and my love he purloin'd away.* [24]

In one season, the Sadler's Wells presented musicals, pantomimes, farces, a number of adaptations from such novelists as Balzac and Dickens, and some stock dramas, as well as vocal performances and comedy routines. One of these routines, performed in 1891, featured one Charles Chaplin, whose son of the same name was two years old at the time.

During the 1890s Sadler's Wells was managed by George Belmont (whose real name was Belchett), known as the Aristocrat of Alliteration because of the alluring advertising slogans he cleverly concocted, making Marie Lloyd "the Divine Droll, the Music Hall Manager's Mascot, the Svengalian Songstress, a Star Supreme in a Sphere of its own Setting, possessing power of hypnotising the largest houses into Deliriums of Delight."

Another hilariously heady headliner was "Sadler's Special Sadness Shifter." Belmont introduced his first cinema show—the Theatrograph invented by Robert W. Paul. Belmont announced that it "Debars Analysis and Delights Audiences because of its Wonderful Simulation of Human Beings in Action. Pictures, Life-size, Life-like, and full of Character and Colour, thrown on a Screen. This Theatrograph is a mighty Mirror of Promethean Photography, and an act of Artistic and Mammoth Magnificence."[25]

Pantomime, too, continued to hold its place, picking up the traditions of the Commedia dell'Arte, the buffoon and clown, harlequin and panteloon, and adding to them the ingenuities of nineteenth-century melodramatic stage business and the delight of nineteenth-century musical entertainment. Even George Bernard Shaw cheered it. "When a Superior Person—myself, for

---

Opposite, Oscar Wilde at the time of his first theatrical successes in London. (Kodak Museum)

Scenes from Henrik Ibsen's Rosmersholm *at the Vaudeville Theatre in 1891 as shown in the* Illustrated Sporting and Dramatic News. *Ibsen was highly controversial with playwrights and audiences who relished traditional plays in which virtue was rewarded and evil punished. But George Bernard Shaw, the critic William Archer, and others fought hard to introduce the Norwegian and his stark "naturalism." By the time* Rosmersholm *was performed in London, Ibsen was well established on the London stage. (Olin Library, Cornell University)*

instance—takes it upon himself to disparage burlesque, opéra bouffe, musical farce, and Christmas pantomime as mere silliness and levities of the theatre, let him not forget that, but for them, our players would have no mimetic or plastic training, and the art of the stage machinist, the costumier, the illusionist and scene-painter would be extinct."[26]

And then there were the "penny gaffs," the theaters for the poor.

A *Sunday Times* correspondent, exploring on a moonlit Sunday evening the Marylebone borough, which stretches from Regent's Park to Oxford Street, left a vivid account of this diversion: "The narrow streets were ablaze with naphtha, and one out of every two shops seemed to be devoted to the sale of rather thin and flabby beef, pork, and mutton. The gutters were lined with an imposing array of cabbages, potatoes, and crockery-ware. In one shop, with a front all open to the frosty air, a rather rough-and-tumble sale by auction was in full swing, and the surrounding cries of 'Porky-rabbit,' 'all-hot-all-hot,' and 'colly flower-er-er' were mingled with the hoarse voice . . . shouting 'going, going, gone!' After floundering about this salubrious spot for upwards of a quarter of an hour I discovered the establishment I was in search of. Considering that it was only a humble 'penny gaff,' its exterior was somewhat imposing. A goodly array of gas jets illuminated the entry, which was a shop with the front window knocked out. The decorations were of the floral type, and decidedly alarming colours, representing numberless young ladies with pink legs and white, airy skirts hanging up in the air, standing on their toes, and in all sorts of impossible and captivating attitudes, above and beneath which it was announced in large letters that the gorgeous ballet pantomime of 'Dick Whittington' was performed every evening. A group of juveniles, ragged and tattered, and painfully lean, were gazing open-mouthed at this extraordinary work of art, and occasionally casting longing glances down the entry, where a narrow strip of green cardboard conveyed the information that the world of wonder depicted on the poster was only to be witnessed by the fortunate possessors of at least one penny of the Queen's money . . .

"I lost much of the performance going on behind the footlights. What I did see of it compels me reluctantly to confess that as a gorgeous ballet pantomime on the subject of Dick Whittington, as per announcements out-side, it was a mild fraud. There was not much of Dick Whittington, and absolutely no gorgeousness 'whatsoever,' as Mrs. Brown would say. As to the ballet, it was conspicuous by its absence; the stage being only about the size of an ordinary third-class railway carriage did not admit to a very grand display of spectacular effect, so the management had wisely concluded to leave it out altogether . . . the pièce de résistance was evidently the panto-mime proper, in which the antics of a clown, pantaloon, harlequin, and policeman—the establishment, I regret to say, was not equal to a columbine —were followed with eager interest. And such laughter I never heard the life of before. The little ladies and gentlemen who make the boxes ring . . . at Covent Garden and Drury Lane must yield the palm for noise to their leather-lunged ragged little brothers and sisters at the 'penny gaff' in Maryle-bone."[27]

4

READERS
AND WRITERS

Some critics insisted that one of the few pleasures High Society denied itself was reading anything but cheap novels. "A great part of the 'best' English people keep their minds in a state of decorous dullness," remarked one social critic.[1]

Wilde sensed that the development of the novel in England was too closely tied to the middle-class demand for amusement and diversion. He saw this in the new fascination for the "naturalistic" novels of writers such as George Gissing, after the model of Émile Zola, novels which conjure dire poverty in the comfortable sitting rooms of the bourgeoisie. He found such novels lacking in grace and form.

"It is only fair to acknowledge," Wilde wrote, "that there are some signs of a school springing up amongst us. This school is not native, nor does it seek to reproduce any English master. It may be described as the result of the realism of Paris filtered through the refining influence of Boston. Analysis, not action, is its aim; it has more psychology than passion, and it plays very cleverly upon one string, and this is the commonplace."[2]

Unless they preferred to devote themselves to serious drinking, the lower classes were eager to improve their minds and read books and magazines, if only to escape the pandemonium of their overcrowded homes in the quiet of library reading rooms. The number of public libraries in London was steadily increasing. Just how many working-class people took advantage of them is hard to tell. While ever more children attended school and learned some reading and writing, few had occasion to use these skills in later life spent in factories and at menial labor. Richard D. Altick reports in

Newsstand at Newgate Street. The printed word was all over London, from the "yellow press" to esoteric literary magazines. Most of the bookstores were concentrated along the Strand. "Read all about it!" the newspaper boys would shout—and most Londoners did. (Guildhall Library)

his *Victorian People and Ideas:* "As libraries multiplied, so did other ways of spending one's leisure: music halls, cheap theaters, sporting matches, choral societies, entertainments at church or chapel, public parks, railway excursions. The printed word had increasingly stiff competition."[3]

As the middle class increased, so did the number of newspapers and magazines—especially, small literary magazines—books, railroad station bookstalls, bookstores, publishers, writers, and words put on paper. Ruskin, all told, produced thirty-nine bulky volumes. The best-selling Margaret Oliphant wrote more than one hundred books, including history and biography.

London's newspapers ranged from the conservative and respectable to what after 1895 came to be known as the "yellow press." The name derives from "The Yellow Kid," the first cartoon character to be printed in color, and appearing that year in a New York newspaper.

Virtually all of London's newspapers, printing plants as well as editorial offices, were located on Fleet Street. Home delivery was rare. Paper boys, chanting their headlines as they darted through rush hour traffic, were as much of the London scene as the bobbies who kept a bemused eye on them.

THE
Labour Prophet
AND LABOUR CHURCH RECORD.

"LET LABOUR BE THE BASIS OF CIVIL SOCIETY."—MAZZINI.

VOL. V.—No. 59.   NOVEMBER, 1896.   PRICE ONE PENNY.

THE IMMORTAL MORRIS.

This phrase, employed by the Socialists of Milan in telegraphing their sorrow at William Morris's death, expresses a feeling that must be shared by all who ever came under the spell of his unique personality. Now that he is dead, his greatness is acknowledged even by those who during his life persistently ridiculed and made light of his most serious aims. It was inevitable that he too should be the victim of that hasty newspaper biography wherein half-knowledge and superficial criticism are eked out with self-advertisement. Those who have known and loved him will take time to estimate what they and the world have lost by his death. This much is certain, that as time goes on his life and work will seem more and more significant and extra-ordinary, and prove him to be, in the possession of enduring fame, indeed immortal. For myself it is impossible to believe that that generous, buoyant, over-flowing individuality was only the result of a curious chemical compound that, with the cessation of physical life, has been resolved into its elements. That is an assumption which would strain my credulity too far.

Morris has been written about from almost every point of view—as artist, craftsman, writer, and Socialist. In this place it will be fitting to consider briefly his religious significance. Regarding religion, he was usually reticent. In this he may have resembled his countrymen as described in his own *Dream of John Ball*: "They did not want others to see how deeply they were moved, after the fashion of their race when they are strongly stirred." Like Whitman, he "argued not concerning God." Among a party of friends, if the discussion turned upon religion, and became heated, as such discussions will, I have seen him quietly get up from the table and walk away. Some three years ago,

WILLIAM MORRIS.

in an article in JUSTICE, he described himself as "care-less of metaphysics and religion, as well as scientific analysis, but with a deep love of the earth and the life on it."

We may truly say that his "deep love of the earth and the life on it" constituted his religion. How much more religious was it than the attitude of the orthodox, professing to regard Nature as the garment of God and Man as his image, yet content to see that beautiful garment defiled, and that glorious image defaced! Nothing can be further from the truth than to treat Morris's Socialism as an accident, a temporary aber-ration, or mere matter of sentiment. His public adoption of it was a direct challenge to Society, and was probably the most de-liberate and serious act of his life. This act itself was the result of a long process of development, and was not entered upon until he had satisfied himself (with that practical sense for which he has not always received due credit) that the historical and economic basis of Socialism was sound. His later ac-tivities as an exponent of Socialism have often been sharply contrasted with his early description of himself in the introduction to *The Earthly Paradise* as "the idle singer of an empty day." But without some ideal of beneficent activity, the singer would not have com-plained of his idleness, nor that his day seemed empty.

Moreover, the famous lines—
> Dreamer of dreams, born out of my due time,
> Why should I strive to set the crooked straight?

show that the call to action in the field of social reform was already felt by him, even though the way was not yet made clear. It is one stage earlier in spiritual evolution than that represented by the voice which was heard by Saul of Tarsus: "It is hard for thee to

---

The Labour Prophet and Labour Church Record, *one of London's countless "little" magazines. The cover story of this issue of November 1896 is an obituary of William Morris. (Guildhall Library)*

The Yellow Book
An Illustrated Quarterly
Volume I April 1894

London: Elkin Mathews & John Lane
Boston: Copeland & Day

Price
5/-
Net

The Yellow Book, *an illustrated quarterly, of April 1894, with a cover drawing by Aubrey Beardsley, who founded the quarterly with Henry Harland. The title alludes to the cover color of the supposedly wicked and decadent popular French novels of the time. (Olin Library, Cornell University)*

The novel as an art form received a new impetus and a wider range of action with the abolition of the old two- or three-volume format. It was unwieldy and expensive and thus, in effect, chained to the circulating libraries. A new kind of novel appeared, a novel of literary frankness, all in one volume priced at six shillings. It instantly and vastly increased book sales.

The leading publishers, such as Macmillan, supplied the Empire with most of its textbooks and conventional reading matter. Small, daring publishers prided themselves in serving the Muses rather than Mammon. One of them was the Kelmscott Press, founded by William Morris. After an early approach to Macmillan while he was at Oxford to work on some translations from Greek, Wilde attached himself to one of these small, more literary publishers, the Bodley Head, which published his *Salome.*

Newspapers and books were not the only reading matter of the cultured middle class. Of equal literary importance were the small literary magazines such as *The Yellow Book, The Savoy, The Sketch, The Pall Mall Budget, The Octopus, The Pick-me-up,* and literally dozens of others which supplemented such established publications as *The Saturday Review* and *Vanity Fair.* Virtually every important poet, critic, or novelist in Britain made his debut in one of them. They treated subjects of interest to the educated mind, to quote Altick, "in a manner that was serious but not heavy, urbane rather than facetious or sedulously 'bright.' The writers in that genre discovered a happy middle way between vulgarization and pedantry, an art almost lost today because evidently there is no demand for it."[4] Magazines were also important because they printed a number of important books as serials. Three of Trollope's novels were serialized in *The Fortnightly Review* before they appeared as books. *The Picture of Dorian Gray* first shocked critics in *Lippincott's Monthly Magazine* installments.

Most London bookstores were located along Charing Cross Road. They were thriving, serious businesses, where a clerk would apprentice for as many as fourteen years before he was considered fully qualified.

Literary tastes ranged from *The Yellow Book* to the yellow press, from the sentimental to the sensational. Most in demand were "penny dreadfuls" and "shilling shockers." Girls and their mothers would swoon and shudder over titillating romances. For the more discerning, authors like Marie Corelli, the Queen's favorite, offered sentimental romance and sensational adventure in elegant prose. Boys and men would get their thrills from novels of fictitious bravery—unless, of course, they went to the Strand or Holywell Street not for bravery but pornography.

Times of drastic change are also times of nostalgia. The time that brought London electricity and telephones was also the time when most of London looked back. Architectural fashion was Gothic grotesquerie and phony Queen Annery. The Tower Bridge, built at about the same time as the Eiffel Tower, and just as advanced in its steel construction, was disguised in Gothic masonry. William Morris founded the Society for the Protection of Ancient Buildings. The arts and crafts he reintroduced were medieval.

Alfred, Lord Tennyson. The most representative poet of the Victorian Age, Tennyson served as Poet Laureate from 1850 to 1890, writing verse for royal events. This posed photograph in Renaissance costume was taken by his friend, the photographer Julia Margaret Cameron. (Kodak Museum)

Thomas Hardy. His novels, such as The Mayor of Casterbridge *(1886), portrayed the lost world of rural England. (Kodak Museum)*

So was much of the literature. It also looked back, aspiring to little more than a polite, romantic atmosphere, beauty, morality and, all too eagerly, immortality. Alfred, Lord Tennyson, the Poet Laureate, although he wrote as sensitively as any writer about contemporary anxieties, also despaired of the promises of materialism and science and reveled nostalgically in the romantic virtues of King Arthur and his court in his *Idylls of the King.*

When Tennyson joined King Arthur in eternal Camelot, Algernon Charles Swinburne, who in his youth had reveled in vices rather than virtues, was considered next in line for the official crown of laurels. But after waiting a decorous period, Queen Victoria appointed Alfred Austin instead.

Though immeasurably more profound, Robert Browning also drew on romantic remembrances of things past, often very grim things. To judge from the number of his fan clubs—by 1884 there were twenty-two Browning Societies around the world, including several in the United States—he was equally as popular as the Poet Laureate. But there were some whose faith was uncertain. When the Browning Society at Girton College, Cambridge, was dissolved, the Girton girls, according to a newspaper account, "not only voted that the balance of funds in hand should be spent on chocolates, but have actually bought the chocolates and eaten them."[5]

Rudyard Kipling offered hearty nourishment to the British soul, not with nostalgia so much as by expressing a national pride on which the sun never set. But there were shadows. He made his era aware of the obligations of empire, of "The White Man's Burden." When pride seemed tarnished by the pomp and pomposity of the Queen's Diamond Jubilee in 1897, he had some qualms:

> *Far-called, our navies melt away;*
> > *On dune and headland sinks the fire:*
> *Lo, all our pomp of yesterday*
> > *Is one with Nineveh and Tyre!*
> *Judge of the Nations, spare us yet,*
> *Lest we forget—lest we forget!*[6]

London's literary avant-garde sensed the tremendous changes to come. It seemed equally imbued with *fin de siècle* decadence and dawning-new-age optimism, unsure whether this was the end or the beginning. Degeneration was at the same time regeneration. The two went hand in hand. What could be more decadent, for instance, than Oscar Wilde and his provocative statement that "sin is an essential element of progress. Without it the world would stagnate, or grow old, or become colourless."[7] Yet Wilde also wrote of Jesus as a model of progressive individualism in "The Soul of Man Under Socialism." It was an essay that even the most skeptical socialists took seriously.

Despite Gothic bridges and pining for King Arthur, then, the new and

Robert Browning. One of the "cult" writers of the late nineteenth century. Browning societies flourished throughout England. (Kodak Museum)

Rudyard Kipling by Sir Philip Burne-Jones, 1899. (National Portrait Gallery, London)

last generation of Victorians—Wilde, the irrepressible Max Beerbohm and others—was keenly conscious of being distinct from the preceding generation, from all preceding generations. Most everything discussed in the literary magazines was proudly and self-consciously "New"—the "New Remorse," the "New Spirit," the "New Humour," the "New Realism," the "New Hedonism," the "New Drama," the "New Unionism," the "New Party," and the "New Woman."

Part of the purpose of these novelties, certainly those of Wilde, Beardsley, et al., was *épater le bourgeois,* to rattle the bourgeoisie. But it was rarely shock for its own sake. It was shock therapy, in a way, a gentle and entertaining way to cure society of the staid, hypocritical, and rotten pomposity of High Victorianism. It was also a typical bourgeois enterprise. "Nothing," said Arthur Symons, "not even conventional virtue, is so provincial as conventional vice; and the desire to 'bewilder the middle classes' is itself middle class."[8]

"It was fashionable in 'artistic' circles," wrote Holbrook Jackson, "to drink absinthe and to discuss its 'cloudy green' suggestiveness; and other hitherto exotic drugs were also called into the service of these dilettanti of sin. Certain drugs seemed to gather about them an atmosphere of romance during these years, and all sorts of stimulants and soporifics, from incense and perfumes to opium, hashish, and various forms of alcohol, were used as means to extend sensation beyond the range of ordinary consciousness, along with numerous well-known and half-known physical aids to passionate experience."[9]

Among the Aesthetes, poetry often substituted as the stimulation. Algernon Charles Swinburne could be found "in the studio of some painter-friend, quivering with passion as he recited 'Itylus' or 'Felise' or 'Dolores' to a semi-circle of worshippers, who were thrilled by the performance to the inmost fibre of their beings. It used to be told that at the close of one such recital the auditors were found to have slipped unconsciously on their knees. The Pre-Raphaelite ladies, in particular, were often excessively moved on these occasions, and once, at least, a crown of laurel, deftly flung by a fair hand, lighted harmoniously upon the effulgent curls of the poet."[10]

There were also more sober movements.

One was inspired by Socialism. The British working class was at last getting restless.

On Monday, February 8, 1886, some twenty thousand dockers and building workers—"their numbers . . . added to by a very great many of the idle class," as *The Times* put it—marched on Trafalgar Square demanding work.[11] Nothing much happened but for a few broken windows, "but the suspicion of danger was sufficient to induce shopkeepers to close their establishments and to secure their valuables with as much care as if an invading army was expected to march through the streets of the English capital," reported *The Morning Post.*

The Socialist League of Hammersmith was one of the early units of the Socialist (and later Fabian) movement. In response to the social inequities in British society, the Fabians, who were primarily middle class, worked for peaceful reform. (Kodak Museum)

The following year, on "Bloody Sunday," November 13, 1887, a demonstration of labor's right to speak up brought out the troops to Trafalgar Square and resulted in two deaths and many arrests. The London Dock Strike, two years later, lasted a month and backed up the growing clamor with a show of real power. Socialist ideas of various hues came and went, including those of the American single-tax advocate Henry George.

The Social Democratic Federation, founded in 1884, with William Morris a leading member, proved of some consequence. More important, perhaps, was the nonrevolutionary Fabian Society, founded that same year by Beatrice and Sidney Webb. Its scholarly ideas on social engineering and political strategy eventually became the action program of the British Labor Party. But the Fabian's great influence on the thought and letters of its time was the work, the genius, the propaganda of George Bernard Shaw.

True, G.B.S. hardly added a new thought to Fabianism. That was the job of the Webbs. Shaw advocated the cause for much the same reason that he advocated the causes of the French Impressionists, Richard Wagner, and Henrik Ibsen. These causes seemed to him real and rational. His ideal, as he put it, was "the sense of fact." In an unromantic, and even antiromantic, way he strove to help Life in its struggle upward. Only an unsentimental view of reality could satisfy his social conscience. In the wake of Baudelaire, Zola,

The first clash between London's impoverished East End and prosperous West End occurred on February 8, 1886. Demonstrators on St. James's Street (above) and rioters looting a wineshop (below), as depicted in the London Illustrated News. *(Olin Library, Cornell University)*

Sidney and Beatrice Webb at home on Grosvenor Road. (Olin Library, Cornell University)

Young Fabians, painted by Bertha Newcombe in 1897. From left to right: George Bernard Shaw, Beatrice Webb, Sidney Webb, and Graham Wallace. (From The Sketch, *Olin Library, Cornell University)*

and Anatole France, socially aware realism became yet another literary genre in *fin de siècle* England.

Another entirely new literary inspiration was science and technology. Discovery of new and mysterious lores and cultures, in the science laboratories as well as the jungles and mountains of distant continents, fired the imagination of poets and writers. Robert Louis Stevenson published *New Arabian Nights* (1882) and *Treasure Island* (1883) and one might argue that his *The Strange Case of Dr. Jekyll and Mr. Hyde* (1886) is a form of science fiction. Sir Richard Francis Burton, an adventurer, explorer, and Arab linguist, enriched world literature with his translation of *Arabian Nights* (1885–88). Scientific reasoning surely served Sir Arthur Conan Doyle to help his famous creation Sherlock Holmes to his relentlessly elementary solutions.

The leading prophetic novelist of the new age of science and technology, however, was H. G. (Herbert George) Wells. His *The Time Machine* appeared in 1895, the year Sigmund Freud, with his associate Josef Breuer, published his first, seminal work, *Studies in Hysteria.* In 1898, the year Wells's *The War of the Worlds* came out, the first dirigible, *Graf Zeppelin,* flew over Germany and the invention of phosphorus sesquisulfide made the manufacture of safety matches possible.

A profound change in the literature of the time, however, was the emerging new attitude toward the city. During the 1890s, in the words of Holbrook Jackson, "art threw a glamour over the town, and all the artificial things conjured up by that word. Poets, it is true, did not abandon the pastoral mood, but they added to it an enthusiasm for what was urban. Where, in the past, they found romance only in wild and remote places, among what are called natural things, they now found romance in streets and theatres, in taverns and restaurants, in bricks and mortar and the creations of artificers. Poets no longer sought inspiration in solitude, they invoked the Muses in Fleet Street and the Strand."[12]

"The future belongs to the dandy. It is the exquisites who are going to rule," said Oscar Wilde. And the awakening interest in urban things found expression in Richard Le Gallienne's

> *Ah, London! London! our delight,*
> *Great flower that opens but at night,*
> *Great City of the Midnight Sun,*
> *Whose day begins when day is done.*
>
> *Lamp after lamp against the sky*
> *Opens a sudden beaming eye,*
> *Leaping alight on either hand,*
> *The iron lilies of the Strand.* [13]

Not that the wonder of London was in any sense new. What was new was the adoration of the artificial, a certain delight in urban bustle and even wickedness.

Painters shared the enthusiasm of the writers. Whistler taught the modern world how to appreciate the beauty of the city not only in pictures but also in magical words: "And when the evening mist clothes the riverside with poetry, as with a veil, and the poor buildings lose themselves in the dim sky, and the tall chimneys become campanili, and the warehouses are palaces in the night, and the whole city hangs in the heavens, and fairy-land is before us . . ."[14] Oscar Wilde nimbly interpreted this to mean that art really reveals to us Nature's lack of design and that "all bad art comes from returning to Life and Nature." With Aubrey Beardsley cheering Wilde on, the discussion quickly turned into a Pagan revolt against Nature and led to Wilde's dictum that "The first duty in life is to be as artificial as possible."

Most literary encounters in Wilde's London were carefully arranged as events. Thus Arthur Conan Doyle, invited to dinner one evening in 1889 by the American publisher J. M. Stoddard, was pleasantly surprised to find himself in the company of Oscar Wilde. It became "a golden evening" for Doyle when it turned out that Wilde was enthusiastic about Doyle's latest novel, *Micah Clarke.* The result of the evening was that both Doyle and Wilde promised to write books for *Lippincott's Magazine.* Doyle contributed *The Sign of the Four,* in which Sherlock Holmes made his second appearance. Wilde sent *The Picture of Dorian Gray.*

Charles Whibley fired the most outrageous shot against Wilde's novel from the anonymous safety of the *Scots* (later the *National) Observer,* which was at the time edited by Wilde's anti-Aesthetic protagonist William Ernest Henley:

"Why go grubbing in muck heaps? The world is fair, and the proportion of healthy-minded men and honest women to those that are foul, fallen, or unnatural is great. Mr. Oscar Wilde has again been writing stuff that were better unwritten; and while *The Picture of Dorian Gray . . .* is ingenious, interesting, full of cleverness, and plainly the work of a man of letters, it is false art—or its interest is medico-legal; it is false to human nature—for its hero is a devil; it is false to morality—for it is not made sufficiently clear that the writer does not prefer a course of unnatural iniquity to a life of cleanliness, health, and sanity. The story—which deals with matters only fitted for the Criminal Investigation Department or a hearing *in camera*—is discreditable alike to author and editor."[15]

Whibley's attack on Wilde's novel prefigured much of the condemnation of the author and his work during the trial and Wilde's conviction for "acts of gross indecency" in 1895.

The dinner party which led to the publication of Wilde's novel was not the only form of literary encounters in Wilde's London. One attempt to revive the eighteenth-century literary tavern was the Rhymers' Club, which gathered at the Cheshire Cheese in the Strand. Members read their poems to one another and discussed the great business of poetry and life. A dozen or so writers belonged. Oscar Wilde came only when the group met in a private

Magazine seller at Ludgate Circus. Photograph by Paul Martin. Reading journals, novels, or pamphlets became a sign of middle-class respectability. (Victoria and Albert Museum)

house. The readings were given in alphabetical order. They would typically begin with Ernest Dowson and end with W. B. Yeats. Dowson might recite his poem to Cynara, the young daughter of a Polish immigrant over whom Dowson mooned, and with whom he played cards every evening in her father's restaurant, until she married an Italian waiter.

There was also literary discussion in what Henry James called "the rumble of the tremendous human mill."[16] "Art lives on discussion," James said, "upon experiment, upon curiosity, upon variety of attempt, upon exchange of views, and the comparisons of standpoints; and there is a presumption that the times when no one has anything particular to say about it, and has no reason to give for practice of preference, though they may be times of honour, are not times of development—are times, possibly, even, a little of dullness."

And yet beyond all the quibbling and the quoting, books mattered. And to Wilde, who knew this—and who knew better than anybody that the serious and the trivial were sides of the same hard coin—the issues which surrounded or inspired books also mattered, in a way that went beyond manners and morals.

In 1900, wrote Yeats, ". . . everybody got down off his stilts; henceforth nobody drank absinthe with his black coffee; nobody went mad; nobody committed suicide; nobody joined the Catholic church; or if they did, I have forgotten."[17] Also in 1900, Henry James shaved off his beard and moustache. Released from Reading Gaol, Wilde, taking the name Sebastian Melmoth after a character in a Gothic novel, died in Paris in 1900.

London—and literature—have never been quite the same since.

5

LONDON'S GROWTH

London not only had soul; it also had a mind of its own.

Eluding dreamers and planners, good intentions and bad, the city kept growing and growing. By 1884, when Oscar Wilde moved into his Tite Street house not far from the just completed Chelsea Embankment, London had grown higgledy-piggledy into a vast and diverse, often inspired, often dismaying jumble of some three hundred independent neighborhoods, villages, and little towns.

This urban hodgepodge clustered around two original centers—Westminster, the center of power, and the square-mile City, the center of money. The total population was nearly five million people. They had no central metropolitan government. Officially, London did not even have a name. It legally became London only when the first London County Council was elected in 1889.

Henry James, who arrived at about the same time as Oscar Wilde, found the city "not a pleasant place . . . agreeable, or cheerful, or easy, or exempt from reproach." He found it "only magnificent . . . the biggest aggregation of human life, the most complete compendium in the world."

In Oscar Wilde's "Lord Arthur Savile's Crime" (1891), Lord Arthur observes the white-smocked carters at Covent Garden at dusk and wonders what a strange London they saw: "A London free from the sin of night and smoke of day, a pallid, ghost-like city, a desolate town of tombs! He wondered what they thought of it, and whether they knew anything of its splendour and its shame, of its fierce, fiery-coloured joys and its horrible hunger, of all its makes and mars from morn to eve."[1]

It was a turbulent time. The machine age was moving in on the lives of

The Thames, 1901. The river was London's "silent highway" and lifeline, bringing in raw materials and shipping out finished goods to the new empire. Rapidly growing along the Thames were London's manufacturing industry and slums. (Kodak Museum)

Bargeworkers on the Thames lived little better than their counterparts in the factories. Work was unsteady and wages often below the minimum needed for survival. Photograph by J. W. Thompson. (Olin Library, Cornell University)

lords and paupers alike, taking over, moving, churning, and changing the city and its people, changing everything unceasingly like the picture in a revolving kaleidoscope.

The railways were laying their network all over the city, burrowing tunnels under the streets, building ostentatious stations, creating new suburbs. Crowded steamboats turned the Thames into a commuter highway. Ever more bridges, tunnels, and thoroughfares were constructed, only to be instantly congested with ever more horse-drawn omnibuses, tramways, and other traffic.

In the West End, the fashionable residential and shopping area between Temple Bar and Kensington, office buildings, department stores, and twelve-story, five-hundred-room "monster" hotels, as they were then called, were jumping the skyline. In the East End, which included the port and London's working-class districts, ever more docks, warehouses, factories, sweatshops, and immigrants from all over the world kept increasing the bustle, the crowding, and the squalor.

With a flick of a switch entire buildings and even streets could be lighted. Electric trains began to move through the tunnels without asphyxiating smoke. People read their newspaper at breakfast to learn what had happened in Hong Kong or Brighton as they went to bed the night before.

One price Londoners had to pay for progress was traffic congestion. "One fall of snow, a single fog," complained the *Star* in 1888, "reduces London to chaos."

"A monstrous nuisance to everybody," another newspaper called it, predicting, as editorials on traffic congestions inevitably predict to this day, that the city would choke to death unless immediate, drastic measures were taken. Just as today, the measures, when finally taken, only made matters worse.

The biggest problem was—and remains—the city's medieval street pattern. But there rarely was—and mercifully still isn't—much inclination toward drastic urban renewal. If London muddles through, it muddles through mostly by intent.

There were exceptions. After the Great Fire of 1666, Christopher Wren drew up a grand plan to rebuild London in the image of the Rome of Pope Sixtus V. Nothing much came of it. On the Continent, authoritarian popes, tsars, or sun kings could arbitrarily slice straight avenues lined with monumental splendor through slums and beloved old neighborhoods alike. London was too independent, or at least too divided between the royalty at Westminster and the merchants in the City, to consider seriously any such thing.

After Waterloo, people, including royalty, compared London with Paris and wondered whether the victors of the Napoleonic Wars should not look as imposing as the vanquished. They argued that Paris was everything London ought to be, but wasn't. Ambitious plans were drawn up but left only

Train entering the station at Kingsbury-Neasden, to the north of London, where the Metropolitan Railroad yards were located. (Kodak Museum)

hints of their envisioned grandeur—Buckingham Palace was one. Others were new bridges, New Oxford Street, Victoria Street, Regent Street, and Trafalgar Square.

Regent Street was never quite completed. The Regent, who later became George IV, had asked his favorite architect, John Nash, in 1813, to improve the area in front of his residence, Carlton House. What he had in mind was slum clearance and the sort of architectural pomposity that would have pleased Louis XIV. What he got, London having a mind of its own, was something both more modest and more useful: the essential, much rebuilt, south-north traffic artery of the West End.

Trafalgar Square, which honors Admiral Nelson with a vast flotilla of pigeons, managed to achieve both some modest splendor and traffic improvements at the intersection of several vital thoroughfares, notably Pall Mall and Whitehall.

Maiden trip of the London Underground Metropolitan line in 1863. At the beginning and end of factory hours, special "workers' trains" were run at reduced fares. They were subsidized by the government to encourage low-income families to move out of the slums into the new suburbs. (London Transport Executive)

The London Underground railway kept expanding. Parts were tunneled, parts were constructed by the "cut and fill" method, in which the trench was dug, then covered. (London Transport Executive)

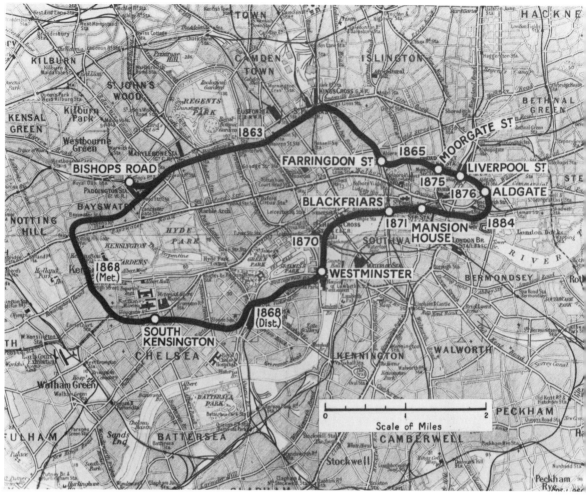

Metropolitan Line of the London Underground, built 1863 to 1884. (London Transport Executive)

In Oscar Wilde's time, the growing traffic problem caused some London planners once more to look enviously at Paris where Baron Haussmann was building his grand boulevards. But London's attempts to combine urban grandeur and traffic relief were made reluctantly and usually ended in failture. *The Architect,* a professional monthly, thought boulevards *à la* Haussmann morally unsuitable for the English. "If in London we possessed such agreeable roads," the journal said, "we might have a vast number of *flaneurs* among us . . . An immense amount of dawdling and frittering away of life must be put down to the broad ways of Continental cities."

The most conspicuous traffic jam then and now was along that "indirect, tortuous, obstructed and narrow lane," the Strand, which linked the City with Westminster.[2] The Board of Works' solution was the Thames Embankment which the *Building News* rightly called "a splendid thoroughfare, reared on foundations of Roman solidity."[3] But neither splendor nor Roman solidity did the job. Then and now heavy traffic agonizes up and down the

"Regent Street Quadrant at Night" painted by Francis L. M. Forster, 1897. London, having a mind of its own, never completed architect John Nash's vision of grandiose Regent Street, but made it the handsome and essential traffic artery between the south and north West End. (London Museum)

Strand, while the Embankment is a lovely place for a solitary walk, all but undisturbed by rushing vehicles.

Until the horseless carriage began to take over early in the twentieth century, all surface transportation within the city was horse-drawn. The advent of railroads, oddly enough, only increased the use of horses. Without carriages, wagons, carts, coaches, broughams, phaetons, hansoms, four-wheelers, buses, and trams, thousands of passengers could never get to their trains or would have been stranded at the station on arrival.

Horses lent rural airs to the city. Water troughs abounded and London's Haymarket actually smelled of hay. Behind most rows of well-to-do houses were rather rustic back alleys, or mews, where the horses, their hay and oats, and vehicles were stabled and where the coachmen and some other servants lived.

In quite a few instances, mews that had fallen into disrepair were promptly invaded by squatters and turned into "rookeries," small, wretched slum islands in placid ponds of affluent respectability. The invaders were laborers, chimney sweeps, tripe sellers, diesinkers, and the like, who serviced the wealthy but were excluded from their neighborhoods. The squatters merely wanted to live closer to their work, trading slightly more miserable living conditions for hours of walking. A two- or three-mile walk to work was quite usual for London workers at the time.

Four-wheelers, which one summoned by whistling once, and the more expensive hansom cabs, for which one whistled twice, "were adorable, with the spanking horse trotting along in front," Lady Charlotte Bonham Carter confided to her diary. "They always had a bell.

"But with all the horse traffic," Lady Charlotte continued, "there was an awful amount of dirt on the streets, some were in dreadful state. There were crossing sweepers, rather oldish men, and if one gave them a coin they would be very pleased to sweep a path across the street in front of one. I remember once I was going to lunch with an officer from the brigade of Guards, and I had to cross at the bottom of St. James's where the King's Guard was, and there wasn't a crossing sweeper. It began to pour with rain, so I rushed across the street, arriving in St. James's Palace looking simply frightful, my lovely white suede shoes utterly ruined for the time being."[4]

The mess on the streets was matched by the grubbiness of the air. There was good cause why Londoners talked about the weather so much. It was hard to ignore. London's climate can be naturally nasty. It became considerably nastier a century ago with the smell of open sewers (of which the Thames was the biggest), the smoke from all those homey hearths, and the sulfurous soot of progress.

Some made the best of it. Henry James thought that "the smoke and the fog and the weather in general, the strangely undefined hour of the day and season of the year, the emanations of industries and the reflection of furnaces, the red gleams and blurs that may or may not be of sunset . . . form the undertone of the deep, perpetual voice of the place."[5]

H. G. Wells found romance in the damp and drizzle and thick fogs. In *Love and Mr. Lewisham* (1899), he wrote: "Grand indeed were these fogs, things to rejoice at mightily . . . it was no longer a thing for public scorn when two young people hurried along arm in arm, and one could do a thousand impudent, significant things with varying pressure and the fondling of a little hand (a hand in a greatly mended glove of cheap kid). Then indeed one seemed to be nearer that elusive something that threaded it all together. And the dangers of the street corners, the horses looming up suddenly out of the dark, the carters with lanterns at their horses' heads, the street lamps, blurred, smoky orange at one's nearest, and vanishing at twenty yards into dim haze, seemed to accentuate the infinite need of protection on the part of a delicate young lady who had already traversed three winters of fogs, thornily alone. Moreover, one could come right down the quiet street where she lived . . . with a delightful sense of enterprise."[6]

The street where she lived might have been in Lisson, Grove, Hoxton, or Earl's Court or any other of many dozens of London neighborhoods, so

---

Opposite, horse-drawn buses provided the predominant means of public transportation because their network was much denser than that of the Underground. Buses traveled even such elegant residential streets as Park Lane (center). And as G. W. Joy's painting of "The Bayswater Omnibus" (below) shows, they were frequented by elegant women and gentlemen of the middle class as much as by blue-collar workers. (London Transport Executive, Guildhall Library, London Museum)

Traffic congestion became a never-ending problem in London's medieval street system. The problem was aggravated (right, below) when a carriage turned over, as happened all too often. (Kodak Museum, Victoria and Albert Museum)

"A London Cabstand," painted by J. C. Dollman, 1888. Despite or, rather, because of London's growing and efficient Underground transit system the number of horse-drawn vehicles increased toward the end of the century. They were needed to take passengers to the train station. (London Museum)

distinct in their character and makeup that they even had their own dialects. George Bernard Shaw amusingly illustrates this in *Pygmalion* (1912).

The scene is at Covent Garden at 11:15 P.M. A small, chatty crowd, including the Flower Girl Liza, has found shelter from a torrent of summer rain under the portico of St. Paul's Church. Everyone is gloomily peering out at the rain, except one man with his back turned to the rest, who seems wholly preoccupied with a notebook in which he is writing busily.

> *The Note Taker* [Professor Higgins]: And how are all your people down at Selsey?
>
> *The Bystander: (Suspiciously)* Who told you my people come from Selsey?
>
> *The Note Taker:* Never you mind. They did. *(To the girl)* How do you come to be up so far east? You were born in Lisson Grove.
>
> *The Flower Girl* [Liza]: *(Appalled)* Oh, what harm is there in my leaving Lisson Grove? It wasn't fit for a pig to live in; and I had to pay four-and-six a week. *(In tears)* Oh, boo—hoo—oo—
>
> *The Note Taker:* Live where you like; but stop that noise . . .
>
> *The Flower Girl: (Subsiding into a brooding melancholy over her basket, and talking very low-spiritedly to herself)* I'm a good girl, I am.
>
> *The Sarcastic Bystander: (Not attending to her)* Do you know where *I* come from?
>
> *The Note Taker: (Promptly)* Hoxton . . .
>
> *The Flower Girl:* Poor girl! Hard enough for her to live without being worrited and chivied.
>
> *The Gentleman:* How do you do it, if I may ask?
>
> *The Note Taker:* Simply phonetics. The science of speech. That's my profession; also my hobby. Happy is the man who can make a living by his hobby! You can spot an Irishman or a Yorkshireman by his brogue. *I* can place any man within six miles. I can place him within two miles in London. Sometimes within two streets.
>
> *The Flower Girl:* Ought to be ashamed of himself, unmanly coward![7]

Horse pollution combined with unpaved roads made street crossing a risky undertaking, particularly for ladies with long skirts and gentlemen with white spats, dressed up for a date. The solution was "crossing-sweepers" of all ages. For a small tip they would clear a path through the smelly muck. (Kodak Museum, London Museum)

Water troughs for horses and humans were all over London. But an adequate supply of drinking water for the growing city was a problem since the Middle Ages. By the end of the nineteenth century, various private and semi-private water companies amalgamated into a single provider of relatively safe water. (Kodak Museum)

If London made no big plans, it often made charming little plans. Many of the "better" center city neighborhoods—the kind that Professor Higgins would have diagnosed as speaking "Cheltenham, Harrow, Cambridge, and India"—are the result.

Early in the sixteenth century, King Henry VII commanded that most of the land on which London was built must be kept in large leasehold estates rather than be divided into small freehold parcels as in other cities. The large leaseholds were owned by either religious institutions, notably the Abbey of Westminster and the London Charterhouse, or the aristocracy, such as the Earl of Bedford, the Duke of Westminster, the Marquess of Northampton, Sir Thomas Grosvenor, the Duke of Norfolk, Lord Southampton, and Lord Portman.

Freeholds, like most city properties elsewhere, were usually bought and sold by speculative builders who might be businessmen, sailors, or chandler's shopkeepers seeking to get rich quick. Their objective, their only objective in leasing freehold land, was to build on it as cheaply as possible, sell it for as much as they could get, take their profit, and be done with it. Friedrich Engels and other social reformers claimed that these jerry-built houses were nicely calculated to last exactly the term of the lease and no longer.

The leasehold estates, on the other hand, were considered permanent family assets whose value must not only be carefully protected but also, if possible, increased. Fortunately, seven times more London houses were built on leasehold estates than on freehold parcels, according to an 1887 estimate.

Leaseholders had absolute power to do with their estates as they wished. Rather than selling them off parcel by parcel to heaven knows whom and what end, most of them followed the precedent established by the Earl of Bedford in the 1630s. Bedford decided to keep control by developing his entire estate, which became Covent Garden and its surrounding area, in accordance with a pleasing plan, drawn up for him by England's greatest architect, Inigo Jones.

The *pièce de résistance* of Bedford's Covent Garden was a piazza framed on two sides by terraces or row houses, on the south by the gardens of Bedford House, and on the west by St. Paul's Church. After some years, among other changes that were part of cultivating the development, permission was obtained to admit vegetable vendors and Inigo Jones's noble piazza rang with street cries and was littered with cabbage leaves. Today's market halls were built in the 1830s—but not before the piazza had become the prototype for the London Square.

The London Square at its best, along with the Royal Crescent at Bath, is the crowning achievement of Classic Georgian architecture, the architecture of gentility. After Covent Garden, London's aristocratic real estate developers discovered that looking out on a bit of nature is the most pleasant way to live in the city. The centerpiece of all London estate developments, therefore, is a square, or sometimes a circle, planted with a park or garden and

"Cabman and Policeman," sketched by Charles Keene, shows both helping inebriated gentlemen home from a night on the town. (The Tate Gallery)

lined with houses. The houses may be freestanding "villas," but are more often row houses, as basically uniform as the proverbial peas in the pod (which, unlike peas in a tin can, do show minor variations). The park or garden is usually enclosed with a handsome wrought-iron fence, and in Queen Victoria's days only the residents and their nannies had keys.

In fact, the entire estate development, the entire small town within the city, was originally quite exclusive. Most of them had gates which were closed to all traffic from 11 P.M. to 7 A.M. to protect the sleep of the residents.

The effect of this exclusivity was that, in contrast with other cities, the rich remained in central London or maintained residences there for use during the Season, while working people were driven out to the suburbs to live. The railroads accelerated this trend by making it possible for professionals, business people, and blue-collar workers to live in semi-rural suburbia and commute to their jobs in town.

London's great parks were even more desirable to live along than the squares. The houses were generally narrow but deep because street frontage was expensive. Architects did not much like these narrow city houses. Robert Kerr, professor of construction at Kings College, told a meeting of the Royal Institute of British Architects in 1894: "Height becomes the substitute for breadth . . . one has to be continually running up and down stairs; the very light of heaven becomes a scarcity; fresh air is an unattainable luxury; and even how to escape from over a fiery furnace is brought only too plainly within the range of practical consideration."[8]

In this house lived not only the family, but the servants as well. A

Opposite, London's police, nicknamed "bobbies" or "peelers," were a commanding presence on the streets. Their high-domed helmets gave citizens a sense of safety. (Kodak Museum)

There was always life on the street, the place where all classes mingled. Some people offered services, like shoeshines. Some offered wares, like lemonade. Some used the street to shop or go from here to there. And some just wanted to be there. (Kodak Museum, Victoria and Albert Museum)

moderately wealthy family might employ two dozen servants, London's largest source of employment. The women on the staff included a housekeeper, lady's maid, nurse, two housemaids, laundry maid, kitchen maid, and scullion. The men included the butler, a valet, house steward, coachman, three grooms, two footmen, gardeners, and possibly a handyman.

The two footmen were needed for more than to escort "a plate of muffins upstairs," as someone alleged. They would also often accompany the lady of the house at her afternoon ritual of calling on friends and potential in-laws and they might be in attendance to daughters at balls and garden parties. Tall ones were preferred. While a footman of average height, according to Charles Booth, made only twenty to twenty-two pounds a year, one over six feet tall could command as much as forty.

Most servants, particularly young women, were recruited in the country, country girls being considered more diligent and honest. They were frequently subject to sexual harassment. If the poor girl was found pregnant, she was instantly dismissed. Dismissal without "a character," as letters of recommendation were called, led many of these girls into prostitution. As many as half of the thousands of prostitutes who plied their trade in the back streets east and south of the City, most visibly on Haymarket, were former domestic servants.

The vast number of prostitutes in all price ranges was, to some measure, also due to the Season. It traditionally begins early in April and ends in August, the period when Parliament is normally in session. It would lure the nobility out of its country houses and attract nearly everybody who is anybody in the Empire to a whirl of balls and other festivities. The main stage set was the West End with its exclusive squares and expansive houses. But it also branched out to state balls, Royal Academy exhibitions, the opera and, of course, Ascot and the Derby.

The London Season served primarily to provide the daughters of the English aristocracy, in their isolated country houses, an opportunity to get out and meet eligible young men. In Oscar Wilde's London, the Season took on a further dimension. It provided the social link between the old landed gentry and the new industrial wealth. In the words of Gavin Weightman and Steve Humphries, the stakes in the upper-class marriage market were often as high as in the money market in the City. Bankers, businessmen, and merchants, eager for an opportunity to mix with and marry into families with some sort of aristocratic pedigree, might spend thousands of pounds to participate in the events of the Season.[9]

Lady Charlotte Bonham Carter, whom we met crossing a street earlier in this chapter, recalled: "In the Season, *The Times* had an enormous list of dances each night, and I'd be invited to one more or less every night. Parents were very particular about the young men their daughters knew, and in your first year in Society you were chaperoned all the time. The mothers sat in elegant gold chairs all round the ballroom floor, whilst the daughters

London's parks, originally hunting grounds of the nobility, became "the lungs of the city." They were (and are) extensively used by young and old, rich and poor, for all manner of recreation. (Kodak Museum)

Covent Garden Market. Originally a select residential quarter designed by Inigo Jones for the Fourth Earl of Bedford, the present market was established in 1661. Here is where Bernard Shaw's Professor Henry Higgins first met Eliza Doolittle. (Guildhall Library)

Covent Garden Market vegetable vendor stands on a box, thus avoiding cold and wet feet. (Kodak Museum)

danced with their young men friends. Parents were very careful because they hoped that their daughters might meet a suitable marriage partner at one of these events. We would meet lots of eligible young men, a few were in the army and navy—they were always awfully nice—some from the diplomatic world, landowners, and City businessmen, young men from the City, there were masses of them, they were almost the only people one saw."[10]

Young, rich American women who came to London to "come out" and, perhaps, also to find a penurious noble husband, were ubiquitous in the more fashionable sections of London. "There is something fascinating in their funny, exaggerated gestures and their petulant way of tossing the head," remarked Oscar Wilde. "Their eyes have no magic nor mystery in them, but they challenge us for combat; and when we engage we are always worsted. Their lips seem made for laughter and yet they never grimace. As for their voices, they soon get them into tune. Some of them have been known to acquire a fashionable drawl in two seasons; and after they have been presented to Royalty they all roll their R's as vigorously as a young equerry or an old lady-in-waiting. Still, they never really lose their accent; it keeps peeping out here and there and when they chatter together they are like a bevy of peacocks. Nothing is more amusing than to watch two American girls greet each other in a drawing room or in the Row. They are like children with their shrill staccato cries of wonder, their odd little exclamations. Their conversation sounds like a series of exploding crackers; they are exquisitely incoherent and use a sort of primitive, emotional language. After five minutes they are left beautifully breathless and look at each other half in amusement and half in affection."[11]

The Season, which struggled on until the 1950s and has now been replaced by London's tourist season, caused peculiar economic hardships. At the end of the nineteenth century, a great deal of "new money" was added to the traditional spending spree of the landed gentry. The millions of pounds spent in just three or four months on food, fashion, and entertainment created an army of almost a million seasonal workers, largely without the skills or opportunity to find work during the remaining eight months of the year. They were predominantly servants for all those parties and seamstresses for all those ball gowns.

Gavin Weightman and Steve Humphries in their *The Making of Modern London, 1815–1914* estimate that during the Season the West End fashion houses employed around twenty thousand women, mostly younger girls who had more nimble fingers than the women over thirty. Their workday had between twelve to fourteen hours and might run to seventeen hours when there were urgent orders for a ball at Court. The wages were minimal and the girls could be fired at a moment's notice when the Season was over.

"We didn't like to hear the girls singing in the streets," recalled May Pawsey, who worked in one of the fashion houses. "They used to sing

"Cheer ap, Keptin, n'baw ya flabr orf a pore gel!" Flower girls, like Eliza Doolittle, were ubiquitous, particularly in front of theaters and restaurants. (Kodak Museum)

'who'll buy my blooming lavender, sixteen branches for a penny.' We hated it because we knew that it was the end of the Season and that we would get short time."[12]

Some girls found work in the East End sweatshops and factories. Some just starved, "eating air pie," they called it. Some drifted to Haymarket.

Although the West End was increasingly surrounded by colonies of the working-class people who serviced it—from lamplighters to laundresses and shop assistants to sweepers—the development and redevelopment of the West End leasehold estates continued until the end of the century. But only a few of the old Georgian Squares and neighborhoods managed to hold on to their "quiet air and aristocratic appearance." The calm Georgian gentility increasingly yielded to the bustling and booming business of "the mother city of the British Commonwealth of Nations."

The Colonial Office, the Admiralty, the War Office, the Ministry of Education, and dozens of other bureaucracies built monumental new offices around Whitehall. Private companies established themselves in the most prestigious West End neighborhoods, such as Belgravia and Mayfair. By 1900, the number of civil servants employed in London reached one hundred and sixty thousand, to say nothing of the rapidly proliferating number of employees of the growing international trading firms, banks, and insurance companies, and the armies of solicitors, businessmen, merchants, and all kinds of other professionals. They all invaded the West End.

All middle-class families had servants. Moderately wealthy ones had as many as two dozen, including tall footmen to "escort a plate of muffins upstairs." Servants were generally underpaid and overworked. (Kodak Museum)

Row houses at Plumstead, Purrett Road, 1890s. London's suburbs provided workers and civil servants with space and comforts they could not afford in the center city. But for a pub at the corner, there were few public amenities. (Borough of Greenwich)

"Koko" promotion riding high through the streets. As consumers took over society, so did advertising. "High and low, on every available yard of wall, advertising clamoured to the eye . . . (selling) all the produce and refuse of civilization," commented novelist George Gissing. (Kodak Museum)

Some moved into new middle-income houses and flats, or apartment blocks, which began to blend in with the select districts. Most lived in the suburbs, but crowded the West End in the evenings or on Saturday afternoons to spend their money and leisure. There was nothing in the suburbs for the expenditure of either. The wealth of the Commonwealth, at the height of its power, gave them the money. The passage of the Bank Holiday Act in 1871 and the gradual introduction of Saturday half holidays thereafter gave them the leisure.

These middle-class consumers took over society. Offices, shops, department stores, museums, opera, concert halls, music halls, restaurants, and hotels took over the center city. So did advertising. "High and low, on every available yard of wall, advertisements clamoured to the eye: theatres, journals, soaps, medicines, concerts, furniture, wines, prayer meetings—all the

"Farmer Bates Cash Butcher," c. 1880. Merchandising changed radically, with tiled and sanitary butcher stores, elegant window displays, chain stores, and huge department stores offering just about everything a customer could hope for. (Kodak Museum)

produce and refuse of civilization commenced in staring letters, in daubed effigies, base, paltry, grotesque," complained novelist George Gissing.[13]

For the rising middle class, shopping became a form of entertainment. Fancy storefronts with artful window displays began to line the Strand, Oxford Street, and Regent Street. Stores stayed open until eight and even ten in the evening. This meant that store clerks worked as much as eighty hours a week, but customers enjoyed shopping by gaslight, and shop owners profited.

The new machine-manufactured, packaged, and trademarked goods were not merely sold; they were merchandised in chain stores. The Maypole Dairies, for instance, featured marble walls and counters to give their products a reassuring sanitary look. One of the earliest chains was Liptons, which combined tea shop and tearoom. Among the most popular West End attrac-

Private room in the Fleece Hotel Restaurant, with the table set for an opulent meal. "Monster" hotels and restaurants became fashionable in the 1880s, outdoing each other with ever more fancy decor. (Kodak Museum)

tions were the big department stores.

The biggest were Harrods on Knightsbridge and Whiteley's in West-bourne Grove. Whiteley's started as a drapery and clothing store in the 1860s. By the time Oscar Wilde shopped there, it had expanded to a full-fledged department store, offering just about everything anybody could hope to get out of life short of love, from perfume to pianos. It featured a retiring room for ladies, a theater ticket agency, a banking department, a refreshment room, and a dry cleaning establishment.

Smart businessmen quickly recognized that what the office workers with their steadily rising income wanted most was a taste of luxurious upper-class life at prices they could afford. One response was the "monster" restaurant and hotels.

The railroad station restaurants, according to one contemporary observer, first discovered "that dirt and discomfort were not absolutely indispensable to economy" and began to feed hungry travelers in comfortable saloons. In time restaurants featured more and more fancy decor, ranging from "fancy French," with lots of gilding, mirrors, and wreathed, bosomy caryatids, to an anticipation of a one-building Disneyland which included Venetian Gothic rooms, Wagnerian Teutonic halls, and Versailles salons.

Some of these restaurants were huge culinary palaces. The Holborn Restaurant included fifteen private dining rooms. Another, the Criterion Restaurant, at Piccadilly Circus, was "one of the best specimens . . . of architecture of this festive class."[14] According to its architect, it included "dining rooms of various capacity, restaurant, grill room, buffet, smoking room, a grand hall (now used as a table d'hôte, but originally intended for a ball room), lavatories, retiring and cloak rooms, and lastly a theatre . . . The average number of dinners and luncheons is 2,000 [served at one time], and on several occasions the enormous number of 4,500 has been reached."[15]

"Ladies shopping without male escort, and requiring luncheon," advised a guidebook of 1879, "can safely visit any of the great restaurants—care being always taken to avoid passing through a drinking bar."[16] The main business of the great restaurants, however, was family outings. At Holborn's Grill Room, in 1888, father, mother, governess, and four children could dine for fifteen shillings.[17]

"One of the greatest changes in London during the last score or so of years is in the matter of hotels," the tourist guide added, asserting that in this respect London was "still far worse provided" than Continental and American cities.[18] But London was at last beginning to catch up. A decade later, London boasted of hotels such as the Grand, the Victoria, and the Metropole.

The vestibule of the Metropole, the *Building News* gushed at length after the opening in 1885, was decorated in the grandest of manners, with *amorini,* festoons, painted flowers, blue skies, and sundry arabesques, "said to be taken from those in the Gallery of Apollo in the Louvre." There were "panels of Mesharebeyeh woodwork and treated in an Arabic manner." And "the Royal suite of rooms, including the Marie Antoinette chamber, which is an exact copy of the Marie Antoinette boudoir at Fontainebleau, are as chastely elegant as they are costly . . ." All in all, there were about six hundred bedrooms. Each had a small semaphore, or railroad signal, outside its door which raised its arm whenever the visitor touched the electric bell, "thereby saving a great deal of unnecessary labour."[19]

Such were the new luxuries enjoyed by those called "the idlers of the globe," the international steamship set of old and new wealth from all over the Empire.

London's West End was their "pleasure lounge."[20]

6

...AND LONDON'S SHAME

West End and East End were separated more by privilege than distance. The West End was dazzling and ostentatious. The East End was deprived and depraved—although, as the century ended, things began to improve a little.

But early in the 1880s, it seemed that as the West End got richer, the East End got ever more wretched. It was considered "a kind of human dustbin overflowing with the dregs of society."[1] The sun, which never set on the Empire, also never rose in the dark alleys north of the Old Port.

The Old Port docks had given the area its livelihood. They attracted vast numbers of people from all over the world. From the rest of the United Kingdom came "decayed and bankrupt master-butchers, old sailors, Polish refugees, broken-down gentlemen, discharged lawyers' clerks, suspended government clerks, almsmen, pensioners, servants, thieves—indeed, every one who wants a loaf, and is willing to work for it," reported Henry Mayhew, the mid-century social investigator.[2]

From the rest of the world, according to the Baedeker guidebook at the time, came "a large and motley crowd of labourers, to which numerous dusky visages and foreign costumes impart a curious and picturesque air." The Baedeker asserted that London housed more Scotsmen than Aberdeen, more Irishmen than Dublin, more Jews than Palestine, and more Roman Catholics than Rome.[3]

Most of these people were laboring at the docks. The men would be loading and unloading, repairing, supplying, and building ships. The women would be laundering for the sailors and cooking and serving in the pubs and lodging houses.

Fore Street, Lambeth. London suffered worse housing conditions than other English cities. The slums, described by Charles Dickens in the 1840s and '50s, had changed little by the end of the century. (Victoria and Albert Museum)

But with the coming of the railroads, work at the docks, always seasonal and underpaid, began to decline. Trains could move coal and other goods cheaper and faster. Steamship and mechanized cranes began to replace sweat and muscle.

Nor did London, being far from the sources of iron and coal, develop the steam-driven manufacturing industries that kept men working in other cities. It produced luxuries rather than necessities, consumer rather than capital goods, silks rather than woolens. London's industry produced garments, watches, pianos, jewelry, fine furniture, beer, spirits, tobacco, and sugar products. Economically even more important than these goods were

Seven Dials, in the East End, was so dangerous that even bobbies feared for their safety and generally left the area unpatrolled. (Guildhall Library)

London's services: hairdressing, education, tailoring, music, drama, domestic service, prostitution. The East End's primary occupation was serving the West End.

The luxuries were produced in miserably small factories and sweatshops. The notorious "stink industries" made soap, rubber, tar, glue, fertilizer made from blood, and matches. These industries contaminated the water and polluted the air and caused nausea, sore throats, and smarting eyes. Workers were hired by the day; more than three consecutive days of work was forbidden as a health hazard.

Working conditions in the sweatshop were only a little better. Rachel Silver, a seamstress, told Weightman and Humphries: "When I first started out, I worked in houses, part of which would be used as a workshop, and we used to go around Stephney looking into house windows to see if there were any hands wanted. My first job was on trousers, doing the buttoning and the fly, that was in a house with bare walls, bare floorboards, and no fire. It was freezing cold, and in the winter you'd work with all your clothes on and a scarf over your head to keep warm. Went in there at eight in the morning and you'd work right up until eight at night, doing piece work, then take

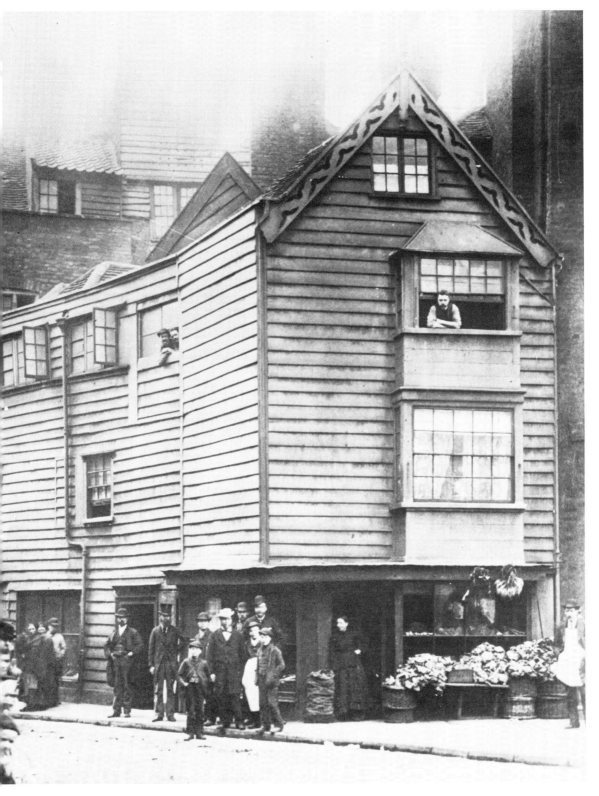

Bartholomew Close, at Smithfield Market, the center of London's meat trade, was a place of illegal traffic in stolen goods and prostitution. (Guildhall Library)

home and keep going for an hour or an hour and a half to make up your money. Sometimes conditions were so bad you'd end up crying. Then after a few weeks you'd get the sack, there was no more work, and you'd go around looking for another job."[4]

The landlords in the East End would subdivide their tenements in ever smaller units so much that often large families were forced to live in one or two rooms, packing as many as four people—children and grownups, male and female—into one bed. Toilets and washing facilities were shared with the rest of the people on the street. Rents were extortionate, a quarter to a half of the family's weekly wage.[5]

In the winter months, fog, rain, and snow often brought the docks and building construction to a complete standstill. This meant serious hunger and often also serious diseases. The full extent of the physical deficiencies became apparent when young East Enders were drafted for service in the Boer War in 1899. The health of a large percentage was so poor that they were rejected.

The deficiencies affected society in many other ways. There was much crime. Garroters and muggers prowled the streets. They would step out of the dark, throw a cord around their victim's neck, and rob them.

The degradations, and above all the overcrowding, of the East End slums led to indiscriminate sexuality, incest, and child abuse. Constantly fighting for their existence and inured to pain and brutality, a shockingly large number of women and even children became night house tarts, courtesans, sailors' whores, dolly-mops (promiscuous servant girls), synthetic virgins (whose hymens were repaired), and catamites (boy prostitutes). Many suffered venereal diseases. (A study at the time found that one fifth of the British Army, including the Brigade of Guards, was infected by venereal diseases. The Navy statistics were even higher.)

London suffered worse working and housing conditions than other British cities, largely because its workers had few, if any, labor unions. This was due in part to the nature of its industries. It is hard to organize domestic servants or seamstresses working in small scattered sweatshops. Recent immigrants, counted among "the lower orders," were too frightened to risk annoying their exploiters, let alone join a protest or, heaven forbid, a labor union.

The East End became ever more crowded. Along with the victims of slum clearance in other parts of London, immigrants kept arriving in a steady stream. Many were Jews from Eastern Europe, where conditions were often worse. The added competition for a limited number of jobs and housing often aroused anti-Semitic feelings, expressed in minor riots against Jews whenever things went wrong—when there were trade slumps, for instance, or at the time of the Jack the Ripper murders (the Ripper was popularly

---

Opposite, Petticoat Lane, in the East End, was and remains the center of commercial life in Whitechapel. This picture was used by Dr. Thomas Barnardo's Home for Working and Destitute Lads, one of the major child rescue organizations in Oscar Wilde's London, to document the horrors of poverty. (Barnardo Photo Library)

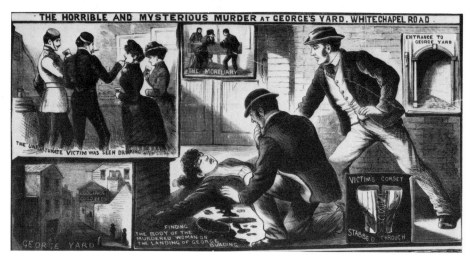

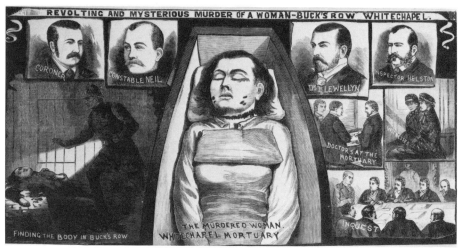

(*The British Library*)

presumed to be a Jew), or when, at the turn of the century, there was unrest because immigration was restricted.

The Jack the Ripper murders, more than anything else, perhaps, brought the plight of the East End slum dwellers to the rest of London.

The Jack, who signed himself "the Ripper" in his mocking notes to the police, committed a series of five gruesome murders. He was never caught. All the gory details of the horrors were, of course, fully reported and imaginatively illustrated in such newspapers as *The Illustrated Police News* from which the drawings here are reproduced.

The first of the murders (later understood not to be of the series) was that of a prostitute, Martha Tarbram, whose lacerated body was found in the East End on August 7, 1888. Unlike the rest of the murders, her body,

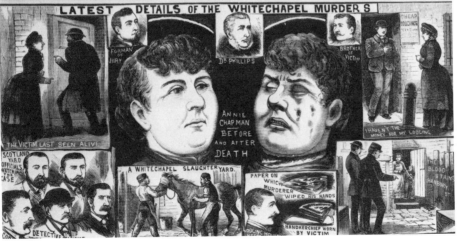

(The British Library)

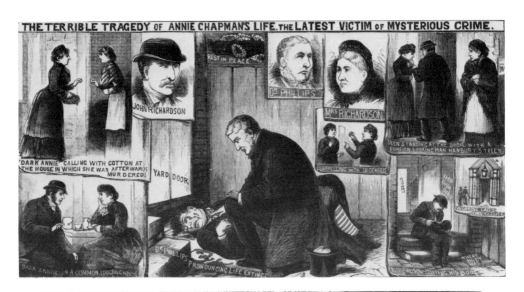

(The British Library)

(The British Library)

although stabbed, was spared mutilation. When twenty-one days later, Mary Ann Nicholls, also a prostitute, was found slashed and eviscerated in Buck's Row, Whitechapel, the Jack the Ripper serial officially began. The serial pattern was confirmed on September 8, when the slashed body of Annie Chapman was found in back of Dr. Thomas Barnardo's children's asylum in Hanbury Street. Miss Chapman's womb was removed from her body "by an expert."[6]

In the night of September 30, Jack struck twice, killing Catherine Eddowes in Mitre Square and Elizabeth Stride in Berner Street. It was over a month until Jack struck again. The bloody remains of the last victim, Mary Jane Kelly, were discovered in Miller's Court, Dorset Street, on November 9, 1888. All of London was in a panic, even though the murders were clearly limited to the most desolate whores in the most poverty-stricken area of the city. But in a way the horror also provided relief. The fear of sexually motivated crime, which pervaded London's middle class, could now be talked

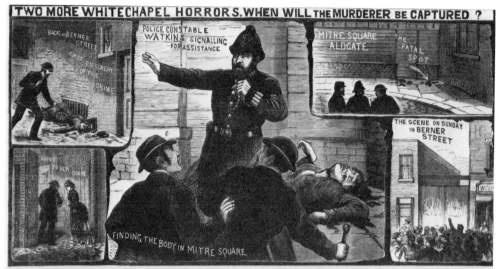

(The British Library)

(The British Library)

about. It happened, after all, not in socially acceptable circles, but in the haunts of the "lower orders."

The murderer was initially depicted as a crude caricature of the Eastern European Jew. As the murders continued and the Ripper eluded arrest, *The Illustrated Police News* depicted him as "degenerate," with a broad nose, lobeless ears, and the workingman's bowler hat. By December 1888, he had become an upper-class fop, with a fur collar, and his butcher tools in a leather bag.

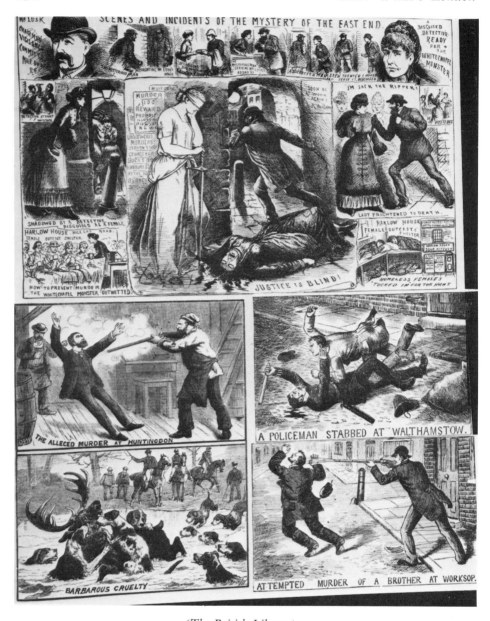

(The British Library)

A year after the first London County Council was installed, London's first electric underground railway line opened between the City and Stockwell. It was nicknamed "the two-penny tube" and within a short seven years had expanded to include three more lines, serving millions of commuters.

London's underground rail system began as the capitalist enterprise of an American, Charles Tyson Yerkes, who has been described as "one of the

(The British Library)

most cynical and unscrupulous of all robber barons of the age." He had also launched and operated public utilities in at least a hundred American cities. Their citizens proved so ungrateful for his manner of serving them that, after several scandals, Yerkes removed himself and his Rembrandt paintings from his Fifth Avenue mansion to seek his profits in London.

Londoners, too, were not altogether charmed by Yerkes's wheeling and dealing. James Whistler led the outcry over the ugly, smoke-belching power station Yerkes placed at the precise bend of the Thames that Turner had made famous. But in the end, Yerkes having died before he could exploit, degrade, and squeeze all profit from his enterprise as he had done elsewhere, Londoners remember him with some gratitude. The London Underground remains exemplary.

To architects the changing cityscape was exhilarating. It had a liberating, indeed a revolutionizing effect on their designs. Much as the twentieth-century Modern style was at first dedicated to the radical overthrow of Victorian eclecticism, so the Victorian style started as a rebellion against the restraints of Georgian Classicism. The great Victorian aesthetes and Gothic revivalists Augustus Welby Northmore Pugin and John Ruskin fulminated against the Bedford Squares and Portland Places. Much of Georgian London, an architecture and ambience we now consider priceless and would, today, lovingly preserve and restore, was deemed hopelessly obsolete and destroyed a century ago.

"This is the age of new creations," is how one architect stated the case.

"Steam, power, and electric communication are entirely new revolutionizing influences. So it must be in Architecture."

The new architecture was soon locked in a ridiculous "Battle of the Styles," that showed none of the revolutionizing technological influences. If London was, as Henry James said, the world's most complete compendium of the human race, Late Victorian architecture was the world's most complete compendium of world architecture of all ages—Flemish, Moorish, Gothic, Roman, Chinese, Baroque, Renaissance, Egyptian, "Queen Anne," Japanese, Alpine, and on and on, at times all in one building, or so it seemed, at times in fierce combat.

Ruskin grumbled that "the peculiar characteristic of the present day [was] that we are acquainted with the history of art"—and deplored it, preferring ignorance. "It does not matter one marble splinter," he fumed, "whether we have old or new architecture. The forms of architecture already known are good enough for us and far better than any of us." He did not care what style architects used, as long as it was Gothic.

"Queen Anne" was what young architects pretended to design when they got fed up with Ruskin's embroidered Gothic. But their creations have almost nothing to do with dear Queen Anne. It was an imaginative and pretty combination of Gothic bones with Classic flesh, as the English architecture historian Mark Girouard puts it. The results are asymmetric structures with Gothic high roofs, gables, bay windows, and turrets, decorated with pediments and little domes and—in the fashionable Aesthetic Manner— sunflowers, pomegranates, lilies, and even touches of Japanese ornament. The acknowledged master of this style, and probably London's busiest architect at the time, was Norman Shaw, a friend of William Morris.[7]

"The greatest change perhaps," noted *Building News* in 1881, was that architecture had given up "the search for beauty, and has entered, instead, on a search for expression."[8]

Among the most effusive expressions of Victorian architectural braggadocio is the enormous St. Pancras railroad station, a concoction of French and Italian Gothic styles on which the architect Sir Gilbert Scott applied the riches of no fewer than fifty sketchbooks of ornaments. The clock tower alone, soaring to three hundred feet, must have achieved the foremost aim of any railroad station of the time: it must have awed the stockholders into believing that the Midland Railway was the most powerful and successful of all railroads in the realm.

Among the most eclectic expressions of the age was the Imperial Institute of Kensington which, save for one tower, did not survive the Empire. It was built to contain exhibitions and research facilities on the Commonwealth nations and when it was conceived, Alfred, Lord Tennyson, the Poet Laureate, urged that the building "speak to the centuries." The architectural language its designer, T. E. Collcutt, chose was an amalgam of French, Flemish, and Spanish styles. "Do the centuries understand Esperanto?" quipped a critic.

Period Architecture typified in the National Liberal Club. (Olin Library, Cornell University)

Other conspicuous landmarks of High Victorian are the sprawling Law Courts (all fairy-tale picturesqueness by architect G. E. Street), Scotland Yard (the famous and dour police palace by Norman Shaw), the Elephant and Castle (once a coaching house, rebuilt in the 1890s into a polychrome whimsy), and—now all but drowned in traffic and miserable, modern mediocrity—Piccadilly Circus. Sculptor Alfred Gilbert's fountain, though, is surely the most lovable and beloved in London. Its central column is graced by an archer standing on one foot, whom Gilbert intended to be the Angel of Christian Charity, but whom Londoners, as happens so often to charitable angels, mistake for "Eros." Soon after the dedication in 1893, the satiric magazine *Punch* showed the missing arrow in the back of a passing cabdriver.

American cities have been compared with doughnuts, with all the dough on the outside and a hole in the middle. London made deliberate efforts to keep the wealthy in the center and let the working class move to the edge of town. The policy had mixed motives. Center-city landlords feared for their investment. They weren't going to have their nice, genteel squares overrun and depreciated by the poor. Politicians in Westminster feared the explosive potential of too great a concentration of a malcontent working class.

Disraeli put it idealistically: "I have always felt that the best security for civilization is the dwelling. It is the real nursery of all domestic virtue and without a becoming home, the exercise of these virtues is impossible." Lord Shaftesbury put it more bluntly: "If the workingman has his own house, I have no fear of revolution."

The workingman's house—or his "cottage," as he usually called it— was, of course, possible only at the edge of town where he could afford the price of the land. Thus, in 1883, a Cheap Trains Act forced the railways to give workers reduced fares so they could commute to work. Several working-class suburbs, like Tottenham and Walthamstow, are built on this subsidized fare structure. The chairman of London Tramways was able to boast a year later: "We have relieved London of an immense number of poor people by carrying them out to the suburbs . . ."

The redeeming virtue of London's suburbs is that they gave all but the most despondent families decent housing. The price for more privacy and living space and fewer rats was that suburbia placed often excessively long distances between people and their work, their shopping, and cultural stimulation and recreation. It also made the Victorian class system even more rigid by segregating people in strictly single-class neighborhoods.

This concentration was exaggerated by the desire of builders and developers to mass-produce suburbia as cheaply as possible. Architecturally, the working-class neighborhoods, with their tightly packed cottages and row houses, were nothing much more than horizontal tenements, except that a few square feet of front garden was touchingly tidy and the doorsteps were well scrubbed.

The middle-class neighborhoods tended more to freestanding or semi-detached villas. Different clusters of a hundred or so were aligned along arrow-straight streets, each cluster built in the same fashionable style.

Suburbia did not enjoy a good press in central London. Newspaper reporters tended to snarl at its social and architectural faults, deploring the architectural *ennui* and the restricted social life and isolation of the housewives after their husbands had gone off to work. *Building News,* in particular, kept complaining. In 1884, the journal said: "We cannot avoid remarking the dull and wearying sameness of treatment . . . as if individuals had tastes precisely the same, or were cast in one mould."[9] In 1893, *Building News* remarked: "Monotonous repetition of features . . . is one of the saddest things in this fearful spreading of tenements and middle-class dwellings."[10] Reporting on "a walk in the suburbs," one architect reported: "North, south, east or west, they are all the same."[11]

Politics was most hotly debated in the London pubs or public houses, as they were officially known. The pubs, in fact, were one of the very few institutions to provide a congenial link between the classes.

London pubs at the time—the last quarter of the nineteenth century—were something quite different from what they were before William Hogarth's days when they tended to be mostly "gin houses," where a good many of the guests seemed intent on drinking themselves into a stupor, if not the grave.

The good old days of the aging Queen Victoria, however, saw the "golden age" of the pubs, according to Mark Girouard, with gilded mirrors, mahogany carvings, and windows glittering with cut and embossed glass.[12] Food was served as well as drink. Customers could sit at tables or stand at a bar. People mingled. The rigid class distinctions relaxed a little.

The pub was also the place where workingmen waited for the horse bus or found solace and sustenance every half mile or so on their long walk home from work. True, the fancy, new restaurants and hotels, to say nothing of temperance zeal, kept the more status-conscious professional and business people at a disdainful distance. "In these days when taverns are voted vulgar, it would be almost the ruin of a barrister's reputation to be seen entering a public house unless it were called a restaurant," commented the *Licensed Victuallers' Gazette* in 1888.[13] But that did not hurt the publicans or make their establishments less ubiquitous. There was a pub for every three hundred and forty-five Londoners.

The glitter of the taverns symbolized the advancement of laborers into a proud industrial working class, a new and powerful force in English social and political life, somewhat akin to the French *petit bourgeoisie.* Pubs were respectable places, despite what the temperance advocates said. Many customers brought their wives and there were groups of women enjoying a drink or two together. Ladies of easy virtue were barred.

The drinking places of the upper classes were places of assignation. During Wilde's trial, testimony was taken from working-class male prostitutes about how and where their meeting with Wilde took place. It was not in the working-class pubs but in the expensive restaurants of Soho, with their private dining rooms, that these encounters occurred. The examination of Charles Parker, a valet out of work at the time of his meeting with Wilde, reveals some of the night life of the upper class:

> *Witness:* I said that if any old gentleman with money took a fancy to me, I was agreeable . . . I was terribly hard up.
>
> *Mr. Gill:* Where did you first meet Wilde?
>
> *Witness:* [Taylor] said he could introduce us to a man who was good for plenty of money . . . He took us to a restaurant in Rupert Street. I think it was the Solferino. We were shown upstairs to a private room, in which there was a dinner table laid for four. After a while Wilde came in and I was formally introduced.
>
> *Mr. Gill:* Who made the fourth?

Witness: My brother, William Parker. I had promised Taylor that he should accompany me.

Mr. Gill: Was the dinner a good dinner?

Witness: Yes . . . we had plenty of champagne with our dinner and brandy and coffee afterwards. We all partook of it. Wilde paid for the dinner.

Mr. Gill: Of what nature was the conversation?

Witness: General, at first. Nothing was then said as to the purposes for which we had come together.

Mr. Gill: And then?

Witness: Wilde said to me, ". . . will you go to the Savoy Hotel with me?" I consented, and Wilde drove me in a cab to the hotel. Only he and I went, leaving my brother and Taylor behind. At the Savoy we went first to Wilde's sitting room.

Mr. Gill: More drink was offered you there?

Witness: Yes, we had liqueurs. Wilde then asked me to go into his bedroom with him.

Mr. Gill: Let us know what occurred there.

Witness: He committed the act of sodomy upon me.[14]

As the century came to an end, Britannia ruled not just the waves but one quarter of the world's population and one quarter of the world's land. Her mother city was prosperous and proud.

Both prosperity and pride were flawed, to be sure. Badly flawed. Under the veneer of Victorian morality, gentility, and propriety was much ruthless and often cruel economic and sexual exploitation. Even in high society—in public school and country houses—there was an obsession with spanking, whipping, birching, flogging, thrashing, and paddling of young bottoms of both sexes in the name of education and character building.

Although work and sanitary conditions unquestionably improved, so many poor flocked into the city from the countryside and from across the seas, that the proportion of London's destitute at the end of Queen Victoria's reign was probably higher than at the beginning.

Victorians knew. Many spoke out passionately and with candor. They knew about the crying need for real reform and for a more honest, realistic morality. As a character in one of Oscar Wilde's plays explains: "A man who can't talk morality twice a week to a large, popular, immoral audience is quite over as a serious politician."

The evil we know about Oscar Wilde's London, we after all know mostly from those who lived with it, who exposed it, who would reform it: from the conservative seventh Earl of Shaftesbury; from Andrew Mearns's fighting pamphlet "The Bitter Cry of Outcast London"; from the wealthy shipowner Charles Booth who compiled an exhaustive seventeen-volume survey of London's social conditions. Booth's survey shows that thirty percent of the total London population lived below the poverty level. It also shows, however, that seventy percent escaped poverty.

Not all who escaped poverty managed to rise much above what Booth called "working-class comfort." But all of them, and virtually all of Oscar Wilde's London, saw a remarkable improvement in the living and working conditions, public health, and human dignity of London's men, women, and children.

7

THE
LOWER CLASSES

There are two nations, wrote Benjamin Disraeli early in the Victorian Age, "between whom there is no intercourse and no sympathy; who are as ignorant of each other's habits, thoughts, and feelings, as if they were dwellers in different zones, or inhabitants of different planets; who are formed by a different breeding, are fed by a different food, are ordered by different manners, and are not governed by the same laws . . . the Rich and the Poor."[1]

By 1891, London's poor had become ever more numerous.

That year, Lord Rosebery, Chairman of the London County Council, complained: "I am always haunted by the awfulness of London: by the great appalling fact of these millions cast down, as it would appear by hazard, on the banks of this noble stream."[2]

The population had grown from 3,215,000 in 1870 to 4,211,000 in 1890. There were two causes: immigration from British farms and mining towns and immigration of Jews from Russia and Poland.

Imports of coal, iron, cotton, and grain from the United States, cheaper than the domestic products, resulted in unemployment and a sense of gloom. "Sunburnt herdsmen of the hill" and "village maiden with dancing eyes and country curls," as poet Ernest Rhys put it, deserted hill and village "to taste of London's Feast."

Too late, dear children of the sun;
For London's Feast is past and gone![3]

General William Booth of the Salvation Army fought for a way out of "darkest England."
(Library of Congress)

Children labored along with adults in this jewelry polishing shop at Whitby, as they did in most workshops and factories. The picture was taken in 1890. (Sutcliffe Gallery, Whitby)

It was, at any event, anything but merry. The average life expectancy in the fresh air of the British countryside was fifty-one years. In London's dark smog it averaged only twenty-eight. One out of three in the working-class districts lived in abject poverty. The "poverty line" according to Charles Booth, the pioneer of social surveys, was eighteen to twenty shillings a week for a family of "moderate size." That barely sufficed for food and lodging.

The "out-of-work," as the unemployed were called, lacked even that. Their number, in London at that time, was officially estimated at twenty thousand. "This vast reservoir of unemployed labor," wrote another Booth, the founder and General of the Salvation Army William Booth, "is the bane of all efforts to raise the scale of living, to improve the condition of labor. Men are hungering to death for lack of opportunity to earn a crust . . ."[4]

"A considerable percentage of wanderers from the country in search of work," wrote General Booth elsewhere in his book *In Darkest England and the Way Out* (1890), "find themselves at nightfall destitute . . .

"[They] betake themselves to the seats under the plane trees on the Embankment . . . Here, between the Temple and the Blackfriars, I found the poor wretches by the score; almost every seat contained its full complement of six—some men, some women—all reclining in various postures and nearly all fast asleep. Just as Big Ben strikes two, the moon, flashing across the Thames and lighting up the stone work of the Embankment, brings into

Some children had nannies (left), but many had to work to survive. (Kodak Museum)

Children, many of them homeless, were the worst victims of London's miseries. (Victoria and Albert Museum, Guildhall Library)

relief a pitiable spectacle. Here on the stone abutments, which afford a slight protection from the biting wind, are scores of men lying side by side, huddled together for warmth, and, of course, without any other covering than their ordinary clothing, which is scanty enough at best. Some have laid down a few pieces of waste paper, by way of taking the chill off the stones, but the majority are too tired even for that, and the nightly toilet of most consists of first removing the hat, swathing the head in whatever old rag may be doing duty as a handkerchief, and then replacing the hat . . .

"In addition to these sleepers, a considerable number walk about the streets up till the early hours of the morning to hunt up some job which will bring a copper into the empty exchequer, and save them from actual starvation. I had some conversation with one such, a stalwart youth lately discharged from the militia, and unable to get work.

" 'You see,' said he, pitifully, 'I don't know my way about like most of the London fellows. I'm so green, and don't know how to pick up jobs like they do. I've been walking the streets almost day and night these two weeks and can't get work. I've got the strength, though I shan't have it long at this rate. I only want a job. This is the third night running that I've walked the streets all night; the only money I get is by minding blacking-boys' boxes while they go into Lockharts' for their dinner. I got a penny yesterday at it, and twopence for carrying a parcel, and to-day I've had a penny. Bought a ha'porth of bread and ha'penny mug of tea.'

"Poor lad! probably he would soon get into thieves' company, and sink into the depths, for there is no other means of living for many like him; it is starve or steal, even for the young. There are gangs of lad thieves in the low Whitechapel lodging-houses, varying in age from thirteen to fifteen, who live by thieving eatables and other easily obtained goods from shop fronts.

"In addition to the Embankment, *al fresco* lodgings are found in the seats outside Spitalfields Church, and many homeless wanderers have their own little nooks and corners of resort in many sheltered yards, vans, etc., all over London. Two poor women I observed making their home in a shop doorway in Liverpool Street. Thus they manage in the summer; what it's like in winter time is terrible to think of. In many cases it means the pauper's grave, as in the case of a young woman who was wont to sleep in a van in Bedfordbury. Some men who were aware of her practice surprised her by dashing a bucket of water on her. The blow to her weak system caused illness, and the inevitable sequel—a coroner's jury came to the conclusion that the water only hastened her death, which was due, in plain English, to starvation."[5]

Jewish immigrants, having fled the pogroms which became more numerous and vicious in Russian-controlled countries after the assassination of Tsar Alexander II, often fared better. Beatrice Potter Webb, the economist, social reformer, and co-founder of the socialist Fabian Society, wrote of them:

"Let us imagine ourselves on board a Hamburg boat steaming slowly up the Thames in the early hours of the morning. In the stern of the vessel we see a mixed crowd of men, women, and children—Polish and Russian Jews, some sitting on their baskets, others with bundles tied up in bright colored kerchiefs. For the most part they are men between 20 and 40 years of age, of slight and stooping stature, of sallow and pinched countenance, with low foreheads, high cheek bones and protruding lips. They wear uncouth and dirt-bespattered garments, they mutter to each other in a strange tongue. Scattered among them a few women (their shapely figures and soft skins compare favourably with the sickly appearance of the men), in peasant frocks with shawls thrown lightly over their head; and here and there a child, with prematurely set features, bright eyes and agile movements. Stamped on the countenance and bearing of the men is a look of stubborn patience; in their eyes an indescribable expression of hunted, suffering animals, lit up now and again by tenderness for the young wife or little child, or sharpened into a quick and furtive perception of surrounding circumstances . . .

"The steamer is at rest, the captain awaits the visit of the Custom House officials. All eyes are strained, searching through the shifting mist and dense forest of masts for the first glimpse of the eagerly hoped-for relations and friends, for the first sight of the long-dreamt-of city of freedom and prosperity. Presently a boat rows briskly to the side of the vessel; seated in it a young woman with mock sealskin coat, vandyke hat slashed up with blue satin, and surmounted with a yellow ostrich feather, and long six-buttoned gloves. She is chaffing the boatman in broken English, and shouts words of welcome and encouragement to the simple bewildered peasant who peers over the side of the vessel with two little ones clasped in either hand. Yes! that smartly dressed young lady is her daughter. Three years ago the father and the elder child left the quiet Polish village: a long interval of suspense, then a letter telling of an almost hopeless struggle, at last passage money, and here to-day the daughter with her bright warm clothes and cheery self-confidence—in a few hours the comfortably furnished home of a small wholesale orange-dealer in Mitre Street, near to Petticoat Lane . . .

"The scenes at the landing-stage are less idyllic. There are a few relations and friends awaiting the arrival of the small boats filled with immigrants: but the crowd gathered in and about the gin-shop overlooking the narrow entrance of the landing-stage are dock loungers of the lowest type and professional 'runners.' These latter individuals, usually of the Hebrew race, are among the most repulsive of East London parasites; boat after boat touches the landing-stage, they push forward, seize hold of the bundles or baskets of the new-comers, offer bogus tickets to those who wish to travel forward to America, promise guidance and free lodging to those who hold in their hands addresses of acquaintances in Whitechapel, or who are absolutely friendless. A little man with an official badge *(Hebrew Ladies' Protective Society)* fights valiantly in their midst for the conduct of unprotected females, and shouts or whispers to the others to go to the Poor Jews' Temporary Shelter in Leman Street. For a few moments it is a scene of indescribable confusion: cries and counter-cries; the hoarse laughter of the dock loungers at the strange garb and broken accent of the poverty-stricken foreigners; the rough swearing of the boatmen at passengers unable to pay the fee for landing. In another ten minutes eighty of the hundred new-comers are dispersed in the back slums of Whitechapel; in another few days, the majority of these, robbed of the little they possess, are turned out of the 'free lodgings' destitute and friendless.

"If we were able to follow the 'greener' into the next scene of his adventures we should find him existing on the charity of a co-religionist or toiling day and night for a small labour-contractor in return for a shakedown, a cup of black coffee, and hunch of brown bread. This state of dependence, however, does not last. For a time the man works as if he were a slave under the lash, silently, without complaint. But in a few months (in the busy season in a few weeks) the master enters his workshop and the man is not at his place. He has left without warning—silently—as he worked without pay. He has learnt his trade and can sell his skill in the open market at the corner of Commercial Street; or possibly a neighbouring sweater, pressed with work, has offered him better terms. A year hence he has joined a chevras, or has become an habitué of a gambling club. And unless he falls a victim to the Jewish passion for gambling, he employs the enforced leisure of the slack season in some form of petty dealing. He is soon in a fair way to become a tiny capitalist—a maker of profit as well as an earner of wage. He has moved out of the back court in which his fellow-countrymen are herded together like animals, and is comfortably installed in a model dwelling; the walls of his parlour are decked with prints of Hebrew worthies, or with portraits of prize-fighters and race-horses; his wife wears jewelry and furs on the Sabbath; for their Sunday dinner they eat poultry. He treats his wife with courtesy and tenderness, and they discuss constantly the future of the children. He is never to be seen at the public-house round the corner; but he enjoys a quiet glass of 'rum and shrub' and a game of cards with a few friends on the Saturday or Sunday evening; and he thinks seriously of season tickets for the People's Palace. He remembers the starvation fare and the long hours of his first place; he remembers, too, the name and address of the wholesale house served by his first master; and presently he appears at the counter and offers to take the work at a lower figure; or secures it through a tip to the foreman. But he no longer kisses the hand of Singer's agent and begs with fawning words for another sewing machine; neither does he flit to other lodgings in the dead of night at the first threat of the broker. In short, he has become a law-abiding and self-respecting citizen of our great metropolis, and feels himself the equal of a Montefiore or a Rothschild."[6]

If the Jews were seen as being upwardly mobile, a function of the nineteenth-century British perception of the Jew as materialist and overachiever, the poor were usually seen as fixed in their place forever. Although their poverty could not be changed, perhaps their condition could be redeemed somewhat by seeing in it a potential for beauty, something like the awful beauty of the grim clouds of soot that hung over London. That is what Oscar Wilde, with his immense sympathy for the plight of the poor, chose to do:

"Poverty and misery," he wrote, ". . . are terribly concrete things. We find their incarnation everywhere and, as we are discussing a matter of art, we have no hesitation in saying that they are not devoid of picturesqueness. The etcher or the painter finds in them 'a subject made to his hand,' and the poet has admirable opportunities of drawing weird and dramatic contrasts between the purple of the rich and the rags of the poor."[7]

Many of London's poor went begging. A beggar could earn as much as two pounds a day, according to H. M. Stanley, an investigative reporter whose story inspired one of Conan Doyle's Sherlock Holmes tales, "The Man with the Twisted Lip."

Another anonymous investigator reported:

"I had been commissioned to join the vagrant band for the day, and, among other adventures in prospect, I had to face the possibility of arrest . . . I comforted myself while ransacking a parcel of old clothing purchased from a Jew dealer in the neighbourhood of Houndsditch. I had not much difficulty in getting a suitable 'rig-out.' There was a buttonless tweed coat, with lacerated sleeves and a ruptured breast pocket; a pair of faded trousers, bearing no trace of the original colour, and as jagged at the extremities as the outline of the Alps; a greasy-looking slouch hat, and a pair of boots that some poor rascal must have thrown aside in despair. I felt I could not do much better than that, so with many strange anticipations I divested myself of respectability for the day . . .

"Oxford Street was the line I decided upon, and for six hours on end did I parade Oxford Street up and down, and through streets and squares adjoining, until I actually found it hard to free myself from the belief that I was really a tramp. The experience of these six hours leads me to believe that begging is much more profitable than people imagine. I knew nothing of the tricks of approach, or of the whining whisper that marks the accomplished mendicant; and yet I netted one and tenpence before the last lingerer in the Circus took pity on my supposed misery. The darkness aided my disguise, and made me bold, and I was utterly astonished at the freedom with which I accosted people, some of them my own acquaintances, and succeeded in exacting coppers from them. I found young men deaf to all my entreaties while standing or walking alone, but when chatting with women they were much more approachable, moved partly, perhaps, by the wish to appear generous, and partly, no doubt, by the desire to rid themselves of so objectionable an interruption. As the evening wore on I made these little groups

Opposite, Emma Cook, one of a family of six children of an unemployed laborer who had died. Her mother, said the case record, was a "respectable woman" but was unable to hold a steady job because of poor health. In 1887, at the age of six and a half, Emma joined two of her sisters at Dr. Barnardo's Home. (Barnardo Photo Library)

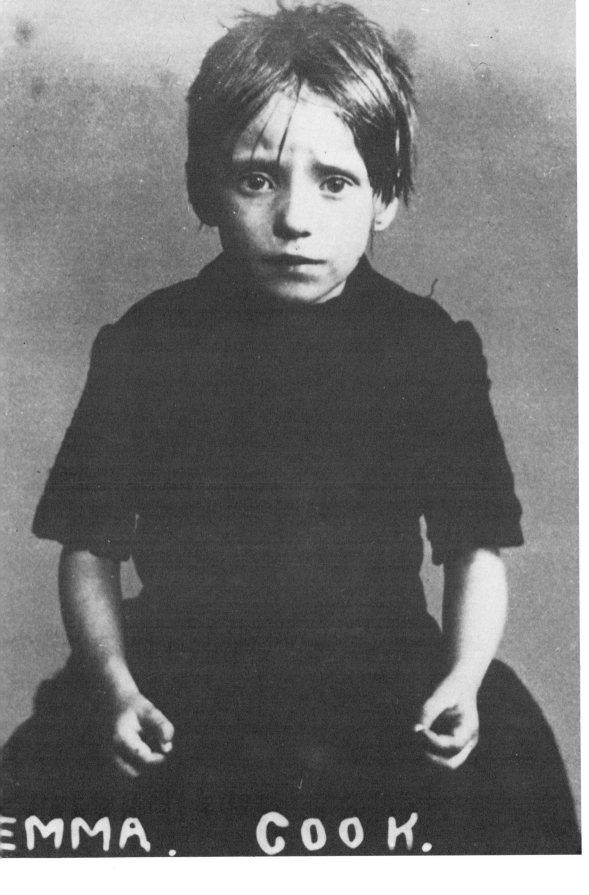

EMMA. COOK.

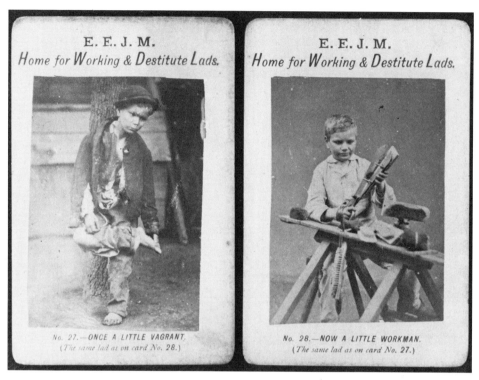

"Once a Little Vagrant" (left), "Now a Little Workman" (right) are two of the many photographs Dr. Barnardo's organization sold to raise funds for his effort to turn street urchins into productive members of society. (Barnardo Photo Library)

Crippled boys in Dr. Barnardo's Home. Many of them were maimed in industrial accidents. The uniform, like that of the Salvation Army, was to help instill pride and a sense of belonging. (Barnardo Photo Library)

Dr. Thomas Barnardo, a London physician, c. 1890. (Barnardo Photo Library)

the chief object of my attacks, and was much struck by the readiness with which the women stood up for me, giving me coppers themselves sometimes when they could not induce their companions to do so. With elderly gentlemen the case was hopeless. They looked at me as if I were a leper, and invariably turned round to see if there was a policeman at hand, so that they might give me in charge. Twice I was so complained of, and was warned that if seen again I would be locked up. I found, though, that the police are not at all anxious to get up cases against beggars. Whenever it is possible they do not see them, and the virtuous young man who becomes at all noisy in his remonstrances is told that he is no better than he should be, which is probably true.

"While wandering about I came across some other beggars, who bemoaned the hard conditions of existence now-a-days. The only way to make a livelihood at begging, they said, was to have a settled place to stand at, and then people get to know one, as they did in any other line of business. But they were for ever moving on from district to district, and made new friends only to lose them. It was all very well for the man who had a wooden leg, or some personal deformity to work on. There was always a living for him. But the hapless being who was sound in wind and limb, and 'had no work to do,' might just as well give up honesty as a bad job. Women are better beggars than men. To begin with, they are less easily discouraged, and one has always more pity for a woman than a man. I saw one late at night in Regent Street, and from the folds of her dress she produced food enough to feed a family. She also told me, confidentially, that she had thirteen shillings stowed away, and her affectionate converse was proceeding with such rapid strides that I thought it advisable to move on, lest she should make me an offer of marriage."[8]

Some, like Charles Parker, one of Wilde's working-class lovers, sold themselves. Others, like Shaw's Eliza Doolittle, sold matches. Still others hawked penny pamphlets describing their misfortunes. Little Alice Moss, who went begging with her blind father until his death, sold both, matches and pamphlets.

Here are some verses of her ballad, *Written and Printed for Her with the Kind Permission of the Authorities* in 1880:

> *Buy a box of matches, sir,*
> *Pray buy a box from me;*
> *The wind is cold, and few we've sold,*
> *My Father's blind, you see.*
> *And Mother, she lies ill at home,*
> *With younger children two;*
> *In whispers said—I bent my head—*
> *"Poor little maid,"*
> *Some lights I'll buy from you.*

Passing gentleman:
But tell me now, unfortunate man,
    How came it thus to be [to the Father]
That, young as yet, you should have met
    This dread calamity?

                        . . .

Blind John Moss replies:
Kind sir, my name it is John Moss.
    A working man I've been;
And tho' even young, I ne'er was strong;
    Some happy days I've seen.

In this Great City I was born,
    Bootmaking was my trade;
But health broke down, confined in town,
    I could not earn my bread.

                        . . .

Yes, Sir, the doctors were most kind.
    They always are so to the blind;
But much I mourn the misery of my poor
        wife and family,
Support for whom 'tis hard to find. [9]

Among London's beggars were numerous "phos" girls without jaws or fingers. They had worked in the Victoria Match Factory, which employed over a thousand women and girls. The typical work day began at 8 A.M. and ended at 9 P.M. The pay ranged from seven to eleven shillings a week. The work consisted of tipping matchsticks into phosphorus, which, after prolonged contact, caused the bones of the worker to decay.

The Factory Act prohibited the employment of children younger than thirteen.

"And who says I ain't thirteen," retorted one of two "hands" in a Highgate factory when asked her age by social reformer James Greenwood. The two "mites of girls" had "dirty faces streaked with the rain that trickled down from their untidy heads of hair; with nothing to cover their thin little shoulders, and . . . feet but ill-protected by woefully dilapidated shoes," Greenwood wrote.

" 'I don't say so,' I replied, 'but you certainly appear younger.'

" 'Then I just ain't,' she said, 'there's my teeth to prove it, and you can go and ask our doctor if you don't believe me.'

"After which she was good enough to explain that if there was any doubt as to the age of a child who applied for work at the factory she was referred to a medical gentleman retained by the firm, who by experience had

*Here and opposite, in contrast to photographs of the period, illustrations published in the Fleet
Street periodicals inevitably romanticized working-class life. (Guildhall Library)*

learnt to rely on the evidence of dental witnesses within a child's mouth
rather than on any oral testimony that might proceed from it.

"The two poor little shivering wretches were in dire distress. They had
not appeared at the factory gate at the exact minute when their dinner-hour
expired, and, as a punishment for the offence, were shut out for half an hour
and fined a penny as well. We grew quite confidential under the shelter of
my umbrella. They were really not to blame for being late. Another girl—
for a 'lark,' as my bonnetless friends now ruefully assumed—had told them
of a certain cookshop in Camden Town where might be bought enormous
penn'orths of pudding, left cold from yesterday. They couldn't go home to
dinner on account of the long distance, but had been provided for the mid-

day repast by their respective parents with a slice of bread and a halfpenny. The penny, therefore, with which the feed of cold pudding was to be purchased was a joint stock affair, and they had set out together to make the investment. They had a run for it—it is at least a mile and a half from the Holloway-road to Camden Town—but no pudding shop was there . . .

"It seemed, legislative wisdom notwithstanding, a sin and a shame that such puny, ill-conditioned little children should be deemed fit for active service in the battle of life.

"It wouldn't have mattered so much—nay, I will go so far, excluding for the moment the moral question—it would not have mattered at all, if these small 'hands' had been warmly clad and plentifully fed; but in by far the majority of cases they were neither. Possibly they were bread-winners for the smaller fry at home, and there is no economy in sending them out to work at all if, in a vulgar manner of speaking, they consume all the grass they cut."[10]

Working in shops was not much better for London's young women than working in sweatshops.

Shops multiplied, as many enterprises began to open chain stores. Singer Sewing Machines had thousands of them at the close of the century. The Boots pharmacy had hundreds.

Women working in bars, millinery shops, "amongst drapery" and similar establishments stood behind counters from eleven to thirteen hours a day, "to the certain injury of their health," reported *Truth,* a muckraking newspaper.

Truth was edited by the member of Parliament for Northampton, whom Queen Victoria called "that wicked Henry Labouchère." Along with several other journalists, Labouchère had led a campaign to stamp out vice, which resulted in the passage of the law under which Oscar Wilde was later convicted. In another of his campaigns, Labouchère published an appeal to employers to allow the "unfortunate counter slaves" to sit, rather than stand, behind their counters:

> *Thank God! the day has ended—the long,*
> *   long day at last;*
> *Through another weary struggle with*
> *   my weakness I have passed.*
> *I need fight with it no longer; now*
> *   with safety I can weep—*
> *'Tis the only comfort left me, for I feel too*
> *   tired to sleep!*
>
> *And yet I've tried my hardest to be brave, and*
> *   not give way,*
> *And I think I have looked cheerful, though my*
> *   heart's ached all the day;*
> *For when I've been most weary, and so faint I*
> *   scarce could see,*
> *I have thought upon my mother—she has no one left but me!*
>
> *'Tis not the work has tired me, though I am*
> *   not strong nor stout,*
> *But the twelve long hours of standing, it*
> *   is that has worn me out;*
> *It is that has made me stagger to my bedroom*
> *   like a ghost,*
> *Why, the strongest girls beside me faint in*
> *   summer time almost . . .*

Down and out in darkest London. (Kodak Museum)

My very hope had left me, as awake I used to lie,
And sometimes—God forgive me!—I have wished
  that I could die!

But that I knew was wicked, and I've fought
    against the thought,
And resolved to do my duty, and be
    patient, as I ought . . .

And now, when all was darkest, there's
    at last a ray of light,
For I'm told there are kind ladies who are
    working with their might
To give us weary shop-girls what we've
    never yet possess't,
I mean seats behind the counter on which all
    of us may rest.[11]

Nor was private employment much of an escape from poverty. There were seats below the stairs, to be sure. But "the staff" was worked and considered much like slaves. The pay was marginal. The servant rooms under the eaves were cold and cheerless. And the food from the servants' kitchen was sparse.

As working conditions for domestic servants improved a little, their number, in proportion to those served, began to decline. Between 1871 and 1888, the number of domestic servants increased only one percent. It totaled a million and a quarter.

An article in *The Fortnightly Review* of 1888 commented on "the disposition of the upper classes towards their social inferiors":

" 'A servant's work,' as has been well said, 'is never done potentially, if even actually.' There is no reason why this should be so. A very little reorganisation in most London homes would enable the servant to have at least four or five hours every day, or if not every day, every other day, to herself. Let a lady or gentleman try to realise how rigorous are the laws which govern the actions of servants, and it will be seen that the intractability of their retainers is not entirely unjustified. Has it ever occurred to the master or the mistress what humiliation and distress attach to the single circumstances that the footman or the housemaid, the cook or the butler, dare not stir beyond the four walls of the house without permission except once or at most twice in a fortnight? Nothing is more bitterly resented below-stairs than to have to ask leave to 'go out' if only for a few minutes. Again, when servants are allowed out, the time at their disposal is ludicrously meagre, and, as a consequence, quarrels because the man or maid is late are frequent. But when a mistress declaims against a servant who does not come in till eleven o'clock, she never stays to think how often that servant may have sat up for her or some member of the family. Beyond doubt little good comes of girls being allowed out very late, but if they visit friends some distance off, it is cruelly inconsiderate to compel them to be back by half-past nine or even ten . . . Another matter, by which masters and mistresses insist on impressing upon their servants the fact that what is right in the drawing-room is wrong in the servants' hall, is dress and general appearance. Why, if he wishes—and for all the master can tell it may be a source of comfort to the man to do so—should the coachman, the butler, or the footman not be allowed to grow his beard and moustache? Why, if she has a particular liking for it, should the housemaid be denied the privilege of a fringe? These things are small but not insignificant. They are positive causes in the alienation from domestic service of the freedom-loving sons and daughters of the democracy. Love of finery, again, is undoubtedly strong in many servants' breasts, as love of good clothes is in the ladies'. And of this love of finery comes infinite evil. But it is not fair to level the charge of plagiarism in apparel against all servants. Some may ape their masters and mistresses, but their number is small, and the constant aim of servants who respect themselves is not to follow the lead of, but to take a line diametrically opposed to, that affected by their employers.

Blind beggars with their alms boxes. The one on the left is guided by his little girl. Blindness and other infirmities were a constant fear of the Victorians. Being unable to work meant to be thrown onto the none too tender mercies of charity, public and private. (Kodak Museum, Victoria and Albert Museum)

"Apart from the question of individual *laissez-faire,* servants are, rightly or wrongly, leavened with the idea that their masters and mistresses are their determined and deliberate enemies. They do not, as they ought in the hour of trouble, look up for guidance to, or seek themselves to remove difficulties from the path of, their social betters. It is a strange truth, that whilst classes were never so close to each other intellectually, socially they were never farther apart . . .

"Servants are no longer willing to follow their masters like sheep, and, unless service is made acceptable to them, servants will disappear altogether. They have a right to claim credit for intelligence, for human feeling, for honesty, and for any other attribute which is the common inheritance of an English subject."[12]

Oscar Wilde saw the poor caught in the web of a society which provided just enough to keep them alive, but not enough to let them live. Poverty was for Wilde a crime, but a crime committed by the state. He wrote in "The Soul of Man Under Socialism":

"The best amongst the poor are never grateful. They are ungrateful, discontented, disobedient, and rebellious. They are quite right to be so. Charity they feel to be a ridiculously inadequate mode of partial restitution, or a sentimental dole, usually accompanied by some impertinent attempt on the part of the sentimentalist to tyrannise over their private lives. Why should they be grateful for the crumbs that fall from the rich man's table? They should be seated at the board, and are beginning to know it. As for being discontented, a man who would not be discontented with such surroundings and such a low mode of life would be a perfect brute. Disobedience, in the eyes of any one who has read history, is man's original virtue. It is through disobedience that progress has been made, through disobedience and through rebellion. Sometimes the poor are praised for being thrifty. But to recommend thrift to the poor is both grotesque and insulting. It is like advising a man who is starving to eat less. For a town or country labourer to practise thrift would be absolutely immoral. Man should not be ready to show that he can live like a badly-fed animal. He should decline to live like that, and should either steal or go on the rates, which is considered by many to be a form of stealing. As for begging, it is safer to beg than to take, but it is finer to take than to beg. No; a poor man who is ungrateful, unthrifty, discontented, and rebellious is probably a real personality, and has much in him. He is at any rate a healthy protest. As for the virtuous poor, one can pity them, of course, but one cannot possibly admire them. They have made private terms with the enemy and sold their birthright for very bad pottage. They must also be extraordinarily stupid."[13]

8

RELIGION, SPIRITS, AND HOSANNA

Religion, which Karl Marx called "the opium of the people," was a time-honored way of easing the pain of poverty. But the Church of England had lost touch with the poor, having become a church of the middle and upper classes. It was still the custodian of some wonderful buildings and grand funerals. Its service—especially its hymn singing—seemed capable of inspiring a lump of clay. But its congregations were dwindling and its authority diminishing in secular, as well as spiritual, matters.

One reason was dissension from rigid doctrines and often staid and dull rituals. Another was the lure of Roman Catholicism, which Oscar Wilde, who was received into the church on his deathbed, had previously described as "the fowler's snare . . . the wiles of the Scarlet Woman." A strong fad was spiritualism, which attracted thousands of Londoners into the Theosophical Society, including Wilde's wife, Constance.

Most of all, however, religious indifference increased among all classes in society.

What troubled the Church of England was, in the words of one clergyman, "the very fact that we have been a Church established by law, and, to a great extent, the Church of the aristocracy and higher classes. While it has given us, in some respects, a great vantage ground, it has, in others, been a snare . . . We have stood upon our dignity. We have a morbid horror of being *vulgar*. Our ministers have not been trained for a work among 'the common people'; and 'the common people' have soon discerned their want of adaptation to their wants and tastes."[1]

Charles Haddon Spurgeon, Baptist minister, and the founder of the great Metropolitan Taber-nacle, the largest Protestant church in London, seating over six thousand. Spurgeon was one of the ministers who recognized that an upper-class church had little to offer to "the common people." (Olin Library, Cornell University)

Another minister put it more bluntly: "If men found what they needed, they would come to the churches. But they do not. Church after church is empty."[2]

Then there were the sermons. They were boring. Sydney Smith once asked whether "sin was to be taken from men, as Eve was from Adam, by casting them into a deep slumber."

A supposed remedy was dictionaries or cyclopaedias of illustrated anec-dotes to assist the hard-pressed clergy. Under "Persons, Noisy," for in-stance, a preacher would find: "It is with narrow-souled people as with nar-row-necked bottles—the less they have in them, the more noise they make pouring out." How much this helped to quiet the "Persons, Noisy," is not on record.

Oscar Wilde's views on preaching are perhaps best represented in his comic portrayal of the Reverend Canon Chasuble, D.D., in *The Importance of Being Earnest:*

"My sermon on the meaning of the manna in the wilderness can be adapted to almost any occasion, joyful, or, as in the present case, distressing. *(All sigh)* I have preached it at harvest celebrations, christenings, confirmations, on days of humiliation and festal days. The last time I delivered it was in the Cathedral, as a charity sermon on behalf of the Society for the Prevention of Discontentment among the Upper Orders. The Bishop, who was present, was much struck by some of the analogies I drew."[3]

The dispute with Roman Catholics was bitter. William Gladstone, who was hardly a militant, asserted that Catholicism "enslaved the intellect." Others argued that it subverted national purpose and constitutional liberty. The Catholics, on the other hand, were determined to achieve emancipation for themselves within a country that prided itself on a tradition of social, economic, and political freedom.

In 1854, the year Oscar Wilde was born, the doctrine of the Immaculate Conception was promulgated. In 1870, papal infallibility was announced. In between these new dogmas came the publication of the "Syllabus of Errors Denouncing Absolute Rationalism, Moderate Rationalism, Indifferentialism, Socialism, Communism, Secret Societies, Bible Societies, and Modern Liberalism." One of its pronouncements was: "Whosoever teaches that the Roman Pontiff can and ought to reconcile and adjust himself with progress,

An official hearse from the Woolwich Arsenal. Funerals were the most spectacular religious events. This hearse was reserved for the workers of the Woolwich munitions factories. (Borough of Greenwich)

liberalism and modern civilisation . . . let him be anathema."[4] Neverthe-less, Wilde felt that Catholicism might wake in him "some earnestness and purity," causing him "to sacrifice and give up my two great gods, 'Money' and 'Ambition.' "

The extremes of Victorian religiosity were extraordinary, ranging from those who wished to bury God to those who worshiped Him in a frenzy. Some, less concerned with Wilde's deities, or the conventional manifesta-tions of faith, for that matter, were attracted by what amounted to the rise of a new, secular religion of scientificality—Darwinism.

If there was one central manifestation of "the warfare between science and theology," as A. D. White, the founding President of Cornell, put it in the title of his 1895 study, it was Darwin's evolutionary theory. It suddenly dominated the discussion. Darwin, a shy and hesitant man, pondered his ideas of biological change on a trip around the world on H.M.S. *Beagle.* In 1859, he finally committed them to paper with his *Origin of the Species.* By his death, in 1882, there were innumerable evolutionary theories competing for space as a new orthodoxy of science. Some of them were variations on Dar-win's original views; some of them were the application of the concept of evolution to areas which Darwin had not even imagined, such as politics and economics. Herbert Spencer's "Social Darwinism," a Darwinism in name only, stressed the necessity of disease, war, famine, and poverty for the "sur-vival of the fittest." Spencer found these natural forces necessary to "de-crease the surplus population," to quote Dickens's Scrooge. By the 1880s such a view was no longer understood as the dyspepsia of a social misfit. It had become a science.

"Darwinism"—or, rather, "Darwinisms"—became the model of sci-ence. It seemed to glorify competition, to stress individualism, to see the importance of strength and conquest. It seemed to prove that the ruling classes had earned their power over colonies and workers because of their innate biological superiority. None of this is found in Darwin himself. It was all "Darwinism." It became a cult which sat well with the rise of colonialism, the ideas of racial inferiority which dominated the Victorian understanding of the biology of the human species. It was the parallel to David Living-stone's sense of mission as he spread the gospel throughout "darkest Africa." Science, like religion, had to bear "the white man's burden."

This new orthodoxy of science, in short, paralleled Victorian organized religion as much as it seemed to contradict it.

On the intellectual fringes of the city, another alternative to Catholicism was spiritualism. There were many ways of making contact with the spirit world. The most common was to find a guide, or medium, available for those not so moved themselves, in shabby places for whatever the traffic would bear. Some seekers of supernatural truth availed themselves of "mes-merism," as the hypnotic techniques invented in the eighteenth century by Vienna-born Dr. Friedrich Anton Mesmer were called.

Charles Darwin. One of the most influential thinkers of the nineteenth century. Darwin's theory of evolution changed the way his contemporaries understood the world. (Kodak Museum)

MAN·IS·BVT·A·WORM·

"Man Is But a Worm," a Punch *cartoon, December 1881. Published a few months before Darwin's death, the cartoon illustrates how Darwin's careful formulations were often distorted by a crude, popular "Darwinism." (Olin Library, Cornell University)*

Charles Maurice Davies, a Church of England clergyman, left a description of "A Mesmeric Seance" administered to a room full of people in a small apartment by a Miss Chandos. Much to Davies's relief, Miss Chandos turned out to be "a very pretty young lady indeed, of not more than eighteen or twenty years of age with a mystic crop of long black curls."

Her first "patient" was an innocent-looking young man at whom "she smiled a fatuous smile as her taper fingers lighted on his head, while the other hand rested on the frontal portion of his face, as though Miss Chandos were going to pull his nose. He was off in a moment, and sat facing the audience in his magnetic trance, looking like a figure at a wax-work show. Miss Chandos then passed to a gentleman, No. 2, who never succumbed during the entire evening, though she made several onslaughts on him." Her results continued to be mixed, "but the audience was an indulgent one and thought it splendid."

On walking home, Davies wrote, "I asked myself whether, if the lecturess had not been a lecturess but a lecturer—if she weighed eighteen stone, or was old and wizen, or dropped her h's—whether I should have stayed three mortal hours in that stuffy room, and I frankly own I came to the conclusion I should *not.*"[5]

Others were less skeptical. Occultism, mesmerism, spiritualism, theosophy were the rage. The most talked-about promoter of the cult was a Madame Helena Blavatsky of New York City, who, in 1875, founded the Theosophical Society. But it was a competitive market. A London rival group announced: "We regard her neither as the mouthpiece of hidden seers, nor as a mere vulgar adventuress; we think that she has achieved a title to permanent remembrance as one of the most accomplished, ingenious, and interesting impostors in history."[6]

This, decided W. T. Stead, the editor of the *Pall Mall Gazette,* merited a review of Madame Blavatsky's enormous, two-volume book, *The Secret Doctrine.* He further decided that Annie Besant should do the reviewing. His "young men," he wrote her, all fought shy of the book's fifteen hundred pages, "but you are quite mad enough on the subject to make something of them."[7]

Annie Besant was already well known to Londoners. In 1877, she and a radical free-thinker, Charles Bradlaugh, had republished an American pamphlet written in 1832 by one Charles Knowlton entitled *Fruits of Philosophy or The Private Companion of Young Married Couples.* It promoted birth control, giving mistaken information about female physiology and correct information about contraceptives, larded with nineteenth-century beliefs about masturbation and aphrodisiacs.

Besant and Bradlaugh were charged with corrupting the morals of youth and inciting and encouraging Her Majesty's subjects to indecent, unnatural, and immoral practices. The jury agreed that the book was calculated to deprave public morals but exonerated the defendants from any corrupt motives in publishing it, and kept the fine small.[8]

The public was outraged, especially since Bradlaugh and Besant were notorious atheists. Mrs. Besant's estranged husband sued successfully to remove their children from her custody. In a cruel judgment, she was deprived of the right to see either of her children until their majority. She turned her energies to social and political activities. When she read Madame Blavatsky's book, she converted.

Bradlaugh was appalled. He considered many Theosophists "very respectable, very good and very mad," but some of them "less mad and less good." George Bernard Shaw told his friend Annie Besant that if she really needed a mahatma, he'd take on the job. One of the few genuine mahatmas around, a twenty-one-year-old Indian law student living in London at the time, professed to be a great admirer of hers. His name was Mohandas K. Gandhi and Annie Besant later joined him in the fight for Indian home rule.[9]

A spiritualist séance. Luminous "spiritual garments" appear to be floating in midair. A "ghost" is revealed to be merely a mortal confederate. (From The Graphic, *1880. Olin Library, Cornell University)*

Charles Bradlaugh also stayed in the news. He did not become a Theosophist but, having won a seat in the House of Parliament as a Liberal, refused to take the oath—refused, that is, to say, "I, Charles Bradlaugh, do swear that I will be faithful and bear true Allegiance to Her Majesty Queen Victoria, Her Heirs and Successors, according to Law. So help me God."

Randolph Churchill denounced him as "an avowed Atheist and professedly disloyal person." Special committees were appointed to explore the matter. Bradlaugh spoke at the Bar of the House—the brass bar opposite the Speaker which, ever since Charles I tried to arrest the "Five Members" in 1642, marked the line beyond which "strangers" could not pass—and was asked to withdraw. He refused, and was led away to be imprisoned in the Clock Tower. His seat was declared vacant, but he won it again and again. As court cases dragged on, the religious issue became less important than the constitutional one.

Another issue that bothered London at the time was what to do about Sunday. The Sabbatarians, as they were called, became a formidable power, deeply rooted in paradox. On the one hand, they did not want the government to meddle in their lives, on the other, they called for state regulations to enforce the Sabbath.

The traditional working-class Sunday began on Saturday at midday, after father had received the week's wages and given the wife her "treating" to run the household. Then father would probably spend the later part of the afternoon, as well as the evening after supper, at the public house. Sunday itself was indeed a day of rest. Breakfast was at about eleven o'clock and of a light nature. Then followed a perusal of the Sunday paper in shirt-sleeves, while preparations were made by the rest of the family for the culinary climax of the week—the Sunday dinner. By about twelve the male population was generally to be seen, shaven but not wholly dressed, taking a constitutional in the streets until the public houses opened at one. Then *exeunt omnes* within them for two hours until the Christian State shut them at three. This was the time for Sunday dinner, which was followed by sleep or talks with a neighbor till the public houses opened and were filled at six.

The background of this life, of course, was the home. With it came an everyday, unending, though half-unconscious sense of confinement. Either two or three rooms, on the average, served as home for father, mother, and a family increasing and growing up. There was seldom privacy and quiet to look forward to during the weariness and strains of toil during the day's work.[10]

The anti-Sabbatarians did not simply want to drink and play games on Sunday. Some of them wanted to go to museums and art galleries or to the Crystal Palace. Charles Bradlaugh helped organize the National Sunday League which was set up to organize Sunday band concerts, rambles, lectures, and discussions of scientific as well as religious truths.

One clergyman who attended a meeting of the Sunday Lecture Society

Advertisement for "the unvarying efficacy of the Electropathic Belt . . . in the alleviation of rheumatism, indigestion, lumbago, sciatica, paralysis, epilepsy, constipation, and nervous debility." With unprecedented scientific, technological, and industrial progress, the end of the Victorian Age also brought widespread faith in snake oil, superstition, and spiritualism. (Olin Library, Cornell University)

The Salvation Army in action. (Salvation Army Archives, New York)

described the audience as "a very large and intelligent one, comprising many eminent scientific men, quite a fair quota of ladies, a sprinkling of the rising generation, and altogether a collection of heads that would have delighted a phrenologist or physiognomist. Surely there is another old prejudice that must be rooted up by such gatherings as this. Whatever else we may be called, the English people must no longer be set down as a race of unmitigated Sabbatarians."[11]

For General William Booth and his Salvation Army, however, religion was not a matter of one liturgy versus another, staying home on Sunday or hearing a concert, nor was spirituality a matter of conversing with ghosts or previewing the afterlife. Booth's army did battle in the slums; its gospel inspired masterpieces of street theater. One observer described in the *Saturday Review:*

> *Hark, hark! my soul, what warlike songs are*
> *swelling*
> *Through Britain's streets and on from door to*
> *door;*
> *How grand the truths those burning strains are*
> *telling*
> *Of that great war till sin shall be no more!*
> *Salvation army, army of God!*
> *Onward to conquer the world with fire and*
> *blood.*

"There was some peculiar quality in these last words which a stranger could not catch. The phrase 'with fire and blood' was sung, or rather roared, again and again, until the perspiration ran down the faces of the soldiery as they clasped one another's hands and beamed. Public attention was particularly drawn to one captain on the lower platform, who vociferated with such zeal as almost to lose the semblance of humanity, and who finally gave his neighbour a hard rub round the head in token of spiritual good-fellowship. This quaint person afterwards recounted his experiences, and delighted the audience by assuring them that he used to be 'a swearing, drunken shoemaker at Merthyr Tydvil,' but that now he was 'a Hallelujah pastor at Whitechapel,' to which the entire hall sympathetically replied 'Hosanna!' "[12]

9

THE SOUNDS OF LONDON

Onward, Christian soldiers,
Marching as to war,
With the cross of Jesus
Going on before!
Christ, the royal Master,
Leads against the foe;
Forward into battle,
See, his banners go.

Hymn tunes were a staple of Victorian music. This one was written by Sir Arthur Sullivan, whose *Patience* of 1881 seemed to set Oscar Wilde—in the character of Bunthorne—to music.

Before *Patience,* Sullivan's career was distinguished by extraordinary feats of musical parody, served in a pastiche of popular favorites such as Mendelssohn, Verdi, Gounod, and Bizet. The best of these were *H.M.S. Pinafore,* produced in 1878, and *The Pirates of Penzance,* which opened the following year. But now Sullivan produced music for some of the greatest English comic operas, including *The Mikado* (1885) and *The Yeomen of the Guard* (1888).

The Queen herself often sang arias from these operas. She thought of Sullivan as her composer and, although she never went to the Savoy Theatre, she commanded two performances of Gilbert and Sullivan operas—*The Gondoliers* at Windsor and *The Mikado* at Balmoral.

Victoria liked operas of all sorts. Of the fourteen performances she saw

Writer Sir William Schwenck Gilbert, left, and composer Sir Arthur Seymour Sullivan, above. To the world, Gilbert and Sullivan, or "G&S," seemed an inseparable team. In fact, they communicated only through their solicitors. (Kodak Museum)

over twenty years at Windsor, ten were operas. The performances at Balmoral were equally divided between opera and theater.

Once an avid theatergoer, Victoria went into long mourning after Prince Albert's death in 1861. In 1881, it had been twenty years since she had seen a performance. But that year the Prince of Wales succeeded at last in persuading his mother to revive her interest. His own was kindled by his involvement with "the Jersey Lily," Lillie Langtry, who made her debut in the 1881 Haymarket production of *She Stoops to Conquer*—and conquer she did. During the next two decades she became one of the most successful actresses on both sides of the Atlantic.

"The three women I have most admired," remarked Oscar Wilde, "are Queen Victoria, Sarah Bernhardt and Lillie Langtry. I would have married any one of them with pleasure."[1] All three liked to be amused.

The first play the Queen saw after she allowed herself this pleasure again was *The Colonel* by F. C. Burnand, who was at the time the editor of *Punch.* "A very clever play, written to quiz and ridicule the foolish aesthetic people who dress in such absurd manner, with loose garments, puffed sleeves, great hats, and carrying peacock's feathers, sunflowers and lilies,"[2] noted the Queen. The play had been chosen not because of any special merit, but because of what had become the surprisingly topical subject. It was an obvious parody of Oscar Wilde and his merry band of aesthetes. *The Colonel* preceded *Patience* on the London stage by two months; indeed, the success of Burnand's play may well have persuaded W. S. Gilbert to change a cleric called the Reverend Lawn Tennison into a poet called Reginald Bunthorne.

Sir Arthur Sullivan's career as an opera composer began when Burnand, in 1866, persuaded Sullivan—at the time best known as a composer of "serious" music—to turn the popular Victorian farce *Box and Cox* into a comic opera called *Cox and Box.* But the prolific Sullivan also continued to write popular songs such as "The Lost Chord," one of the most widely sung melodies of the era.

> *Seated one day at the organ,*
> *I was weary and ill at ease,*
> *And my fingers wandered idly,*
> *Over the noisy keys.*
> *I knew not what I was playing,*
> *Or what I was dreaming then,*
> *But I struck one chord of music,*
> *Like the sound of a great Amen.*

Between its introduction in January 1877 and the end of the century, more than half a million copies of "The Lost Chord" were sold.

What counted was not just sentimentality, but skillful musical rendition

Richard D'Oyly Carte. The owner of the Savoy Theatre and the producer of most of the Gilbert and Sullivan comic operas during the closing decades of the century. (Kodak Museum)

of sentimentality. At that the Victorians excelled. It was, in particular, a great time for religious music, on the streets, in Methodist chapels, and in the cathedrals.

Foremost among the religious composers was Villiers Stanford. He composed anthems and settings for the Anglican service that are still often heard. His orchestral pieces, however, did not meet with universal acclaim. "When Professor Stanford is genteel, cultured, classic, pious, and experimentally mixolydian, he is dull beyond belief," wrote George Bernard Shaw. "His dullness is all the harder to bear because it is the restless, ingenious, trifling, flippant dullness of the Irishman, instead of the stupid, bovine, sleepable-through dullness of the Englishman, or even the aggressive, ambitious, sentimental dullness of the Scot . . . According to all classic precedent, it should end in hopeless gloom, in healing resignation, or in pathetic sentiment. What it does end in is blue murder . . ."[3]

Another remarkable musician of the period was Herbert Parry—a prolific songwriter, an accomplished composer of choral works and church music, a writer of incidental music for the stage and of oratorios. He is credited with inaugurating the so-called English musical "renaissance" during this period with his choral composition based on Shelley's poem *Prometheus Unbound*. It is an enthusiastic piece of dramatic music showing the marks of Parry's admiration for Wagner and Brahms. His stage music was primarily for the revivals of Greek plays, something of a fashion during the period. Parry did settings of Aristophanes's plays *The Birds* and *The Frogs* that became quite well known—for ingenuity, among other things. He even found a way of setting to music the Frog's cry, "Brekekekex koax koax."

He belongs right in the dull center of a Victorian phenomenon—the oratorio, a kind of secular wallow in sacred water. Oratorios were astonishingly popular and their popularity kept choirs and musicians in work. Dvořak, Gounod, and Brahms provided some variety to a tradition that essentially belonged to Handel and Mendelssohn, and the English composers took to it in part because it seemed to be *the* great musical form. Shaw, among others, detested it, and he took out his irritation on Parry's oratorios *Judith* and *Job*.

"In so far as these are not dull imitations of Handel, they are unstaged operettas on scriptural themes, written in a style in which solemnity and triviality are blended in the right proportions for boring an atheist out of his senses or shocking a sincerely religious person into utter repudiation of any possible union between art and religion. However, there is an intermediate class in England which keeps up the demand in the oratorio market. This class holds that the devil is not respectable (a most unsophisticated idea); but it deals with him in a spirit of extraordinary liberality in dividing with him the kingdom of the fine arts. Thus in literature it gives him all the novels, and is content to keep nothing but the tracts. In music it gives him everything that is played in a theatre, reserving the vapidities of the drawing room

The Royal Albert Hall of Arts and Sciences, designed by architects Fowke and Scott in the Italian Renaissance style, was completed in 1871 as a public memorial to the late Prince Consort Albert. It soon became (and continues to serve as) the foremost center of London's musical life. (Guildhall Library)

and the solemnities of the cathedral for itself. It asks no more in graphic art than a set of illustrations to its family Bible, cheerfully devoting all other subjects to the fiend . . . I hope [Parry] will burn the score, and throw Judith in when the blaze begins to flag."[4]

Of course, oratorios were not blown away by Shaw's blast. Sir Edward William Elgar, perhaps the greatest English composer of the century, in fact, produced a notable example in 1900, *The Dream of Gerontius.* But Elgar's great genius was much more expansive, and found its form in his remarkable orchestral works, especially the *Enigma Variations* of 1899.

Yet, the music of Oscar Wilde's London was in large measure a music of songs and of concerts. The Queen's Hall Promenade Concerts, begun by Henry Wood in 1895, provided a new opportunity for orchestral works, continuing a tradition begun in 1855 at the Crystal Palace.

London's music delighted audiences far away, especially in North America. London was also an enthusiastic consumer of Continental music,

especially opera, which was caught somewhere between a dogmatic assumption that good opera is Italian opera, and a growing enthusiasm for Wagner.

Earlier in the century, opera had been dominated by singers such as the contralto Marietta Alboni, the sisters Giuditta and Giulia Grisi, the tenor Giuseppe Mario, and—above all others—the immensely popular soprano Jenny Lind, "the Swedish Nightingale." By the 1880s new talent had emerged—especially Adelina Patti and, later, Nellie Melba—but there was no singer to match Mario until the Polish brothers Édouard and Jean de Reszke began to share the limelight. Jean de Reszke was a tenor greatly admired by Shaw, and dominated the scene from the moment the curtain fell on his London debut in *Aïda* in 1887. (Actually, he had sung twelve years earlier at Drury Lane—but that was as a baritone.)

Reszke's success coincided with the consolidation of London opera in 1888 under the management of Augustus Harris, who had run Drury Lane for nearly a decade. Harris took over Covent Garden, then called it the Royal Italian Opera. Harris soon changed it to the Royal Opera and gave London a polyglot opera fare—a variety of French, German, and, of course, Italian opera.

The possibilities of *English* opera were tried by Carl Rosa and his company in the 1880s, but with slim success. Rosa, however, was instrumental in establishing Wagner in London. *The Flying Dutchman* was performed in 1870 at Drury Lane—in Italian. *Lohengrin* was presented at Covent Garden in 1875, and *Tannhäuser* in 1876, both also in Italian. It was not until the Bayreuth company presented the entire Ring cycle at Her Majesty's Theatre, in 1882, that London heard Wagner in German. When Wilde's first son was born in 1885, Wilde praised the baby as having "a superb voice, which it freely exercises: its style is essentially Wagnerian."[5]

Not all critics were enthusiastic. The *Standard* described the Ring as "a monument of industry and power—misdirected," and described listening to it as most fatiguing because of the "total absence of human interest, the gross contradictions and inconsistencies, the trivialities of the plot—to say nothing of its repulsive incidents—the introduction of childish dragons, bears, alligators, horses, real and pasteboard."[6]

Of *Die Walküre,* the *Standard* critic said that "the loathsome subject upon which the whole of *Die Walküre* is based altogether places it beyond the pale of human sympathy . . . When the poem is full of the most revolting incidents, which are reiterated again and again, and dwelt on persistently by all the personages of the drama, what must be the effect of the music upon the hearer?"[7]

But the *Times* critic was enthusiastic: "There were defects of detail, but the entire rendering was instinct with a spirit of artistic earnestness too rarely found on the operatic stage. There was here no striving for cheap effect, no

---

Opposite, Hans von Bülow. German conductor and pianist and the most famous Wagnerian conductor of his age. His wife, Cosima, a daughter of Franz Liszt, left him for Richard Wagner. Von Bülow, nevertheless, remained the foremost interpreter and promoter of Wagner's music throughout the Continent and the British Isles. (Kodak Museum)

shouting of high notes at the audience, no undue self-assertion on the part of the prominent singers. Everyone was intent only upon doing justice to the requirements of his part, and the result was a high standard of excellence sustained throughout."[8]

Punch had some "Wagnerian Waggeries" for the enterprise. "Of course it is utterly bad taste to declare that we would far rather hear *The Flying Dutchman* or *Lohengrin* than the whole of the *Ring des Nibelungen.* After four nights of the *Ring,* with the *Ring* of it still in our ears—which makes us look and feel quite savage,—we deliberately say, 'Never again with you, Wotan, Siegfried, and Co!'

"It appears to our untutored and uncultivated taste that the *Ring* taken as an 'all round' work, is just what might be expected from an impulsive musician after seeing a melodrama and a pantomime for the first time, and struck by the happy thought of combining the effects and setting them to music."[9]

Theater songs, the product of the music halls, were less complicated. So were the music halls. Music halls had their origin in a combination of musical and social ventures, from the traveling shows and pleasure gardens of the early part of the century to the glee clubs, song and supper clubs, and taverns that flourished in Queen Victoria's time.

The first building designed specifically as what we would now term a music hall was called the Canterbury Arms and was built in London in 1852 by Charles Morton, who became one of the great music hall entrepreneurs. By 1860, there were over two hundred and fifty halls in London, and the building boom continued till the end of the century, with larger halls and eventually music hall chains, the Empires and Hippodromes of the 1890s.

The patrons of the music halls were originally from the lower and working classes, with a sprinkling of gentlemen slummers. In time, however, they became all but classless. Changes in licensing laws in 1878, requiring a "certificate of suitability" on the buildings themselves, closed down some of the shabbier establishments, and the best music hall performers were becoming so well known that the respectable middle class wanted to be part of the scene. At the Christmas pantomime at Covent Garden in 1879, two of the music hall stars of the day, Herbert Campbell and G. H. ("The Great") MacDermott, were included in the cast, and the next year Drury Lane brought in its own recruits from the halls. From then on, the traditionally lower-class music hall would become more and more available to the middle-class audiences of pantomime, and more and more caught up in the artistic anarchy, but wonderful delights, of the "variety" stage. And there was no matching the sheer variety of music hall entertainment, as described by a writer in *Harper's New Monthly Magazine* in 1891:

"London music halls might be roughly grouped into four classes—first, the aristocratic variety theatre of the West End, chiefly found in the immedi-

Marie Lloyd. A star of the music halls, she helped make them respectable and they, in turn, made her a star. (Kodak Museum)

ate neighbourhood of Leicester Square; then the smaller and less aristocratic West End halls; next, the large *bourgeois* music halls of the less fashionable parts and in the suburbs; last, the minor music halls of the poor and squalid districts. The audiences, as might be expected, correspond to the social scale of the particular place of entertainment, but the differences in the performances provided by the four classes of music halls are far less strongly marked . . .

"Both externally and internally the *bourgeois* and suburban music hall

Poster by Dudley Hardy for A Gaiety Girl, *which played the Prince of Wales's Theatre in 1895. The showgirl became the stuff of comedy. (Victoria and Albert Museum)*

differs considerably from its more fashionable rival. For one thing, it is generally dingier and gaudier of appearance; the entrance is covered with huge posters and adorned with tea-garden plaster statues bearing colored lamps . . .

"There are no dress-coats and caped cloaks, no dashing toilets, to be seen here; but the vast majority are in easy circumstances and eminently respectable. You will see little family parties—father, mother, and perhaps a grown-up daughter or a child or two—in the stalls. Most of them are probably regular visitors, and have the *entrée* here in return for exhibiting bills in their shop-windows; and these family parties all know one another, as can be seen from the smiles and handshakes they exchange as they pass in or out. Then there are several girls with their sweethearts, respectable young couples employed in neighboring workshops and factories, and a rusty old matron or two, while the fringe of the audience is made up of gay young clerks, the local 'bloods,' who have a jaunty fashion in some districts of wearing a cigar behind the ear. Large ham sandwiches are handed round by the cooks in white blouses, and when a young woman desires to be very stylish indeed, she allows her swain to order a glass of port for her refreshment . . .

"After a song and some feats by a troupe of acrobats, came an exhibition by a young lady in a large glass tank filled with water. She was a very pretty and graceful young lady, and she came on accompanied by a didactic gentleman in evening dress, who accompanied the announcement of each new feature of her performance by a little discourse. 'Opening and shutting the mouth under water,' he would say, for example. 'It has long been a theory among scientific men that by opening the mouth while under water a vacuum is created, thereby incurring the risk of choking the swimmer. Miss So-and-so, ladies and gentlemen, will now proceed to demonstrate the fallacy of that opinion, by opening and shutting her mouth several times in succession while remaining at the bottom of the tank.' Which Miss So-and-so accordingly did, to our great edification. Then came 'gathering shells under water,' which was accomplished in a highly elaborate manner, so that there could be no mistake about it. 'Sewing' and 'writing under water.' 'Eating under water,' when the lady consumed a piece of bread with every appearance of extreme satisfaction. 'Drinking from a bottle under water. Most of you,' remarked the manager, sympathetically, 'are acquainted with the extreme difficulty of drinking out of a bottle under *any* circumstances.' Then a cigar was borrowed from the audience, lighted, and given to the lady, who, shielding it with her hands, retired under the water and smoked vigorously for a minute or two, reappearing with the cigar still unextinguished. Lastly the manager announced, 'Ladies and gentlemen, Miss So-and-so will now adopt the position of prayer'; whereupon the lady sank gracefully on her knees under water, folded her hands, and appeared rapt in devotion, while the orchestra played 'The Maiden's Prayer,' and the manager, with head reverently bent, stood delicately aside, as one who felt himself unworthy to intrude upon such orisons. Then the lady adopted a pose even more implor-

Above and opposite, sheet music covers for "How London Lives" and "Quite too Utterly Utter." The insatiable demand for the lyrics and score of the new musical hits both reflected and promoted the popularity of the music halls. Their success rested mainly on their stars, the lions comiques, *and their hit songs were sung or hummed in all the London pubs and parlors. (Victoria and Albert Museum)*

QUITE TOO UTTERLY UTTER.

New Æsthetical Roundelay,
Written & Composed by
ROBERT COOTE.
LONDON. HOPWOOD & CREW 42. NEW BOND ST

ing, and a ray, first of crimson and then of green light, was thrown into the tank, presumably to indicate morning and evening prayer respectively. After some minutes of this, the fair performer, a little out of breath from her spiritual exertions, rose, sleek and dripping, to the surface, hopped nimbly out, and bowed herself off . . ."[10]

At the Empire Theatre of Varieties on Leicester Square, the entertainment might be of a slightly different character; whatever the entertainment, its promenade at the rear of the orchestra provided one of the best chances for a pickup in London.

"Its exterior is more handsome and imposing than that of most London theatres, even of the highest rank. Huge cressets in classical tripods flare between the columns of the façade, the windows and *foyer* glow with stained glass, the entrance hall, lighted by softened electric lamps, is richly and tastefully decorated. You pass through wide, airy corridors and down stairs, to find yourself in a magnificent theatre, and the stall to which you are shown is wide and luxuriously fitted. Smoking is universal, and a large proportion of the audience promenade the outer circles, or stand in groups before the long refreshment bars which are a prominent feature on every tier. Most of the men are in evening dress, and in the boxes are some ladies, also in evening costume, many of them belonging to what is called good society. The women in other parts of the house are generally pretty obvious members of a class which, so long as it behaves itself with propriety in the building, it would, whatever fanatics may say to the contrary, be neither desirable nor possible to exclude. The most noticeable characteristic of the audience is perhaps the very slight attention it pays to whatever is going on upon the stage . . .

"[The] ballets are magnificent enough to satisfy the most insatiate appetite for splendor. There are two in one evening, and each lasts about half an hour, during which time the large stage is filled with bewildering combinations of form and color. Company after company of girls, in costumes of delicately contrasted tints, march, trip, or gallop down the boards, their burnished armor gleaming and their rich dresses scintillating in the limelight; at each fresh stroke of the stage-manager's gong they group themselves anew or perform some complicated figure, except when they fall back in a circle and leave the stage clear for the *première danseuse* . . . At last the end comes; the ballet girls are ranked and massed into brilliant parterres and glittering pyramids, the *première danseuse* glides on in time to appropriate the credit of the arrangement, and the curtain falls on a blaze of concentrated magnificence."[11]

Serious dramatic ballet, such as was the pride of Paris, Copenhagen, and St. Petersburg, was prohibited in London establishments because of the license laws, which prescribed *either* music and dance *or* dramatic entertainments but brooked no combination.

The songs of the music hall ranged from sentimental ballad to nonsense parody, and were often enormously popular. Events of the moment provided the occasion for some, especially of the patriotic variety. The Great MacDermott's famous song, for example, caught the national anti-Russian mood in the midst of the Balkan crisis of 1877, and added a new word to the language:

> *We don't want to fight,*
> *But, by Jingo, if we do—*
> *We've got the ships, we've got the men,*
> *We've got the money, too.*
> *We've fought the Bear before*
> *And while we're Britons true—*
> *The Russians shall not have Constantinople.* [12]

Cockney (or "coster") songs such as "I'm Henery the Eighth I Am" were often part of the repertoire, as were minstrel (or "coon") songs performed by such black-faced comedians as Eugene Stratton, often coming to the music hall stage from the minstrel troupes. Stratton's successes were in songs such as "The Whistling Coon," "The Dandy Coloured Coon," and "My Little Octoroon."

Then there were the so-called "swell" or "masher" songs, the songs celebrating the good life. Nobody was better at these, and nobody's career better exemplified the high life, than George Leybourne, whose "Champagne Charlie" was an early success, with its tub-thumping chorus:

> *Champagne Charlie is my name!*
> *Yes, Champagne Charlie is my name!*
> *Good for any game at night, my boys—*
> *Yes, good for any game at night, my boys—*

Some of his songs had more of a comic side:

> *One night last week I went up in a balloon;*
> *On a voyage of discovery to visit the Moon,*
> *Where an old man lives, so many people say,*
> *For cutting his toe-nails on a Sunday!* [13]

There was no substitute, of course, for sing-along songs, and the music hall specialized in such favorites as "Pack Up Your Troubles," or the somewhat racier "Ta-ra-ra-boom-de-ay," first sung by Lottie Collins in a Dick Whittington pantomime, and then brought onto the music hall stage.

The poet John Davidson gave a portrait of a music hall singer that catches the spirit of it all:

A fur-collared coat and stick and a ring,
And a chimney-pot hat to the side—that's me!
I'm a music-hall singer that never could sing;
I'm a sort of a fellow like that, do you see?
I go pretty high in my line, I believe,
Which is comic, and commonplace, too, maybe.
I was once a job-lot, though, and didn't receive
The lowest price paid in the biz, do you see?
For I never could get the right hang of the trade;
So the managers wrote at my name, "D.B.,"
In the guide-books they keep
Of our business and grade,
Which means—you'll allow me—damned bad,
Do you see? . . .
I'm jolly, and sober, and fond of my wife;
And she and the kids, they're happy at me.
I was once in a draper's; but this kind of life
Gives a fellow more time to himself,
Do you see?[14]

One of the greatest of music hall performers was Marie Lloyd, "Our Marie" as she was affectionately called. On her death in 1922, T. S. Eliot paid extraordinary tribute:

". . . nor is it always easy to distinguish superiority from great popularity, when the two go together . . . Although I have always admired her genius I do not think that I always appreciated its uniqueness; I certainly did not realize that her death would strike me as the most important event which I have had to chronicle in these pages. Marie Lloyd was the greatest music-hall artist in England: she was also the most popular. And popularity in her case was not merely evidence of her accomplishment; it was something more than success. It is evidence of the extent to which she represented and expressed that part of the English nation which has perhaps the greatest vitality and interest . . .

"Among all of that small number of music-hall performers, whose names are familiar to what is called the lower class, Marie Lloyd had far the strongest hold on popular affection . . . The middle classes have no such idol . . . The middle classes, in England as elsewhere, under democracy, are morally dependent upon the aristocracy, and the aristocracy are morally in fear of the middle class which is gradually absorbing and destroying them. The lower classes still exist; but perhaps they will not exist for long. In the music-hall comedians they find the artistic expression and dignity of their own lives; and this is not found in the most elaborate and expensive revue . . . With the dwindling of the music-hall, by the encouragement of the cheap and rapid-breeding cinema, the lower classes will tend to drop into the

"Sit Down in Front." The annual Christmas pantomime at the Royal Victoria Coffee Music Hall drew young and old, but particularly the young. (From The Graphic *of 1882. Olin Library, Cornell University)*

same state of amorphous protoplasm as the bourgeoisie. The working-man who went to the music-hall and saw Marie Lloyd and joined in the chorus, was himself performing part of the work of acting; he was engaged in that collaboration of the audience with the artist which is necessary in all art and most obviously in dramatic art. He will now go to the cinema, where his mind is lulled by continuous senseless music and continuous action too rapid for the brain to act upon, and will receive, without giving, in that same listless apathy with which the middle and upper classes regard any entertainment of the nature of art. He will also have lost some of his interest in life . . ."[15]

Whatever else the variety stage was, it was surely not boring, and it was enhanced by the musical comedies which derived from the old burlesque routines. In the hands of entrepreneurs, such as George Edwardes, musical comedy thrived, with the delights of *A Gaiety Girl*—and then, on the basis of that success, *A Shop Girl, The Circus Girl,* and *A Runaway Girl*. Most famous of all was the enormously popular *The Geisha,* with its score by Edwardes's favorite Sidney Jones, the composer of such songs as "Linger Longer Loo."

But not everybody liked this new development. W. S. Gilbert, who was acid-tongued at the best of times, had an exchange in court (during a minor libel suit he initiated) with the lawyer Edward Carson (who would later take on Oscar Wilde in his terrible trial).

Asked about the direction of current dramatic taste, Gilbert answered:

"In the direction of musical comedy; bad musical comedy, in which half a dozen irresponsible comedians are turned loose on the stage to do as they please."

"Will you mention one of them?"

"Oh, there are plenty of them!"

"I wish you would mention one."

"Well, take the pantomime at Drury Lane Theatre with the great Dan Leno." (Loud laughter.)

"But that only goes on a short time in the year."

"It goes on for a long time in the evening." (Laughter.)

"Do you really describe a pantomime as a bad musical comedy?"

"No, but I would describe a bad musical comedy as a pantomime." (Great laughter.)

"That is very clever," said Carson when the laughter had subsided. "But I would like to know what you mean by bad musical comedies. Give me the name of one."

"There are fifty of them."

"Give me one."

"I would say such a piece as *The Circus Girl.*"

"Would you call it a bad musical comedy?"

"I would call it bad. I believe the manager calls it musical comedy." (Laughter.)

"Have they half a dozen irresponsible low comedians turned loose in *The Circus Girl?*"

"I do not know how many there are." (Laughter.)[16]

Others who lamented the new popular music were more academic in their anxiety, and contrasted the gaudiness of popular songs with the purity of folk songs. Herbert Parry was one of the mourners, speaking at the inaugural meetings of the Folk Song Society in 1898:

"In true folk-songs there is no show, no got-up glitter, and no vulgarity . . . and the pity of it is that these treasures of humanity are getting rare, for they are written in characters of the most evanescent you can imagine, upon the sensitive brain fibres of those who learn them, and have but little idea of their value. Moreover, there is an enemy at the doors of folk music which is driving it out, namely the common popular songs of the day; and this enemy is one of the most repulsive and most insidious . . ."[17]

But the difference was not so much between the true and the sham as it was between urban and rural cultures, and the new music was to a large

---

Opposite, Adelina Patti. One of the leading coloratura sopranos of her day, Patti made her debut in 1861 at the Covent Garden Royal Opera House. Her repertoire included works by Rossini, Bellini, Donizetti, Verdi, Gounod, and Meyerbeer. The highest-paid opera star of her time, she earned two hundred guineas a performance. (Kodak Museum)

The dawn of consumerism. Endorsements by singer Adelina Patti and actress Lillie Langtry, mistress of the Prince of Wales, say more about the popularity of opera and theater than about the quality of Pears' Soap. (Olin Library, Cornell University)

extent popular in a traditional "folk" sense—except that the folk now lived in London and Manchester and other great nineteenth-century towns. It was a simple fact that during the nineteenth century the proportion of the population living in towns rose from twenty percent to seventy percent.

Some of these townsfolk now took to choral singing as well, a movement which was encouraged by a new development in music education, in which the traditional relationship of the note names (do, re, me, fa, sol, la, ti) to the key of C major was replaced with the "solfa" system based on a movable tone base. It was called "tonic solfa," and it meant that a sense of note relationships could now be taught to people otherwise unfamiliar with music. The rise of choral groups, both sacred and secular, and of choral competitions, was given considerable impetus by this and other aspects of music education—though many still held to Lord Chesterfield's advice that music wasted a man's time and took him into odd company.

Popular interest in classical music was erratic during this period. It was fashionable to be enthusiastic about its effects, as Gilbert is in Wilde's dialogue, "The Critic as Artist," when he rises from the piano, having been ignored in his suggestion that he play some Chopin, or "some passionate, curious-coloured thing" by Dvořak.

"After playing Chopin, I feel as if I had been weeping over sins that I had never committed, and mourning over tragedies that were not my own. Music always seems to me to produce that effect. It creates for one a past of which one has been ignorant, and fills one with a sense of sorrows that have been hidden from one's tears. I can fancy a man who had led a perfectly commonplace life, hearing by chance some curious piece of music, and suddenly discovering that his soul, without his being conscious of it, had passed through terrible experiences, and known fearful joys, or wild romantic loves, or great renunciations."[18]

Out on the streets, meanwhile, there seemed no end to the sounds of bands—large and small, British and increasingly German. There was also the relentless mechanical music of the barrel piano, the barrel organ, and the hurdy-gurdy. A writer for *Chambers's Journal* in 1881 described the organ-grinder as "spread[ing] musical culture even among the dregs of the people."[19] The culture in question included a polka, "Adeste Fideles," "Champagne Charlie," the "Marseillaise," a sailor's hornpipe, an extract from a Handel oratorio, and the "Blue Danube" waltz.

From a hospital bed, W. E. Henley described the poignant effect of these sounds of London:

> *Down the quiet eve,*
> *Thro' my window with the sunset*
> *Pipes to me a distant organ*
> *Foolish ditties; . . .*
> *O, the sign and scent,*
> *Wistful eye and perfumed pavement!*
> *In the distance pipes and organ . . .*
> *The sensation*
> *Comes to me anew,*
> *And my spirit for a moment*
> *Thro' the music breathes the blessed*
> *Airs of London.*[20]

10

VIRTUES OF SPORT

Cecil John Rhodes's famous scholarships to Oxford University require more than "literary and scholastic achievements." To be eligible, the candidate must also show a "fondness for, and success in, manly outdoor sports such as cricket, football and the like." The English, as Lloyd George remarked, were a "nation of footballers, stock-exchangers, public-house and music-hall frequenters."[1] But in the end, manly games, games such as football, rather than the other pursuits, were what mattered most to male Victorians. Sports were the nation's virtue and the nation's youth needed to be instructed in them, as they were instructed to love Queen and country.

"The self-reliance of the individual football player and the cohesiveness of the team are of almost as much value in the battles of life" as they are in the game of football, noted *The Times* in its leading article on Monday following the Football Association Cup Final in 1899.[2] Thus, England's public schools, that is to say, England's elite, stood squarely on what Lytton Strachey described as "the worship of athletics and the worship of good form. Upon these two poles our public schools have turned for so long that we have almost come to believe that such is their essential nature, and that an English public schoolboy who wears the wrong clothes and takes no interest in football is a contradiction in terms."[3]

But not everyone was actively virtuous or showed good form. There were crowds of lads, as Lord Baden-Powell remarked in his *Scouting for Boys,* who did not play the games themselves "but were merely onlookers at a few paid performers . . . thousands of boys and young men, pale, narrow-chested, hunched-up, miserable specimens, smoking endless cigarettes, numbers of them betting, all of them learning to be hysterical as they groan or cheer in panic unison with their neighbours . . ."⁴

Others took a more charitable view of spectators. "What would the devotees of athletics do if their present amusements were abolished?" asked F. E. Smith (later Lord Birkenhead). "The policeman, the police magistrate, the social worker, the minister of religion, the public schoolmaster and the university don would each, in the sphere of his own duties, contemplate such a prospect with dismay. It is to be supposed, for instance, that the seething mass of humanity which streams every Saturday at midday out of the factories and workshops of our great towns would ever saunter in peace and contentment through museums and picture galleries, or sit enraptured listening to classical concerts . . . or spend his leisure studying botany or horticulture . . . The poorer classes in this country have not got the tastes which superior people or a Royal Commission would choose for them," Smith reflected, adding that were cricket and football to be abolished, "it would bring upon the masses nothing but misery, depression, sloth, indiscipline, and disorder."⁵

Football (which Americans call soccer) and cricket were *the* national games. They also engendered a national controversy about the place of professional athletics v. amateur sports that became quite heated in the last decades of the nineteenth century. Football had seen the benefits of importing semiprofessional players, especially from Scotland, who were paid expenses and something more. Among other things, this had been an important element in improving the quality of soccer in the industrial midlands, and breaking the London monopoly on the sport. But many people worried about the consequences of using professionals. There were professionals in other sports, such as walking and boxing, but these sports were notorious for dishonest practices. Cricket, however, which was under the upper- and middle-class eye of the country clubs and the Marylebone Cricket Club, was combining amateur and professional sport in an orderly way. So, in its way, was the Football Association.

The members of the Association were amateurs, and knew what sport was all about. They were also, in the main, Londoners, and so they knew what life was about. Under guidelines established by the Association, amateurs and professionals played together; though, of course, they dined separately, because the professionals were servants, after all. In 1886, professionals were even allowed to play in the England v. Scotland match, although they wore different shirts from the rest. Football players originally wore long trousers. When they shortened them, they were accused of discrediting the game. There was some class conflict here, although ex-public school men could be found on both sides. More significantly, there was also a conflict between south and north, between established London-based amateur clubs and the newer northern clubs. Regional pride and a lot of money were tied up in these games, as sport became heavily capitalized.

"Aesthetics v. Athletics." The Aesthete (obviously Oscar Wilde) complains in this 1881 cartoon: "This is indeed a form of death, and entirely incompatible with any belief in the immortality of the soul." Most Britons, however, considered Aestheticism unmanly. (William Andrews Clark Library, University of California at Los Angeles)

But over and above all these disputes stood some larger matters, matters of style. The Scots changed things by introducing a passing style of play to a game which through the 1860s and '70s had been characterized by individual players dribbling down the fields providing much of the excitement. The most important early football club sponsors were churches and chapels. The great Aston Villa team, for example, had its beginnings at the Aston Villa Wesleyan Chapel in Birmingham. Then the pubs got into the game, providing changing and dining facilities, and sometimes even fields, along with the beer. Also, there was the workingplace—the (Woolwich) Arsenal and West Ham United (originally called Thames Ironworks after the shipyard) being the most famous of the teams to originate in this way.

Rugby football, undoubtedly the most famous product of the Rugby School, was until the 1870s a confused and confusing game widely played in London without rules or organization. Only the growing brutality of "hacking" opponents with iron-capped boots finally forced the formation of a Rugby Union and some rules. One Association member complained, however, that the Rugby Union's ban of hacking would do away with "all the courage and pluck of the game" and might "bring over a lot of Frenchmen who would beat you with a week's practice."[6]

Cricket was ubiquitous, and even more highly praised than football for

"The self-reliance of the individual football player and the cohesiveness of the team are of almost as much value in the battles of life as they are in football." (London Museum)

Were football to be abolished, "it would bring upon the masses nothing but misery, depression, sloth, indiscipline, and disorder." (From The Graphic. *Olin Library, Cornell University)*

the way in which it held the mirror up to English nature, and for the virtues
it supposedly inculcated:

> *There's a breathless hush in the close*
> *tonight,*
> *Ten to make and the match to win,*
> *A bumping pitch and a blinding light,*
> *An hour to play and the last man in.*
> *And it's not for the sake of a ribboned*
> *coat,*
> *Or the selfish hope of a season's fame,*
> *But the Captain's hand on his shoulder*
> *smote*
> *"Play up! Play up! and play the game."*
>
> *The sand of the desert is sodden red,*
> *Red with the wreck of a square that broke;*
> *The Gatling's jammed and the Colonel dead,*
> *And the regiment blind with dust and smoke.*
> *The river of death has brimmed his banks,*
> *And England's far, and Honour a name,*
> *But the voice of a schoolboy rallies the*
> *ranks:*
> *"Play up! Play up! and play the game!"*[7]

Cricket gave to the language some of its familiar phrases: "It isn't
cricket," or "Play a straight bat." P. G. Wodehouse called his famous butler
Jeeves after a Warwickshire cricket player. The Reverend Thomas Waugh
gave it an even more significant place in the scheme of things when he wrote
about *The Cricket Field of the Christian Life* (1894).

"Put your whole soul into the game, and make it your very life. Hit
clean and hard at every loose ball. 'Steal a run' whenever you safely can, for
the least bit of work that helps anyone nearer to God is blessed work, and
gladdens the Captain's heart. Be alert and ready, and you will keep up your
end. Lay on hard, and you will run up a grand score. And when 'time' is
called you will 'bring out your bat,' your conscience will say, 'Well done,'
and those you have cheered and helped will say, 'A good man! Thank God
for such an inning!' Aye, and when on the resurrection morning you come
out of the pavilion, leaving your playing clothes behind you, and robed like
your glorious Captain-King, you and all the hosts of God will see and understand your score as you cannot now, and your joy will be full as you hear the
Captain, 'the innumerable company of angels,' and the whole redeemed
Church of God greet you with the words, "Well played, sir!" ' "[8]

Prince Ranjitsinhji, one of the great cricketers of the period, described

"Play up! Play up! and play the game." (Kodak Museum)

with typical enthusiasm, in *Blackwood's Edinburgh Magazine,* the kind of man who played cricket, at least at Ranji's level. "A cricketer is just a man with a clear eye, bronzed face, and athletic figure. He is usually somewhat lacking in general information, and is sometimes a poor conversationalist upon any but his own subject. He does not read much. On the other hand, he does not talk much about things he does not understand, which is a good trait. He gives the impression of having led a free, unconstrained life—he might be, in fact, anything from a trooper in the Rhodesian Horse to a Californian orange-grower. He is simple, frank, and unaffected; a genuine person, with plenty of self-respect, and no desire to seem what he is not: on the whole, not a bad sort of man at all—quite the reverse."[9]

British lists of "Eminent Victorians" usually include at least one sportsman—cricket player William Gilbert Grace. "He enjoyed the proper authority," wrote Neville Cardus. "To catch the popular sense of dramatic fitness, Grace simply *had* to be big, for he stood for so much in the history of cricket at a time when hardly any other game challenged it as the national out-of-door sport and spectacle . . . Alone he conquered—with his bat and (this is certain) by his beard . . . Everybody understood exactly who he was and what he signified in the diet of the day's news. From time to time, *Punch* used him as the subject for a cartoon; the Royal Family occasionally inquired after his health. When he was reported not out at Lord's at lunch, the London

William Gilbert Grace. His skill at cricket, Britain's foremost outdoor sport and spectacle, placed him high on the list of eminent Victorians. "Alone he conquered— with his bat and by his beard," said a contemporary, "and everybody understood exactly who he was and what he signified in the diet of the day's news." (Olin Library, Cornell University)

clubs emptied, and the road to St. John's Wood all afternoon was tinkling with the . . . happy noise of the hansom cab. Sometimes he would play, at the height of his fame, in a country cricket match in some village in the West of England. And from far and wide the folk would come, on foot, in carriages, and homely gigs.

"On one of these occasions Grace had made a score of twenty or so when he played out at a ball and missed it. The local wicket-keeper snapped up the ball in his gloves triumphantly, and swept off the bails and—seeing visions of immortality—he screamed to the umpire: 'H'zat!'

"The umpire said: 'Not out; and look 'es 'ere, young fellow, the crowd has come to see Doctor Grace and not any of your monkey tricks . . .'

"Nobody thinks of Grace in terms of the statistics recorded of his skill; like Dr. Johnson, he endures not by reason of his works but by reason of his circumferential humanity. I always think of him as the great enjoyer of life who, after he had batted and bowled and fielded throughout the whole three days of a match between Gloucestershire and Yorkshire, was at the end of the third afternoon seen running uphill from the ground, carrying his bag, in haste for the train to London—running with a crowd of cheering little boys after him, and his whiskers blowing out sideways in the breeze."[10]

The Bishop of Hereford put it all in perspective: "Had Grace been born in ancient Greece, the Iliad would have been a different book. Had he lived in the Middle Ages he would have been a crusader and would now have been lying with his legs crossed in some ancient abbey, having founded a family. As he was born when the world was older, he was the best known of all Englishmen and the king of that English game least spoilt by any form of vice!"[11]

In his career, from 1863 to 1908, Grace scored nearly fifty-five thousand runs and took over twenty-five hundred wickets. At the beginning of the season in 1895, when everyone thought he was over the hill—he was forty-seven, after all—he scored one thousand in twenty-two days.

The new interest in sports was in many ways the product of new leisure time, especially Saturday half-holidays and what was referred to as "Saint" Monday. So as not to be led into temptation—idleness was the specter—Londoners became as earnest about their leisure activities as about their work. If you had a lawn, you could play croquet, a most earnest endeavor. As Disraeli described it in one of his novels, *Lothair,* the game was very much a social performance:

"Lord Montairy always looked forward to his summer croquet at Brentham. It was a great croquet family, the Brentham family; even listless Lord St. Aldegonde would sometimes play with a cigar never out of his mouth. They did not object to his smoking in the air. On the contrary, 'they rather liked it.' Captain Mildmay too was a brilliant hand, and had written a treatise on croquet—the best going.

"There was a great croquet party one morning at Brentham. Some neighbours had been invited who loved the sport. Mr. Blenkinsop, a grave young gentleman, whose countenance never relaxed while he played, and who was understood to give his mind entirely up to croquet. He was the owner of the largest estate in the county, and it was thought would have very much liked to have allied himself with one of the young ladies of the house of Brentham; but these flowers were always plucked so quickly, that his relations with the distinguished circle never grew more intimate than croquet. He drove over with some fine horses and several cases and bags containing instruments and weapons for the fray. His sister came with him, who had forty thousand pounds, but, they said, in some mysterious manner dependent on his consent to her marriage; and it was added that Mr. Blenkinsop would not allow his sister to marry because he would miss her so much in his favourite pastime . . .

"It seemed to Lothair a game of great deliberation and of more interest than gaiety, though sometimes a cordial cheer, and sometimes a ringing laugh of amiable derision, notified a signal triumph or a disastrous failure. But the scene was brilliant: a marvelous lawn, the Duchess' Turkish tent with its rich hangings, and the players themselves, the prettiest of all the spectacle, with their coquettish hats, and their half-veiled and half-revealed under-raiment, scarlet and silver, or blue and gold, made up a sparkling and modish scene."[12]

Lawn tennis came to prominence in the 1870s, as a more congenial and less earnest version of indoor rackets and Real Tennis. It was "invented" by Major Clopton Wingfield, who called it Sphairistikie or Lawn Tennis; he thought of it as a garden recreation. He took out a patent on it, and sold boxed sets complete with equipment and rules. The Marylebone Cricket Club, which controlled Real Tennis as well as cricket, formulated a set of rules derived from Wingfield, but the game became fully established in 1875 when Henry Jones persuaded the All England Croquet Club to set aside part of its grounds for a tennis court, and put together a new set of rules.

The first tournament in 1877 at the All England Croquet and Tennis Club, Wimbledon, took a two-day break, in keeping with sporting priorities, to allow spectators to attend the Eton-Harrow cricket match at Lord's. The winner at Wimbledon that year was Spencer Gore, with a volleying game that was so successful that there were calls for changes in the rules. The next year, a tea planter back on leave in England from Ceylon beat Gore in the final by countering his volleys with lobs. The game was on, and has changed very little since, though it was not quite strenuous enough for some tastes. The sort of people who were still in favor of hacking and mauling would call it "pat-ball." Tennis, nevertheless, became a popular sport, even—indeed, especially—for women.

Many people, to be sure, still considered women physically unsuited for sports, particularly since their clothes were a serious impediment. Women, therefore, began to change their clothes in line with the new interest in a

Lawn tennis championship meeting at Wimbledon in 1881. The sport had been "invented" by Major Clopton Wingfield as a garden recreation a decade earlier. The first Wimbledon tournament was played in 1877. (From The Graphic. *Olin Library, Cornell University)*

more "rational" dress for both sexes. Tennis and archery were popular with women, but it was bicycling that became the real craze.

Women, it might be said, pedaled to liberation. As one magazine put it, "woman has taken her stand, and her seat in the saddle, and like the author of the historic phrase, we men can only say—This is not a revolt, it is a revolution. I am tolerably certain that the net result will be that woman will take her true position as man's equal."[13]

The bicycle gave women a new mobility and a new place in the public eye. To help her ride it, the "new woman" was advised "to cultivate an erect and alert, though easy carriage in the saddle . . . not [to] hang forward over the handlebars, nor shuffle in the saddle."[14]

Another writer concentrated more specifically on the ankle, of which titillating glimpses were now available. "Neat ankle action is one of the chief points of graceful and expert riding. Don't sit like a stupid duck on the saddle and require the pedals to push up and down your limbs: raise the leg naturally when on the upward curve and learn to drive from the thighs with a clawing rather than a thrusting action. Remember that you have a most beautifully formed ankle, which separates the human foot from the clumsy appendages of the waddling tribes."[15]

And nobody who wanted to be a somebody in London could ignore the subject of dress, a subject "as important to the woman who cycles as to the woman who dances," counseled Mrs. Pennell, writing an article on cycling

Right, archery was the first popular public sport for women until bicycling came into vogue. (Olin Library, Cornell University)

Below, women's bicycling was "not a revolt, it [was] a revolution." It liberated not only fashions, but also attitudes, giving them not only new mobility, but also a new place in the public eye. (London Museum)

for Lady Grenville's collection of written "sketches on sport," entitled *Ladies in the Field.* "A grey tweed that defies dust and rain alike, makes the perfect gown; if a good, strong waterproof be added, a second dress will not be needed. For summer, a linen or thin flannel blouse and jacket—perhaps a silk blouse, for evening, in the knapsack—and, for all seasons, one of Henry Heath's felt hats complete the costume. For underwear, the rule is wool next to the skin, combinations by choice. Woolen stays contribute to one's comfort, and each rider can decide for herself between knickerbockers and a short petticoat. There is something to be said for each. This is practically the outfit by the Cyclists Touring Club for its women members. As for style, an ordinary tailor-made gown, simple rather than elaborate, answers the purpose of the tricyclist. The bicyclist does not get off so easily. Even with a suitable dress-guard, and, no matter what the makers say, the dress-guard should extend over the entire upper half of the rear wheel, there is ever danger of full long skirts catching in the spokes and bringing the wearer in humiliation and sorrow to the ground . . .

"For the tourist, who carries but one gown, and who objects to being stared at as a 'freak' escaped from a side show, it is awkward, when off the bicycle, to be obliged to appear in large towns in a dress up to her ankles; she might pass unnoticed in Great Britain, but on the Continent she becomes the observed of all observers . . . The device by which I make my own cycling gown long and short, as occasion requires . . . is a row of safety hooks, five in all, around the waistband, and a row of eyes on the skirt about a foot below. In a skirt so provided, I look like every other woman when off the machine. Just before I mount, I hook it up, and I wheel off with an easy mind, knowing that there is absolutely nothing to catch anywhere."[16]

The desire for appropriate clothing was also a mark of the Aesthetes, who, along with the rest of nature, wished to shape the body into an idealized aesthetic form. Wilde was at the forefront of this reform in his capacity as the editor of *Woman's World,* for which he wrote in 1887:

"And yet how sensible is the dress of the London milkwoman, of the Irish or Scotch fishwife, of the North-Country factory girl! An attempt was made recently to prevent the pit women from working, on the ground that their costume was unsuited to their sex; but it is really only the idle classes who dress badly. Wherever physical labour of any kind is required, the costume used is, as a rule, absolutely right, for labour necessitates freedom, and without freedom there is no such thing as beauty in dress at all."[17]

Wilde's views were clearly in line with the pragmatic intentions of the clothing reformers, but they also had an Aesthetic side. Function defines beauty for Wilde, in a way which the clothing reformers could only applaud:

"There is a divine economy about beauty; it gives us just what is needful and no more, whereas ugliness is always extravagant; ugliness is a spendthrift and wastes its material; in fine, ugliness . . . as much in costume as in anything else, is always the sign that somebody has been unpractical."[18]

For others, such as Mrs. Harcourt Williamson, it was more a matter of fashion. "I have laid it down, as a rule, that only small women look their best upon wheels, but this, like every other rule, has brilliant exceptions. Few women ride more gracefully than Mrs. W. H. Grenfell. I have seen her dressed all in soft green, a tweed skirt and velvet blouse, with gold belt and velvet Tam-o'-Shanter, looking more distinguished than anybody else as she passed through the throng in Hyde Park. At Battersea, which was always the most fashionable venue, Lady William Nevill and her tall husband were often seen riding together; and Lady William, always neat and well-dressed, looked her very best in navy blue, with a white sailor collar and cloth toque. Lady Minto, who bicycles nearly as well as she skates, and Lady Griffin, who is also a very pretty rider, are both generally seen in navy blue and white, with sailor hats . . . Lady Archibald Campbell, an authority upon such subjects, has laid it down as a law that no costume can look equally well when walking and when upon wheels: but in speaking of cycling dress it is impossible to ignore the divided skirt. A young lady who took part in many of last season's musical rides looked particularly well . . . as it naturally fell into equal folds on each side of the wheels; and even walking quietly about one did not notice the division, which was only at the back, and hidden among the pleated folds . . ."[19]

There were personal touches. "It is certainly the exception nowadays to see a bicycle with ordinary black or unembellished paint," reported Mrs. Williamson. "Most women and many men have their machines painted in their own particular colours. Lady Archibald Campbell is generally dressed in drab, and her smart machine is painted to match . . . Lady Huntingdon has her machine painted green with primrose lines upon it; Miss Cornwallis West's colours are crimson and blue; Princesse Henry of Plessee has the prettiest white machine that ever was seen; and no expense was spared in the finishing off of General Stracey's machine, which is done in the well-known red and blue of the Guards."[20]

Bicycle *racing,* however, was not a matter of primrose lines. Some thought it was headed downhill, as it were. At first it was carried on under the same amateur laws that controlled foot racing because the competitions were principally part of athletic meetings. Soon, however, gentlemen dropped out, the inter-university contests were abandoned, and bicycle racing ceased to be an amateur sport.

Rowing was another matter. It attracted many fine athletes as well as enthusiastic crowds. So did serious track and field sports. The establishment of the modern Olympic Games by Baron de Coubertin in 1896 gave them added importance. Swimming was also becoming popular and received a boost when Captain Matthew Webb first swam the English Channel in 1875. (Eight years later, he died trying to swim the Niagara Rapids.) Mountaineering, too, was much discussed in fashionable circles. Sometimes it was even tried. Judge Alfred Wills, who sentenced Oscar Wilde to two years' hard

Opposite, rowing regatta on the Thames, and onlookers. (Kodak Museum)

Wrestling at a county fair. (Kodak Museum)

labor in 1895, had earlier in his life climbed the Wetterhorn, and written one
of the most memorable mountaineering books of the nineteenth century,
Wandering Among the High Alps. And Lord Francis Douglas, brother to
Wilde's nemesis the Marquess of Queensberry, had fallen to his death after
making the first ascent of the Matterhorn.

The lower classes fancied boxing—or the prize-ring, as it was originally
called—although until 1892 it was basically illegal and notoriously corrupt.
In the 1870s and early '80s, matches were held at places which one could
only reach on special trains by tickets with "There and Back" printed on
them.

The crowds were rowdy—though by no means exclusively lower-class—
and the rules were uncertain. They were reformed by one John Graham

Chambers and his friend from Cambridge, the Marquess of Queensberry. In 1866, they had traveled together to America, where boxing flourished. On their return, they drafted a new set of regulations which were promoted under Queensberry's name.

The old-timers first scorned the new rules as effete and as interfering with the good old robust manner. It was not until 1892, when "Gentleman Jim" Corbett, fighting under the Queensberry Rules, defeated the awesome John L. Sullivan in New Orleans, that the new code was fully accepted. Sullivan's words are famous: "The Marquess of Queensberry must govern this contest, as I want fighting, not foot racing, and I intend keeping the championship of the world." Sportsmanship and Queensberry were, in some minds, nearly synonymous.

John L. Sullivan was a formidable figure. He fought his first exhibition in London in 1888, and was challenged by England's heavyweight champion Charlie Mitchell. Since prizefighting was still illegal in England, the match was scheduled for Chantilly, France. It was a big event. William Randolph Hearst ordered his top reporter, Arthur Brisbane, to drop the Jack the Ripper story and cover it.

The new boxing regime of the 1890s was in large measure the product of the National Sporting Club, formed in 1891 as a replacement for the notorious Pelican Club. The National Sporting Club was upper-middle-class and respectable, a somewhat diminished version of horse racing's Jockey Club; the Pelican Club was Bohemian and aristocratic, and (despite the fact that Queensberry himself belonged to it) did little to make boxing respectable, but it played its part nonetheless. In a celebrated case, deliberately provoked by the Pelican Club, those organizing a fight were charged with "breaching the peace." The case was dismissed after some careful legal strategy designed by Lord Lonsdale and Sir Charles Russell (who later became Lord Chief Justice of England) and their friends. The aristocracy, to be sure, had an interest in the sport of the lower classes.

Horse racing, the sport of kings, was another enterprise altogether. There was money on the racetracks—mainly money to be spent—and the greatest of the owners were very wealthy men. The four key figures of this period were the first Duke of Westminster, the sixth Duke of Portland, the fifth Earl of Rosebery, and of course H.R.H. the Prince of Wales, later King Edward VII. The Prince of Wales's horse won the Derby in 1896, and the Triple Crown in 1900, when he was leading owner and breeder for the year, winning nearly thirty thousand pounds. (There have been only twelve Triple Crown winners in the history of the English Turf; six of them ran between 1885 and 1900.) Rosebery won the Derby two years in a row, 1894 and 1895, while he was Prime Minister. He was criticized for paying too much attention to the ponies and too little to Parliament.

Derby Day was a great social occasion, a day when everyone enjoyed the festive occasion. Considerations of class and rank were temporarily sus-

At Hyde Park, 1895. While the nobility showed off its thoroughbred horses, the middle class showed off its bicycles. (Guildhall Library)

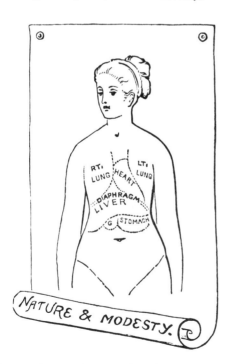 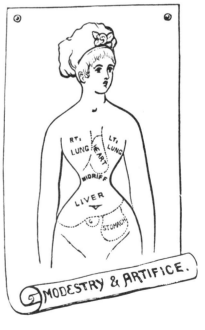

The new interest in sports brought on a new awareness of the body. Pamphlets like Luke Limner's Madre natura v. the Moloch of Fashion *(1870), from which these diagrams are taken, show how fashionably tight corsets cause lasting skeletal damage, to say nothing of frequent (and equally fashionable) fainting spells. (Mann Library, Cornell University)*

Horse v. penny-farthing. A race at London's Agriculture Hall in 1887. (From Illustrated London News. *Olin Library, Cornell University)*

pended. "Good humor and unreserved merriment," wrote the Frenchman Hippolyte Taine. "Classes mingle; P-, one of our party, has met his usual coachman at table with a gentleman, two ladies, and a child. The gentleman had employed and then invited the coachman; the coachman introduces P-, who is amicably compelled to drink port, sherry, stout, and ale. In fact, today it is hail fellow well met; but this lasts for a day only, after the manner of the ancient saturnalia. On the morrow distinctions of rank will be as strong as ever, and the coachman will be respectful, distant, as is his wont."[21]

As with music halls, racetracks became fewer and larger. In 1874, there were a hundred and thirty race courses in England; a decade later, there were half as many. Good railway transportation brought in large crowds, and investments (of about 1.5 million pounds between 1880 and 1900) in race courses and grandstands usually paid good returns. Betting was the key. An expanding sporting press, appealing also to the music hall fans, supplied the growing demand for news and views. Most of the sports papers were based in London.

Sports fans also watched the rapid development of a new age: the Derby was filmed. In California, the first sequence of photographs of a horse in motion was made to prove that in a gallop its four feet were simultaneously off the ground. In 1895, Birt Acres took the first sequence of an entire race. And in 1896, Robert Paul, who had become well known for his "Theatrograph" moving pictures, was commissioned by the Alhambra Music Hall to film the Derby. The winner was Persimmon, owned by the Prince of Wales. The two-and-a-half-minute film was ready for showing the following evening.

11

JUMBO AND SUNDRY DIVERSIONS

By the 1890s, traveling peep shows paled by comparison to a new wonder, the first moving pictures. Cinematographs or theatrographs, they were called.

Dancing bears or monkeys stomping on the back of a hurdy-gurdy grinder, once upon a time an exciting marvel, now seemed merely quaint compared to the new three-ring circus, with its wild animals, clowns, and trapeze artists—"the greatest show on earth."

Her Majesty's "most delicate honors," as *Punch* put it, were showered on an entertaining dwarf. And, next to the Queen, London's most beloved creature was, for a while, a temperamental elephant, named—what else?— Jumbo. The beast nearly caused not only a popular uprising but also an international incident.

In short, the number of diversions increased with leisure time. There was more to entertain people than music halls and racetracks; much more. Not all of it was wholesome.

The Bartholomew Fair, back in 1825, had amazed and delighted audiences with peep shows, in which hand-painted scenes of historical and topical interest—such as Daniel in the lions' den, the Battle of Waterloo, or the Coronation of George IV—were viewed through magnifying lenses. The scenes were mounted on the rim of a turning disk to give a sense of motion. Traveling peep shows were very popular in England, especially those taken around by a colorful figure named James Sanger, who showed pictures of the Battle of Trafalgar (in which he had fought) to an audience of six people at a time—all looking through holes fitted with lenses around a large box on a trestle.

Dancing bear on a city street—a quaint diversion that continued to hold its own as the super-extravaganzas of three-ring circuses became ever more extravagant. (Kodak Museum)

By the end of the century, there were "moving pictures" rather than peep shows. They showed scenes from battles in the Boer War rather than Waterloo and Trafalgar. The appeal was roughly the same, but the marvels of photography gave it all a novel magic.

Sanger's son George was the great circus showman of nineteenth-century England. He called himself Lord George Sanger and, in 1871, established his circus at Astley's, an amphitheater originally built by Philip Astley near the south end of Westminster Bridge. (When it was demolished in 1893, London lost its only permanent circus building.)

Astley was the original founder of the circus. It began in the 1760s as a display of equestrian feats. Soon tumbling and acrobatics on the tightrope were added, and eventually the circus shows included ring and stage, animals and actors. Sanger was a master at extravagant circus delights and his pantomime "Lady Godiva" was a spectacular demonstration of this. Sanger's parades were extraordinary.

In 1899, George Sanger—accompanied by his horses, wild animals, and wagons—was commanded to appear before the Queen at Windsor Castle. After the parade, Sanger was presented to her.

"So you are Mr. Sanger?" the Queen said.

"Yes, Your Majesty," George replied.

Then, with a smile, the Queen added: "Lord George Sanger, I believe?"

"Yes, if Your Majesty pleases," George stammered.

"Very amusing," remarked the Queen. "But I hear that you have borne the title very honourably."[1]

Other circuses of the time included exotic animals, unusual or freakish people, clowns, and a variety of acts of skill and daring.

Some were shabby affairs. "The elephant, a very small one, and three camels or dromedaries came shuffling and splashing along the muddy road in heavy rain looking cold and miserable and shivering as if they were wet through," says one account of a passing circus parade. Accompanying them were a lion, a wolf, a laughing hyena, a black sheep, and a three-foot dwarf whose main role was to poke the animals with a pole to make them roar.[2]

At their most extravagant, however, Victorian circuses were extravaganzas indeed. In its way, the elaborate production of the American showman, Phineas T. Barnum, was indeed the "greatest show on earth."

Barnum came to London in 1844 with his dwarf Tom Thumb, whose real name was Charles S. Stratton and who was six years old at the time. Tom Thumb immediately had an audience with Queen Victoria at Buckingham Palace. Two subsequent command performances turned him into a superstar.

Punch commented: "Continental monarchs stop short in their royal favours at full-grown authors and artists; but the enthusiasm of Her Majesty Queen Victoria, not content with showering all sorts of favours and rewards upon the literary and artistic spirits of her own country and age, lavishes with prodigal hand most delicate honours upon an American, Tom Thumb, whose astounding genius it is to measure in his boots five-and-twenty inches!"[3]

Some forty years later Barnum's role in the "Jumbo affair" rocked the British Isles. Here is how *The Graphic* told the story:

"There is great lamentation in juvenile circles just now, for Jumbo, the large African elephant at the Zoological Gardens, has been sold to the great American showman, Barnum, who intends to take him on a starring tour through the United States. It will be difficult to understand the Zoo without Jumbo and his cargo of merry children, ranging from the tiny tot of two, more than half afraid of the unwieldy monster, and only quieted by the care of the keeper, who seemed to be as skilful in managing children as in controlling his huge steed, to the bold youngster of six, with whom Jumbo was a familiar friend, or the sedate damsel of thirteen, who mounts more for the sake of old times than for the actual enjoyment of the ride.

"Jumbo was an universal favourite, and as gentle with children as the best-trained poodle dog, taking the proffered biscuit or lump of sugar with an almost incredible delicacy of touch, so that the most nervous child, having once overcome his alarm, never hesitated to hand a morsel to the waving

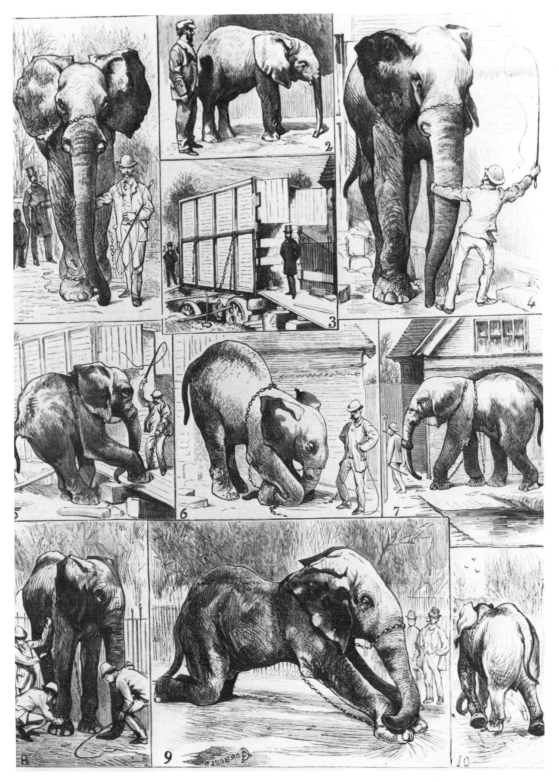

Jumbo, the huge, popular African elephant at the Zoological Gardens in Regent's Park. In 1882, the zoo sold him to the American showman P. T. Barnum, but Jumbo refused to leave. All of London sympathized, and the temperamental elephant's trials and tribulations became an international cause célèbre. *(Olin Library, Cornell University)*

trunk a second time. Jumbo, however, when in his house displayed a very uncertain temper at times, and this has induced the Society to part with him . . . The price offered was £2,000, and Mr. Barnum agreed to take all risks of removal. Mr. Barnum, however, had reckoned without asking Jumbo, who, up to the time we are writing, has firmly declined to consent to the arrangements, and has resisted all the blandishments of Scott, his favourite keeper, who has been told off to accompany him throughout the voyage. Saturday last had been fixed for his removal to the docks, and chains having been passed round his legs and body Jumbo soon felt that something was wrong, and gave vent to loud trumpetings of dismay and anger, while vigorously trying to free himself. The other elephants hearing his cries joined in the chorus, and the female, Alice, or, as she is called, Jumbo's 'little wife,' was almost beside herself with anxiety. By and by, however, Jumbo calmed down, and Scott and the well-known American expert, Mr. William Newman, otherwise known as 'Elephant Bill,' who had been sent to superintend the removal, attempted to induce him to enter the box on wheels, in which he was to be conveyed to the dock. This, however, he absolutely refused to do, and finally he was left quiet for the night.

"Next day it was decided to attempt to lead him through the streets. Jumbo walked calmly enough to the entrance, but then, feeling a different soil under his feet, became once more alarmed, and refused to proceed further. 'Then ensued,' states a writer in the *Daily Telegraph,* 'one of the most pathetic scenes in which a dumb animal was ever the chief actor. The poor brute moaned sadly, and appealed in all but human words to his keeper, embracing the man with his trunk, and actually kneeling before him. Jumbo's cries were soon heard by his "little wife," who quickly responded with loud trumpetings, at the sound of which Jumbo became frantic, and flung himself down on his side.' It now became evident that he could not be induced to march through the streets, and so Scott, to his great joy, led him back to his house, where Alice received him with gambols and great glee."[4]

Public lament soon rose to indignation. "I have found my disgust at this sale intensified by the pathetic and almost human distress of the poor animal . . ."[5] said one of the many letters to *The Times* suggesting a public fundraising campaign to buy Jumbo back from Barnum.

All England seemed to run mad about Jumbo. P. T. Barnum wrote later in his autobiography: "Pictures of Jumbo, the life of Jumbo, a pamphlet headed 'Jumbo-Barnum,' and all sorts of Jumbo stories and poetry, Jumbo Hats, Jumbo Collars, Jumbo Cigars, Jumbo Neckties, Jumbo Fans, Jumbo Polkas, etc., were sold by the tens of thousands in the stores and streets of London, and other British cities.

"Meanwhile the London correspondents of the leading American newspapers cabled columns upon the subject, describing the sentimental Jumbo craze which had seized upon Great Britain. These facts stirred up the excitement in the United States, and the American newspapers, and scores of letters sent to me daily, urged me not to give up Jumbo."

At the height of the excitement, Barnum cabled the editor of London's *Daily Telegraph:* "Jumbo's presence here imperative. Hundred thousand pounds would be no inducement to cancel purchase. My largest tent seats 20,000 persons, and is filled twice each day. It contains four rings, in three of which full circus companies give different performances simultaneously."

Thereupon, Barnum recalled, the English Society for the Prevention of Cruelty to Animals threatened his agent with imprisonment if he used force to induce Jumbo to enter a huge iron-bound cage constructed to move Jumbo to the ship to New York. Questions about the safety of the other passengers were raised in Parliament. Jumbo, remarked the American ambassador only half jokingly, is "the only burning question between England and America."

Barnum's America prevailed and after a rough passage the elephant arrived in New York on Sunday morning, April 9, 1882, in good condition. According to Barnum, "he created an immense sensation, and augmented our receipts during two weeks to such an extent as to considerably more than repay us for his purchase and subsequent expenses, amounting in all to nearly $30,000." Three years after his forced immigration, Jumbo died in a collision with a locomotive in Chatham, Ontario.[6]

London's Zoo, however, lost none of its popularity and, weather permitting, the city's amusement parks were packed. "As the dusk descends," wrote an observer of the Crystal Palace, "there is a general setting of the throng towards the open air; all the pathways swarm with groups which have a tendency to disintegrate into couples . . . Vigorous and varied is the jollity that occupies the external galleries, filling now in expectation of the fireworks; indescribable the mingled tumult that roars heavenwards. Girls linked by the half-dozen arm-in-arm leap along with shrieks like grotesque maenads; a rougher horseplay finds favour among the youths, occasionally leading to fisticuffs. Thick voices bellow in fragmentary chorus; from every side comes the yell, the catcall, the ear-rending whistle; and as the bass, the never-ceasing accompaniment, sounds myriad-footed tramp, tramp along the wooden flooring. A fight, a scene of bestial drunkenness, a tender whispering between two lovers, proceed concurrently in a space of five square yards. —Above them glimmers the dawn of starlight."[7]

Of all the Victorian diversions, drinking was the most common—and most thoroughly denounced. Pamphlets, songs, and slogans were only part of the campaign to obliterate demon drink. Temperance provided a focus for political activity, ranging from the exercise of "local options" to keep neighborhoods dry to the organization of women's groups. Temperance unions gave women an opportunity for social and economic solidarity without coming directly to terms with the larger issues of women's rights in a man's world—a world all too often reeking of alcohol.

In 1898, there was one public drinking house for every two hundred people in the quarter-square-mile district of Soho. Those who made it their business to denounce temptation—led by the Evangelical churches—saw pubs as the breeding grounds of all corruption. A book called *Tempted London,* published in 1888, gives a typically melodramatic description:

". . . In the Clapham Road there is a public-house ingeniously constructed for the convenience and comfort of the young man from the city. From the proprietor's point of view it is all that money and business tact could desire. A convenient range of private bars with cushioned seats and mahogany partitions, silver-plated tankards with a piece of looking-glass at the bottom as a warning to replenish, are the attractions of the lower portions. Above are billiard and cardrooms with a concert-room, which is kept especially select, none but decently dressed persons being admitted. Here drink is not rudely forced upon the visitor; he may take his seat in a comfortably furnished and nicely decorated room without being pestered by a worrying waiter. He will ring a bell when he requires refreshment, and it will be brought to him. There is a piano, and a prepossessing, well-dressed young lady attends from 7 to 11, who cheerfully accompanies any song or renders a piece at intervals. The young lady may be a perfectly modest young lady, but it is not her policy to insist too much upon this, and when a lot of half-educated youths find a woman amongst them they vie with each other in the rudeness of their attentions.

"This is the sort of place which first inveigles the respectable young man into an atmosphere of drink, the place that a drinking man would select to prove the harmlessness of a little amusement to a timid acquaintance, or for the introduction of a young teetotaler with no worse a motive than a sincere desire to give him the least harmful chance of amusement, after the confinement of a long day's work in the city. There is always a friendly young man in each business house, who will take an interest in the new-comer and show him about. He may chance to be a good, sensible, open-hearted, religious young man, or he may, as is more often the case, be the thoughtless or vicious leader of all sorts of dissipation. This is evidence of the care necessary in the selection of first acquaintances. Few young men will take to drink from any particular liking for the liquor itself; in fact, to one wisely restrained by his parents from any indulgence whatever in alcoholic beverages the flavour is at first distasteful. What is jokingly known as 'the whiskey shudder' is a frequent complaint with embryo drinkers. People unused to spirits cannot repress a shiver when taking them, and this it is the aim of every weak-minded youth to overcome. It is laughed at as a sign of a novice, and is proportionately distasteful to the boy who wishes to appear a man."[8]

Drink did not make the wretched lives of London's poor only more wretched. It turned many of them to violence. Journalist George Sims invited his readers to "come into the hovels—the places where men, women, and children herd together like animals" to witness the destitution caused by intemperance. At a school, he let the children, "of whom we have such hopes," tell their own stories of the effect of an alcoholic parent on their future:

M.L.: Father drunk; struck mother and hurt her skull. Mother went raving mad, and has been in a lunatic asylum ever since. Father slipped off a barge when he was drunk and drowned. Poor old grandmother has to keep the children.

R.S.: Father gets drunk and beats mother. Is in prison now for assaulting her. Children dread his coming back, he is so cruel to them when he's drunk.

S.H.: He has a fearful black eye. Mother and father both drink, and hurl things at each other. Missiles often bruise and injure the children.

C.S.: Mother drinks "awful." Dropped baby on pavement; baby so injured it dies. This is the second baby she had killed accidentally.

M.A.H.: Came to school with broken arm. "Father didn't mean no harm, but he was tight."

S.S.: Bright, lively girl of seven. Mother drinks. Shoulders and neck black with bruises. There is curious domestic arrangement in this case which is worth recording. S.'s mother lived with a man, and had several children. The man deserted her. Mrs. S.'s sister was married to man named D., and had also several children. One day, Mrs. D. gets eighteen months for assaulting the police. Then D. takes compassion on his wife's sister, and has her to live with him, and the children of both families herd together. How the family will rearrange itself when the legitimate Mrs. D. comes out remains to be seen.[9]

The degradations of drink were surpassed by those of drugs, especially opium. Cocaine addiction was remarkably common in this period, and nowhere in the world could gloomy hell have been worse than in the opium dens in the port area along the Thames.

"Tiger Bay—or, more properly speaking, Blue Gate Fields—is in the very heart of the Bay, and from end to end it presents an unbroken scene of vice and depravity of the most hideous sort. Almost every house is one of 'ill-fame.' It was not quite late enough for the tigresses to make themselves sleek and trim, preparatory to going on their customary prowl through their hunting ground; and there they sat, or lolled, or squatted at their doors, bleareyed and touzle-haired from last night's debauch. There, too, lounged, and smoked short pipes, and drank out of tavern measures the convenient resting-place of which was the window sills, the males of the tribe—the thieves and bullies, who, quiet enough now, would be wide awake and ready to show their quality when dark came, and the tavern gas was flaring . . . I entered the little public house, and, inquiring of the barmaid—who, all among the pots and glasses, and in fair view of several customers, was 'changing her frock' as coolly as if she were in her private chamber—I was at once directed to the court where the opium-master resided . . .

"After a while the sound of ascending footsteps was heard on the stairs, and the next moment the door was opened. 'Here he is! I thought he wouldn't be long,' said the woman. It was the opium-master; and he has brought home with him two customers of his own nation. Once again was I doomed to disappointment. I had pictured to myself an individual of commanding aspect, richly costumed as a mandarin; but here came a shabby, shambling, middle-aged Chinaman, into whose apparel, if I mistake not, vulgar corduroy entered, and who wore his pigtail over a sort of stableman's smock. He had on Chinese boots, however, and a Chinese cap, which, on seeing me, he removed, bowing with great cordiality and politeness, as gracefully as his lame leg would permit . . .

"With much gravity, the opium-master commenced operations. Out of a cupboard he produced his tools—the two pipes, a sort of a tinder-box of the old-fashioned pattern, a slender iron bodkin fixed in a little handle, and a small brass lamp. The pipes were not a bit like ordinary tobacco pipes. Let the reader imagine a sixteen-inch length of dark-coloured bamboo, as thick as a man's forefinger, hollow, and open at one end. There was no 'mouthpiece,' except the wide, open bore; while, at the closed end, an inch or so from the extremity, was a screwhole. Into this was screwed the tiny bowl, made, I think of iron, and shaped like a pigeon's egg. The opium-master lit the little brass lamp, and stepping up on the bed, squatted tailorwise between his customers, with his tools ready at hand . . . and presently there was a pretty pair. I never should have supposed the human countenance capable of wearing an expression so sensuous, so bestial and revolting. Faintly and more faintly still they sucked, till a gurgling sound in the pipe-stems announced that the opium in the bowl was spent; then the pipes fell from their lips, and they lay still as dead men; . . . Now the opium-master was at my service. I would have given more money than I had about me to have postponed my initiation in the art of opium smoking; but the demon on the bed was politely beckoning me, and I dared not say him nay. With tremulous heart I mounted the mattress, but was firm in my resolve to take my pipe sitting, and not reclining. Direful qualms beset me in a rapidly rising tide; but I was an Englishman, and the eyes of at least one of the sleepy barbarians by the fire were blinking on me. The dose was toasted, and I took the great clumsy pipe-stem between my jaws, and sucked as I had observed the Chinamen suck. I swallowed what I sucked, or desperately endeavoured to do so, and the result was precisely what might have been expected. Without doubt I was stupefied, or I never should have ventured on another pull. That did it! Before I ventured on my perilous expedition I had a vivid recollection of what came of smoking my first cigar; but that dismal remembrance is now quite eclipsed by one a hundred times more dreadful. 'Sispince, please!' said the still polite opium-master, extending his hand; but I hastily pressed on his acceptance the whole of the half-crown I had brought for the purpose, and was glad enough to find myself once more breathing the free and delicious air of Shadwell."[10]

There was another, more amusing world of social drug and drink, a counterpart to the workingman's pub and opium den. This was the world of

The stereoscope was among the most popular home entertainments, offering not only three-dimensional wonders of the world, but also the thrills of soap-opera-like picture stories. But the lure of moving pictures on a silver screen soon made the stereoscope obsolete. (London Museum)

the club. There had long been famous clubs in London—the Carlton, the Reform, the Garrick, the Marlborough, the Guards, the Army and Navy, White's, and the Albemarle (where Queensberry left his infamous message "for Oscar Wilde posing as a sodomite," misspelling the word). These clubs catered to various groups among the upper classes. Some, such as the Jockey Club, the Royal Thames Yacht Club, the Four-in-Hand or the Marylebone Cricket Club, were sporting clubs. The common denominator of all the clubs was that each, in its own way, was exclusive.

George Augustus Sala, who had helped found the Savage Club in 1857, and who was one of the most extraordinary figures of the period, with a writing career that included weekly contributions to Dickens's *Household Words* in the 1850s, and following on that two articles a day for the *Daily Telegraph* for almost a quarter century, gives a whimsical description of an election in a London club:

"About a dozen candidates are up for election, and with divining-rod finger one runs down the list in order to ascertain whether the catalogue contains any people whom you like or would like to know, and for whom you propose to vote; as against others whom you don't know, and consequently hate, or whom you do know, and logically detest, even more bitterly. Aha! Here is old Bilberry, the millionaire manufacturer of vegetable-

London's first "cinematographs," or moving pictures, were shown in the Egyptian Hall in 1896. (London Museum)

ivory button-shanks, at Fogley-in-Furnace. For a long time you have been aware of Bilberry; for is he not one of your fellow-members at the United Fogies', in King Street, St. James's? Bilberry is the man who goes to sleep during his dinner, and wakes up with a snort between the *entrée* and the roast. He has a habit, too, of snoring in the library; of monopolising as many of the evening papers as he can sit upon, or tuck under his arms, while he is reading his *Globe,* as a whet or relish to the others; and sometimes he takes off his shoes in the reading-room, and examines his socks, curiously. Away with Bilberry! so far as your individual negative is concerned.

" 'Sir Hubert Stanley. No occupation, Guards', Beefsteak, Garrick, Bachelors', Polyanthus, White Kid-Glove clubs. Proposed by Sir Roger de Coverley, Bart.; seconded by Lord Nozoo.' Why, of course! A more eligible young fellow of seven-and-forty, with a delightful house in Park Lane, and who is noted for his snug little dinners, and his sprightly little whist parties afterwards, it is difficult to imagine. You will vote for Stanley without hesitation; but, ha! whom have we here! 'Admiral Grumps. K.C.B.' No; Admiral Grumps, this is no place for you—your repute has spread through Club-land. You were a very valiant sea-captain no doubt, in the days of Blake, Sir Cloudesley Shovel, Boscawen, Rodney, and the like. But that was so very long ago. Commander Grumps, although a strict disciplinarian, was the most courageous and smartest of captains. Admiral Grumps, K.C.B., is about as peppery, cantankerous, quarrelsome, and generally disagreeable an old gentleman as can well be met with on a foggy day in Long Acre. He belongs to about half a dozen clubs, apparently for the purpose of making himself and other people uncomfortable at the institutions in question. The Admiral is continually bullying the waiters; harrying the steward; making the butler's life a torment to him; and bombarding the Committee with letters of complaint. The club stationery, the newspapers and magazines subscribed for, the books added to the library, please him no more than the tomato soup, the fried soles, the pickles, and the claret-cups. He is altogether the kind of Admiral to write a nice complimentary little obituary about when he departs this life, but to give a very wide berth to when you meet him in club circles.' "[11]

Along with the clubs, there were the fashionable, often Bohemian, café-restaurants. The first well-known example was Verrey's, followed by the very popular establishment run by the Gatti brothers, and the Café Royal and Romano's. It was the Café Royal that Oscar Wilde and Bosie frequented during the early 1890s. Max Beerbohm described its Domino Room in suitably extravagant terms: "There, in that exuberant vista of gilding and crimson velvet set amidst all those opposing mirrors and upholding caryatids, with fumes of tobacco ever rising to the painted and pagan ceiling, and with the hum of presumably cynical conversation broken into so sharply now and again by the clatter of dominoes shuffled on marble tables, I drew a deep breath, and 'This indeed,' said I to myself, 'is life!' "[12]

Yarmouth Beach. On summer weekends, a long train ride was rewarded by walks along the crowded seashore. lazing on the gravelly beach, wading ankle-deep into the water, and, for the

brave, "the bathing machine," in which people could change into their bathing suits and be pushed a few yards out into the deep. (Kodak Museum, Victoria and Albert Museum)

An amateur chorus line at a borough fair. (Kodak Museum)

Donkey-drawn hurdy-gurdy enlivens the fun. (Kodak Museum)

Many of the upper class liked outdoor recreation with an equal passion, and the various hunting and fishing field sports were very popular. Leading the pack was the Prince of Wales. He was originally a keen fox hunter, but when he became overweight, pheasant hunting took its place.

Social dancing, to be sure, was another of life's serious endeavors. The popularity of fashionable dances, such as the polka, prompted George Grossmith to write a lively song of celebration:

> *You should see me dance the Polka,*
> *You should see me cover the ground;*
> *You should see my coat tails flying*
> *As I jump my partner round.*

The waltz—the name derives from a word meaning to turn—was highly popular, although earlier in the century it had been roundly criticized. The annual Court Gala at Buckingham Palace was the most important of a number of balls held during the season, although the Queen, finding no amusement in dancing, never attended.

What did amuse Victoria were performances of magic. And magicians, of course, loved the publicity that command performances of their showmanship brought them. One of them, who gave a conjuring show at Balmoral, Victoria's castle in Scotland, advertised afterwards:

"Dr. Holden, the Queen's Magician, has the honour to announce that he is prepared to repeat, either in private or in public, the Marvelous Entertainment entitled "CHARMATION" as given by him at Balmoral Castle before Her Most Gracious Majesty THE QUEEN-EMPRESS, who personally complimented him on his success."[13]

Victorian magic provided amusement of a special sort to all classes of Londoners. There was sleight of hand, thought reading, ventriloquism, marvelous inventive escape and transformation routines such as John Nevil Maskelyne's "Box Trick." Maskelyne and his partner George Alfred Cook took up quarters in the 1870s at the Egyptian Hall, on the south side of Piccadilly.

Another famous magician was "Dr. Lynn," the pseudonym of Hugh Washington Simmons, who had a trick to which he gave the curious name "Palingensia." Lynn provided a whimsical description:

"How to take a man to pieces and restore him to his original self by installments.

"You first invite a gentleman to come upon the stage who has never been cut up before, and having made some preliminary observations relating to those persons who are accustomed to be cut up, etc., you commence operations by tying the gentleman to a stake; you cut off one of his arms, after this one of his legs, then remove his head, which you pass around the audience for examination. After this (provided life is not quite extinct) you take off the other leg and arm, throw the remains in a basket, and request the victim to put himself together again—and *that is how it's done."*[14]

Movable shooting gallery entertains a crowd in a city where even the bobbies never carry firearms. (Kodak Museum)

Lemonade stand at the Battersea Park fair, 1892. Photograph by Paul Martin. (Kodak Museum)

"Escape artist." Street performers of all kinds entertained Londoners at the numerous fairs held in every borough of the city. (Kodak Museum)

One of the most common forms of recreation was watching some of the most eminent Victorians make fools of themselves in a court of law. Maskelyne went to court a number of times in disputes ranging from libel actions to questions of proprietary rights to particular tricks. In 1876, the renowned Darwinian zoologist E. Ray Lankester initiated a prosecution for fraud against an American medium, Henry Slade; Maskelyne appeared for the Crown as an expert witness, in a case which did much to generate an interest in spiritualism. There were celebrated libel cases such as James Whistler's action against John Ruskin for saying that he was an impudent coxcomb who didn't know how to paint, or the Tranby Croft slander case in which the Prince of Wales was required to appear as a witness.

The two trials of Oscar Wilde were the most sensational of all. Watching them was somewhat like watching public executions, which had been abolished in 1868.

12

JULIETS
OF A NIGHT

Oh! dear girls, I love you more than honey.
London is a funny place,
But costs a lot of money.
Yes, London is a funny place
Where rummy things are done,
For in London Town they all must go
The whole hog or none. [1]

The rummy things that were done were also known as "the Great Social Evil." Pornography and prostitution were rampant and much of it was sordid.

While Victorian women were supposed to behave themselves, large numbers of Victorian men seem to have made whoring a favorite pastime.

The aristocracy, led by the Prince of Wales, proudly displayed its expensive *grandes horizontales.* If Lillie Langtry was "a professional beauty," Catherine (Skittles) Walters, or, before her, Laura Bell, were clearly beautiful professionals.

The semi-demimondes were admired far beyond the extensive circle of their customers. Londoners would line the trails in Hyde Park to watch them ride horseback. They were celebrities. They would have been entreated to give autographs and blow kisses to the crowd, had that been the fashion of their day.

The intelligentsia often romanticized prostitutes, even the less expensive ones, "the chance romances of the streets," as Arthur Symons called them. Symons was a poet inspired by Baudelaire and other French "decadents." He proudly confessed:

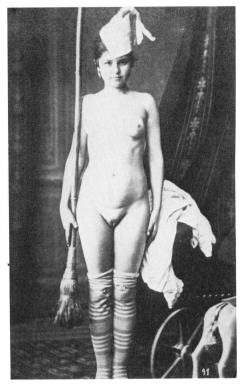

Certain bookstores in London, such as that owned by Oscar Wilde's publisher, Leonard Charles Smithers, sold "artistically posed" photographs of prepubescent girls. Child pornography was a blatant manifestation of the cult of "the little girl." (Private Collection)

"Little girl" cult photographs by Frank M. Sutcliffe and Lewis Carroll. (Sutcliffe Gallery, Whitby)

I too have sought on many a breast
The ecstasy of love's unrest,
I too have had my dreams and met
(Ah me!) how many a Juliet. [2]

And Dante Gabriel Rossetti wrote a long poem to:

Lazy laughing languid Jenny,
Fond of a kiss and fond of a guinea,
Whose head upon my knee to-night
Rests for a while, as if grown light
With all our dances and the sound
To which the wild tunes spun you round.

. . .

Poor shameful Jenny, full of grace
Thus with your head upon my knee;—
Whose person or whose purse may be
The lodestar of your reverie?

. . .

If of myself you think at all,
What is the thought?—conjectural
On sorry matters best unresolved?—
Or only is each grace revolved
To fit me with a lure?—or (sad
To think!) perhaps you're merely glad
That I'm not drunk or ruffianly
And let you rest upon my knee. [3]

Oscar Wilde defended his Romeos—a sordid lot of blackmailing "rent-
ers," or male prostitutes, whom he plied with champagne dinners and silver
cigarette cases—as worthy objects of his affection because of their youth and
"all the joy, hope, and glamour of life" that still lay before them. [4]

"We are all in the gutter," Wilde said on another occasion, "but some
of us are looking at the stars."

Most middle-class Englishmen, however, were not looking at the stars
but at a multitude of self-indulgent pleasures. For out-of-towners, there was a
variety of "pocket books" and guides to every conceivable kind of erotic
titillation and gratification. They offered flowery descriptions and addresses
of strip-tease shows, known as *"Tableaux Vivants," "Poses Plastiques,"* and
"mythological divinities." They listed public houses, where a "sleeping
room for self and lady" could be had for the night, while "for a short visit
the mere calling for wine is deemed sufficient." They led to "introducing
houses" and brothels, some modestly yet transparently disguised as "mas-

Lewis Carroll, the author of the Alice in Wonderland *books, whose fantasies of little girls created fantasies about little girls. (National Portrait Gallery, London)*

sage rooms," "baths," or even "foreign language schools," in every price range and specialty.

They also listed solo performers, whose charms were vividly described. Miss Jane Wilmott, her advertisement said, had a mouth that "looks when closed like a rose when it begins to bud." Miss Merton had "sister hills" that were "prominent, firm, and elastic." In the event that she also had a venereal disease, some books provided hints for the prevention of infection and remedies for cure. On occasion, Ronald Pearsall tells us, guidebooks included a pocket for French letters made of animals' intestine.[5]

The lower classes picked up streetwalkers, sometimes also known as "motts." There were said to be some 80,000 in the 1880s when London had a population of 2,362,000. (General William Booth of the Salvation Army, which set out to rescue prostitutes, called this figure "a monstrous exaggeration" if meant to apply "to those who make their living solely and habitually by prostitution.") By all accounts, however, Juliets of a Night could be found all over town from fashionable Bond Street and Burlington Arcade to the sleazier vicinities of the Strand in the West End area to the red-light districts along the docks, notably on Ratcliffe Highway.

Pornographic literature made no class distinction and was available without much difficulty to any male with the desire and money to be entertained by it. Some wealthy gentry collected erotica. One passage in the 1879 Christmas annual of *The Pearl, A Journal of Facetiae and Voluptuous Reading* even included the Queen. The voluptuous reader is told by one Frank Jones that he dreamed of seeing a wall poster with his name on it. The dream poster begins:

FRANK JONES
Who has had the
HONOUR
to
SHOW HIS VIRILE MEMBER
TO
HER MOST GRACIOUS MAJESTY, QUEEN VICTORIA,
And all the
LADIES OF THE ROYAL FAMILY,
By Her Majesty's
SPECIAL COMMAND,
At the Garden Party held at
WINDSOR CASTLE,
Where he appeared in a state of
NUDITY,
In order to give and receive the utmost
possible amount of satisfaction from every
possible variety in touching and handling
every part of their lovely bodies,

. . .

The invitation to this royal orgy ends with the statement:

No Girls admitted who have not yet
commenced their Courses. No Boys admitted
who are incapable of being frigged.

NOTICE.
The profits of this Exhibition will be
divided between the Society for the Encouragement of
Incest and Sodomy throughout the World, and the
Society for the Maintenance of Female Foundling
Children for the Pleasure of the Nobility and
Aristocracy of the British Empire.
By Royal Command,
PALMERSTON . . .[6]

Viscount Henry Temple Palmerston, the Queen's Prime Minister during the Crimean War, and then again during the American Civil War, was fourteen years dead when this *lèse-majesté* was printed.

Prime Minister at that time was William Ewart Gladstone, "the Grand Old Man" of British politics, who took an abiding interest in rehabilitating "fallen angels," particularly those who worked the high rent districts. The angels, however, were, for the most part, suspicious of "Old Glad-eye," as they called him.

Even the evangelistic General Booth knew it took more than friendly persuasion to lead errant young women back on the path of virtue. What did it, what induced many girls to seek the rigors of salvation in General Booth's Rescue Homes, was their imminent ruin due to disease, gin, abject poverty, and often all three.

"The question of the harlots," General Booth said, is quite insoluble by the ordinary methods. "For these unfortunates no one who looks below the surface can fail to have the deepest sympathy. Some there are, no doubt, perhaps many, who—whether from inherited passion or from evil education —have deliberately embarked upon a life of vice, but with the majority it is not so. Even those who deliberately and of free choice adopt the profession of prostitute, do so under the stress of temptations which few moralists seem to realize. Terrible as the fact is, there is no doubt it is a fact that there is no industrial career in which for a short time a beautiful girl can make as much money with as little trouble as the profession of a courtesan. The case recently tried at the Lewes assizes [a court in a small English town], in which the wife of an officer in the army admitted that while living as kept mistress she had received as much as £4,000 a year, was no doubt very exceptional. Even the most successful adventuresses seldom make the income of a Cabinet Minister. But take women in professions and in businesses all round, and the number of young women who have received £500 in one year for the sale of their person is larger than the number of women of all ages who make a similar sum by honest industry. It is only the very few who draw these gilded prizes, and they only do it for a very short time. But it is the few prizes in every profession which allure the multitude, who think little of the many blanks. And speaking broadly, vice offers to every good-looking girl during the first bloom of her youth and beauty more money than she can earn by labor in any field of industry open to her sex. The penalty exacted afterwards is disease, degradation, and death, but these things are first hidden from her sight.

"The profession of a prostitute is the only career in which the maximum income is paid to the newest apprentice. It is the one calling in which at the beginning the only exertion is that of self-indulgence; all the prizes are at the commencement. It is the ever-new embodiment of the old fable of the sale of the soul to the Devil. The tempter offers wealth, comfort, excitement, but in return the victim must sell her soul, nor does the other party forget to exact his due to the uttermost farthing. Human nature, however, is short-sighted. Giddy girls, chafing against the restraints of uncongenial industry, see the glittering bait continually before them. They are told that if they will but 'do as others do' they will make more in a night, if they are lucky, than they can make in a week at their sewing; and who can wonder that in many cases the irrevocable step is taken before they realize that it is irrevocable, and that they have bartered away the future of their lives for the paltry chance of a year's ill-gotten gains? . . ."

Booth cited several cases from Salvation Army registers. Here is one:

"A girl was some time ago discharged from a city hospital after an illness. She was homeless and friendless, an orphan, and obliged to work for her living. Walking down the street and wondering what to do next, she met a girl, who came up to her in a most friendly fashion and speedily won her confidence.

" 'Discharged ill, and nowhere to go, are you?' said her new friend. 'Well, come home to my mother's; she will lodge you, and we'll go to work together, when you are quite strong.'

"The girl consented gladly, but found herself conducted to the very lowest part of Woolwich and ushered into a brothel; there was no mother in the case. She was hoaxed, and powerless to resist. Her protestations were too late to save her, and having had her character forced from her she became hopeless, and stayed on to live the life of her false friend." A "character" is a letter of recommendation from a respectable person, such as a middle-class employer or minister, without which a member of the lower classes could not hope to obtain respectable employment in Victorian society.

"The very innocence of a girl tells against her," Booth commented. "A woman of the world, once entrapped, would have all her wits about her to extricate herself from the position in which she found herself. A perfectly virtuous girl is often so overcome with shame and horror that there seems nothing in life worth struggling for. She accepts her doom without further struggle, and treads the long and tortuous path-way of 'the streets' to the grave."

Seduction of a lower-class girl, under whatever circumstances, was something more often bragged about than condemned by Victorian sports. As Booth observed, it was only the victims who were "crushed beneath the millstone of social excommunication, while the men who cause their ruin pass as respectable members of society to whom virtuous matrons gladly marry—if they are rich—their maiden daughters."[7]

The attitude of the authorities can perhaps best be summed up as benign neglect.

What concerned Her Majesty's government about prostitution was that it tended to spread gonorrhea and syphilis among soldiers and sailors. The Contagious Diseases Acts, passed 1864–1869, however, led only to what Ronald Pearsall called "a certain climate of hunting the whore"[8] in which the Morals Policemen had their fun badgering innocent women, self-righteous clergymen found new spice for their sermons, and liberals had a great time protesting infringements of human rights and dignity. But administering medical examinations to women loitering near army posts and ports produced little more than a ferocious debate, mountains of meaningless statistics, and—the only sensible result—admonitions to the troops to wash their private parts after trysts with enticing strangers.

But the police did their best, as will be seen from the following excerpts from a report by the Commissioner of Police of the Metropolis for 1875 on the Operation of the Contagious Diseases Acts to the Home Secretary:

"Sir, . . .

"One hundred and ten young girls between the ages of 12 and 18, and 80 women between the ages of 18 and 30, and 12 above that age, who have been found in bad company and improper places, have been rescued.

"The following cases may be mentioned in illustration of the working of the Acts:—

"On the 22nd March, Mary . . . , wife of a seaman who was at sea, took her daughter Sarah, aged 16, and another girl, Laura . . . , aged 13, to a brothel in Henry-street, Plymouth, where they were found by police constable Disberry; he also found the mother with a man in another brothel in Raleigh-street. Mr. . . . , the father of the girl Laura, a highly respectable man, residing at . . . , on being informed by the police where his daughter had been found, stated that she was only 13 (she looked older), had been permitted to spend a week with the . . . 's [family], who he believed to be respectable people. He heartily thanked the inspector for rescuing his daughter, and the woman . . . , who was thoroughly ashamed of her conduct, left the district a few days afterwards . . ."[9]

A few years later, in 1885, a debate every bit as ferocious as that over

"Reading of the Period," an illustration from Leisure Hour. *Reading of popular novels was considered one of the causes of the fall of young women.* The Times *asserted that the British* paterfamilias *complacently admits "demireps, forgers, bigamists, petty murderesses, and the ladies of equivocal reputation into his drawing room, provided they are done up in the pages of fiction." (London Museum)*

the Contagious Diseases Acts, was launched by a racy bit of investigative reporting. The articles by William Thomas Stead in the *Pall Mall Gazette* caused Parliament to raise the age of consent for British females from twelve to sixteen. Being old enough to consent meant that a girl was legally entitled to enter contracts or marriage and to engage in sexual intercourse. Before what some called "Stead's Act" was passed, it was legal for twelve-year-olds —who, for some reason or another, gave what could be taken for their consent—to be exploited by factory and brothel owners.

Child labor was part of the exploitation of "the lower classes" which characterized the early industrial age and gave rise to Marxism. Child prostitution, furthermore, may have been justified by the Victorian cult of the little girl of which Lewis Carroll's *Alice's Adventures in Wonderland* (1865) and its sequel *Through the Looking-Glass* (1871) are the best-known expression.

Sexual abuse of children was no deeply hidden perversion. It was just another version of illicit sex—fairly openly discussed and fairly openly available in London and other English industrial cities. The center of child prostitution, however, was Brussels. Many stolen, kidnapped, or betrayed English girls of twelve to fifteen years were sold to Brussels brothels.

The aforementioned pornographic fantasy of an orgy in Windsor Gar-

Servant and mailman flirt, being suspiciously watched by the maid's employer. The "servant problem" was largely a question of who controlled the servant's body. (Victoria and Albert Museum)

Catherine (Skittles) Walters, one of London's famous grandes horizontales, *who commanded huge incomes and were considered celebrities. (Victoria and Albert Museum)*

dens was thus not too farfetched in its opening scene in which "the smallest girl, barely eleven years old, would insist upon my gamahuching and fucking her, for a wind-up."[10]

A clandestine catalogue advertised photographs of a seven-year-old and a ten-year-old whose "secret charms are completely devoid of hair as nature has not yet given them these revolting tokens of puberty. Like grown-up ladies these little girls indulge in all debauchery."[11]

The London Society for the Protection of Young Females had all it could do to keep up with the affliction. In 1881, a committee of the House of Lords called for testimony on the matter. One of the witnesses was Joseph Dunlap, a Superintendent of the Metropolitan Police.

> *Chairman:* Do you agree . . . that there is a great deal of juvenile prostitution in the district with which you are more particularly acquainted?
>
> *Dunlap:* I do.
>
> *Chairman:* When you use the term "juvenile," what ages do you speak of particularly?
>
> *Dunlap:* I should say as young as 12 years of age; I should be quite within the bounds of prudence in saying so. Some of them are quite children that are soliciting prostitution in my division.
>
> *Chairman:* Are these children, of the age of which you speak, living with their parents?
>
> *Dunlap:* In many instances they are, there is no doubt. I form that opinion from the fact that, when we have been able to charge any of them, they have requested their parents to be informed, or their mothers have sometimes brought them their breakfast to the station; and I have also taken a certain amount of interest in this question, especially with regard to the children, and I have spoken to the mothers when they come, and said to them, "Cannot you get these children out of their wretched life; you know what they are charged with?" They treat the matter, as a rule, indifferently, and will say, "I cannot help it; I have to go out to work; what am I to do?" Then I say, "Then why do you encourage them; why do you not leave the law to deal with them?" They have offered to bring blankets to wrap them up in, which I have invariably refused, and they have offered them every indulgence . . .
>
> *Chairman:* Generally speaking, where is the prostitution carried on?
>
> *Dunlap:* In the brothel; there is a low description of brothel in my division, where the children go. I had a warrant to execute a short time ago, to arrest some brothel-keepers, and I went with my chief inspector, and in each of the rooms in that house I found an elderly gentleman in bed with two of these children. I asked their ages, and got into conversation with them. They knew perfectly well that I could not touch them in the house; and they laughed and joked me, and I could not get any

direct answer whatever. I questioned them, in the presence of the brothel-keeper, as to what they had been paid, and so on. They were to receive 6 s. each from the gentleman, two of them; and the gentleman had paid 6 s. for the room. It was 4 s. if there was only one girl, but 6 s. if there were two girls for the room. The brothel-keeper was committed for trial.

Chairman: The children were paid by the man?

Dunlap: Yes.

Chairman: And he also paid the brothel-keeper for the room?

Dunlap: Just so.

Chairman: Were the children brought there by the men, or did the children take the men to the particular house?

Dunlap: No doubt the children took the men there.

Lord Penzance: Did the children reside in the house?

Dunlap: No.

Chairman: But they frequented the house?

Dunlap: Yes . . .

Earl Belmore: The other inhabitants of the houses are respectable people, are they not?

Dunlap: Yes, working people; but if they knew that such persons lived there, the difficulty of getting any lodgings is so great that they would have to wink at it a great deal . . .

Lord Alberdare: What is the general cause of the fall of these girls; are they deliberately sent out for this purpose by their parents, or are they procured as customers to particular houses by women in the habit of frequenting the houses?

Dunlap: I do not think it is so. It is only an option; but it appears to me that influence has much to do with it. There are a lot of little servant girls about my division in lodgings, and in other places; they are of every kind; they get small wages; they come out on errands; they see these girls walking about the streets, their equal in social standing; they see them dressed in silks and satins; they do not think of the way they get the money; they say, "You can go and dress in silks and satins while I am slaving"; they talk to the girls, and they are influenced . . .

Lord Leigh: Are they not brought up, the two sexes together, in the same room?

Dunlap: Yes.

Lord Leigh: And the girls originally came from many of those lodgings?

Dunlap: No doubt.

Lord Leigh: Where several boys and girls mix together?

Dunlap: Yes. There was a case this morning. We had two lads charged at my station with attempting to steal from a carriage in Bond-street, and I saw the "Dialonians," as they are called amongst us, waiting round the station for the police van to come. Amongst them was a little child that had high boots buttoned halfway up her legs; she had very short petticoats, her hair was down her back, and she wore a tight-fitting polonaise. I went outside and endeavoured to get into conversation with her. She thought I had something to do with the police; she said she was waiting to see her man go down. I said, "Has your young man got into trouble; will you come round the street and talk with me?" I thought I might get out some useful information for your Lordships today. She said, "Oh, no." She had her fingers covered with rings; a child of that age.

Chairman: What age did she appear to be?

Dunlap: I should say not above 13. Her fingers were covered with rings. She found I was trying to get information; she laughed, ran down the passage, and waited till "her man" went away in the van, and then hurried up to the police court to see him there.[12]

Most, if not all, of these girls came from families who lived in cheap lodging houses where as many as eight or twelve persons—children and adults of both sexes—slept in one bed.

Beatrice Webb, who took various jobs as "a plain trouser hand" to study the life of the poor at close hand, was shocked about sexual promiscuity, perversion, child molestation, and incest in these lodgings. But she found the sexually active young girls in no way mentally defective, but often as keen-witted and generous-hearted as her own friends and the promiscuity "almost unavoidable."[13]

The women who ran brothels at least clothed their girls and fed them. As Mother Willit of Gerrard Street put it, "So help her kidnies, she al'us turned her gals out with a clean arse and good tog; and as she turned 'em out, she didn't care who turned 'em up, 'cause 'em was clean as a smelt and as fresh as a daisy—she wouldn't have speck'd 'un if she know'd it." The fruits of vice were, in fact, what should have been the fruits of virtue—reasonably clean living conditions, food, and good clothing. The fact that the girls had to open their legs to a succession of strange men was a matter of minor importance. The morality of prostitution was at no time so ambiguous as it was in the nineteenth-century brothel, where the madam was an all-pervading mother figure both to the inmates and to the visitor.[14]

W. T. Stead's series in the *Pall Mall Gazette,* later published as a pamphlet entitled "The Maiden Tribute of Modern Babylon," is evidence that the Victorian Age was not as ridiculously and hypocritically prudish as the first post-Victorian generation made it out to be. Its vices, far from being swept under a moralistic rug, were sensationally exposed. Then as now, prurient interest was transparently wrapped in moral indignation. Then as now, "new journalism" meant that mere objective fact was "enlivened" and "interpreted" by the reporter's personal view of "human interest" and a dime-novel style of writing.

W. T. Stead, one of the most active and influential investigative reporters of his day. His story about "£5 Virgins" helped to raise the "age of consent"—which had aided child prostitution —from twelve to sixteen. (Kodak Museum)

Stead's installment of July 6, 1885, read:

A CHILD OF THIRTEEN BOUGHT FOR £5

"Let me conclude the chapter of horrors by one incident, and only one of those which are constantly occurring in those dread regions of subterranean vice in which sexual crime flourishes almost unchecked. I can personally vouch for the absolute accuracy of every fact in the narrative.

"At the beginning of this Derby week, a woman, an old hand in the work of procuration, entered a brothel in __ St., M____, kept by an old acquaintance, and opened negotiations for the purchase of a maid. One of the women who lodged in the house had a sister as yet untouched. Her mother was far away, her father was dead. The child was living in the house, and in all probability would be seduced and follow the profession of her elder sister. The child was between thirteen and fourteen, and after some bargaining it was agreed that she should be handed over to the procuress for the sum of £5 . . .

"The next day, Derby Day as it happened, was fixed for the delivery of this human chattel. But as luck would have it, another sister of the child who was to be made over to the procuress heard of the proposed sale. She was living respectably in a situation, and on hearing of the fate reserved for the little one she lost no time in persuading her dissolute sister to break off the bargain. When the woman came for her prey the bird had flown. Then came the chance of Lily's mother. The brothel-keeper sent for her, and offered her a sovereign for her daughter. The woman was poor, dissolute, and indifferent to everything but drink. The father, who was also a drunken man, was told his daughter was going to a situation. He received the news with indifference, without even inquiring where she was going to. The brothel-keeper having thus secured possession of the child, then sold her to the procuress in place of the child whose sister had rescued her from her destined doom for £5—£3 paid down and the remaining £2 after her virginity had been professionally certified. The little girl, all unsuspecting the purpose for which she was destined, was told that she must go with this strange woman to a situation . . .

"The first thing to be done after the child was fairly severed from home was to secure the certificate of virginity without which the rest of the purchase-money would not be forthcoming. In order to avoid trouble she was taken in a cab to the house of a midwife, whose skill in pronouncing upon the physical evidences is generally recognized in the profession. The examination was very brief and completely satisfactory. But the youth, the complete innocence of the girl, extorted pity even from the hardened heart of the old abortionist. 'The poor little thing,' she exclaimed. 'She is so small, her pain will be extreme. I hope you will not be too cruel with her'—as if to lust when fully roused the very acme of agony on the part of the victim has

Opposite, Lord Alfred Douglas and Oscar Wilde. (William Andrews Clark Library, University of California at Los Angeles)

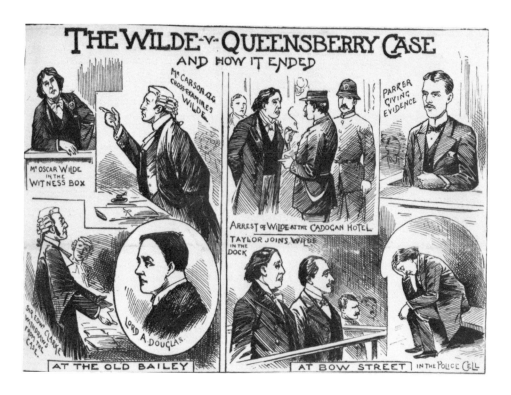

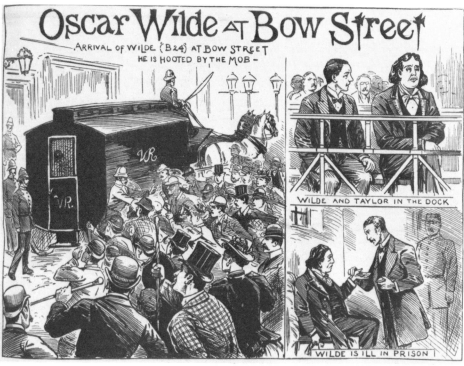

The Wilde trial as seen by The Illustrated Police News. *The proceedings at the Old Bailey on April 5, 1895, ended with Queensberry's exoneration from Wilde's charges of libel because Queensberry called him a "sodomite." Wilde is shown with the homosexual prostitutes who testified against him. Wilde was arrested. With the second trial, April 26, 1895, the popular resentment against the Aesthetes erupted. The illustrations trace Wilde's fall from the height of fashionable grace to the depth of public contempt. They show, in two parallel ovals, young Oscar, lecturing in America, and the convicted Oscar. The bottom picture shows all his possessions—which included his children's toys—being auctioned off to pay his debts. The oval on the right is Wilde's residence on Tite Street. (Olin Library, Cornell University)*

THE ILLUSTRATED Police News
LAW COURTS AND WEEKLY RECORD
ESTABLISHED 1864.

No. 1628. [REGISTERED FOR CIRCULATION IN THE UNITED KINGDOM AND ABROAD.] SATURDAY, MAY 4, 1895. Price One Penny.

CLOSING SCENE AT THE OLD BAILEY.
TRIAL OF OSCAR WILDE

OSCAR WILDE AS A LECTURER 1882 AMERICA.

OSCAR WILDE AS A PRISONER 1895 BOW STREET

JURY

SALE OF OSCAR WILDE'S EFFECTS

OSCAR WILDE'S HOUSE 16 TITE STREET.

not a fierce delight. To quiet the old lady the agent of the purchaser asked if she could supply anything to dull the pain. She produced a small phial of chloroform. 'This,' she said, 'is the best. My clients find this much the most effective.' The keeper took the bottle, but unaccustomed to anything but drugging by the administration of sleeping potions, she would infallibly have poisoned the child had she not discovered by experiment that the liquid burned the mouth when an attempt was made to swallow it. £1 1s. was paid for the certificate of virginity—which was verbal and not written—while £1 10s. more was charged for the chloroform, the net value of which was probably less than a shilling. An arrangement was made that if the child was badly injured Madame would patch it up to the best of her ability, and then the party left the house.

"From the midwife's the innocent girl was taken to a house of ill fame, No. ____, P____ street, Regent-street, where, notwithstanding her extreme youth, she was admitted without question. She was taken up stairs, undressed, and put to bed, the woman who bought her putting her to sleep. She was rather restless, but under the influence of chloroform she soon went over. Then the woman withdrew. All was quiet and still. A few moments later the door opened, and the purchaser entered the bedroom. He closed and locked the door. There was a brief silence. And then there rose a wild and piteous cry—not a loud shriek, but a helpless, startled scream like the bleat of a frightened lamb. And the child's voice was heard crying, in accents of terror, 'There's a man in the room! Take me home; oh, take me home!' . . .

"And then all once more was still.

"That was but one case among many, and by no means the worst. It only differs from the rest because I have been able to verify the facts. Many a similar cry will be raised this very night in the brothels of London, unheeded by man, but not unheard by the pitying ear of Heaven—

> *"For the child's sob in the darkness curseth*
> *deeper*
> *Than the strong man in his wrath."*[15]

It was, as Pearsall puts it sternly, a pseudo-event, "the death knell of responsible journalism."[16] It was also effective.

The same year, 1885, Parliament raised the age of consent to sixteen, made procuration a criminal offense, and imposed a penalty of whipping or penal servitude for assault on a girl under thirteen.

Never mind, then, that Stead was put up to virgin-buying by Bramwell Booth, the son of the Salvation Army general. Booth wanted to raise both the image of his "Hallelujah Lasses" and the age of consent. As prearranged, Stead did not, of course, ravish Lily, whose real name was Eliza Armstrong, and who was inadequately chloroformed and awoke when Stead entered the room. Instead, he whisked her off to Paris without asking her father's permission. Mr. Armstrong sued and Stead went to jail for two months, which he enjoyed immensely due to first-class treatment and much publicity as a "modern Galahad."

Besides, Stead's "Maiden Tribute" vastly increased the circulation of the *Pall Mall Gazette.* Controversial but influential, Stead kept riding the crests of journalistic sensations until he went under in the *Titanic* disaster in 1912.

Stead was instrumental in the passage of the Criminal Law Amendment Act, but it was another muckraking journalist, Henry Labouchère, who persuaded Parliament to make homosexual practices "in public or private" a criminal offense. It was recognized only later that the phrase "or private" was an invitation for blackmail.

A rich man, Labouchère was no missionary do-gooder like Stead, but a witty journalist and an eccentric Member of Parliament, concerned not so much with personal morality as the morality and justice of government. His interest in what came to be known as the Cleveland Street Scandal was not so much the corruption of young boys but the corruption of the Old Boys in government and the Marlborough Club, the favorite hangout of Edward, Prince of Wales. The Old Boys managed to get away with it, while their lower-class playmates were sent to jail.

The scandal first came to light on July 4, 1886, when money was found missing in London's Central Telegraph Office. Suspicion fell on one of the messenger boys, fifteen-year-old Charles Thomas Swinscow, who seemed to possess a lot more money than he could have earned delivering messages. The boy protested that he earned the extra shillings "for private work away from the office." Further pressed, he reluctantly admitted that his "private place of work" was at 19 Cleveland Street, near the West End, and that it consisted of "going to bed with gentlemen."

Police discovered that some of the gentlemen who called on the house at Cleveland Street, a thriving male brothel, included prominent members of the aristocracy. One was Lord Arthur Somerset, superintendent of Prince Edward's stables, another the Earl of Euston, eldest son of the Earl of Grafton. There were also published reports that Prince Albert Victor, the eldest son of the Prince of Wales, visited Cleveland Street. But then, there had also been allegations that in his darker moments Prince Eddie, as everyone called him, was also Jack the Ripper. What seems to have happened is that Prince Eddie, who, as Lady Waterford asserted, "was straight as a line," once ventured to Cleveland Street under the impression that naked females in *"poses plastiques"* were to be shown there.

After most of the telegraph boys had been tried, convicted, and sent off to jail, Labouchère and other journalists slowly but persistently exposed the cover-up and obstruction of justice employed to protect prominent reputations. It turned out that Lord Somerset's lawyer paid tidy sums to two key witnesses to go to America. Only one did. The other stayed to tattle. When

Exercise yard in a London prison. Drawing by Gustave Doré. (Olin Library, Cornell University)

his story could no longer be suppressed, someone in Whitehall tipped off Lord Somerset, who managed to set sail for France before the arrest warrant was delivered. If Oscar Wilde, a decade later, had followed Somerset's example and his friends' advice and left the country, he would not have spent two long years in Reading Gaol.

Yet another journalist, Ernest Parke, implicated the Earl of Euston and other prominent persons "by the score." The Earl sued for libel and won. Parke was sentenced to twelve months without hard labor. But no one really believed him guilty. Parke's key witness, one of the telegraph boys, was made out to be a liar but was never prosecuted for perjury. The moral victory was his and Labouchère's.

In the March 20, 1890, issue of *Truth,* Labouchère summed up the affair:

"I observe that I am now charged with 'gross impertinence' in Tory newspapers for having raised the question of the action of the Government in the case of Lord Arthur Somerset, and I make no doubt that there are many persons who really think that it was an impertinence of the grossest kind. That there should be one law for a nobleman and another for a man of low estate is so rooted in the mind of every flunkey and lickspittle, that he is unable to understand how anyone can take a different view. I can only say that if I again catch Lord Chancellors, Attorney-Generals, and Prime Ministers putting their heads together, with the result that, whilst poor men are sent to prison, a warrant against a nobleman, charged with the same offence, is held over for months, and then only issued when it is known that he has escaped from the country, I shall expose this perversion of justice."[17]

There is no evidence that Oscar Wilde visited the house on Cleveland Street. But there was gossip. Later that year, Wilde published *The Picture of Dorian Gray.* One of his reviewers wrote: "Mr. Wilde has brains, and art, and style, but if he can write for none but outlawed noblemen and perverted telegraph boys, the sooner he takes to tailoring (or some other decent trade) the better for his own reputation and the public morals."[18]

Wilde's retort was: "There is no such thing as a moral or an immoral book. Books are well written or badly written. That is all."[19]

EPILOGUE

There was, of course, another side to it, but the aging Alfred Tennyson summed up much of Oscar Wilde's London in his poem "Locksley Hall Sixty Years After":

> *Is it well that while we range with Science,*
> *   glorying in the Time,*
> *City children soak and blacken soul and sense*
> *   in city slime?*
>
> *There among the glooming alleys Progress*
> *   halts on palsied feet,*
> *Crime and hunger cast our maidens by the*
> *   thousands on the street.*
>
> *There the master scrimps his haggard*
> *   sempstress of her daily bread,*
> *There a single sordid attic holds the living*
> *   and the dead.*
>
> *There the smouldering fire of fever creeps*
> *   across the rotted floor,*
> *And the crowded couch of incest in the*
> *   warrens of the poor.* [1]

Foremost among those who also saw the other side was Prime Minister William Ewart Gladstone, who was no stranger to the seamy side of the city.

He responded to Tennyson with an article in the periodical *Nineteenth Century* in which he stated clearly that the shameful defaults Tennyson listed were not to be denied.

As to "incest in the warrens of the poor," he remarked, however, that "I am not sure that [they] have more to fear from a rigid investigation than other and more spacious habitations." As to the city child's "blackened soul and sense," Gladstone noted: "For one such child now there were ten, perhaps twenty, fifty years back. A very large, and a still increasing proportion of these children have been brought under the regular training and discipline of the school. Take the maidens, who are now, as they were then, cast by the thousands on the street. But then, if one among them were stricken with penitence and sought for a place in which to hide her head, she found it only in the pomp of paid institutions, and in a help well meant, no doubt, yet carrying little of what was most essential, sympathetic discrimination, and mild, nay even tender care. Within the half-century a new chapter has opened. Faith and love have gone forth into the field. Specimens of womankind, sometimes the very best and highest, have not deemed this quest of souls beneath them.

"Scrimping of wages, no doubt, there is and was. But the fair wage of to-day is far higher than it was then, and the unfair wage is assumably not lower.

"Miserable and crowded dwellings, again, and fever as their result, both then and now. But legislation has in the interval made its attempts in earnest; and if this was with awkward and ungainly hand, private munificence or enterprise is dotting our city areas with worthy dwellings . . . Will it be too audacious to submit to the Prophet of the new *Locksley Hall* that the laws and works of the half-century he reviews are not bad but good?

"I will refer as briefly as may be to the sphere of legislation. Slavery has been abolished. A criminal code, which disgraced the Statute Book, has been effectually reformed. Laws of combination and contract, which prevented the working population from obtaining the best price for their labour, have been repealed. The lamentable and demoralising abuses of the Poor Law have been swept away. Lives and limbs, always exposed to destruction through the incidents of labour, formerly took their chance, no man heeding them, even when the origin of the calamity lay in the recklessness or neglect of the employer: they are now guarded by preventive provisions, and the loss is mitigated, to the sufferers or their survivors, by pecuniary compensation.

"The scandals of labour in mines, factories, and elsewhere, to the honour, first and foremost, of the name of [noted social reformer Earl Anthony Ashley Cooper] Shaftesbury, have been either removed, or greatly qualified and reduced.

"The population on the sea coast is no longer forced wholesale into contraband trade by fiscal follies; and the Game Laws no longer constitute a plausible apology for poaching.

"The entire people have good schools placed within the reach of their children, and are put under legal obligation to use the privilege, and contribute to the charge . . . In [the] establishment of cheap communications, England has led the world. Information through a free press, formerly cut off from them by stringent taxation, is now at their easy command . . . Their interests at large are protected by their votes; and their votes are protected by the secrecy which screens them from intimidation either through violence or in its subtler forms. Their admission into Parliament, through the door opened by abolishing the property qualification, has been accomplished on a scale which, whether sufficient or not, has been both sensible, and confessedly beneficial.

"Upon the whole, among the results of the last half-century to them are, that they work fewer hours; that for these reduced hours they receive increased wages; and that with these increased wages, they purchase at diminished rates almost every article, except tobacco and spirits, of which the price can be affected by the acts of the Legislature."[2]

Gladstone's enthusiasm here is clearly restrained. Pax Britannica, to be sure, was not as peaceful as one would have liked, but it sustained a huge and powerful Empire and, for all its haughty insolence, the Empire gave Britons, including all the inhabitants of Oscar Wilde's London, more security and prosperity than any people had ever known.

What is more, the frightening shortcomings of the modern, industrial metropolis gave rise to a new urban idealism, to hopes and plans of applying science and technology to building the ideal community. "Instead of fog, smoke, congestion, soot-blackened buildings, poverty and huge populations," the late Victorian dreamers and schemers, inevitably influenced by Ruskin and Morris, "offered clear air, sun, openness, greenery, moderate prosperity for all, and populations of at most 60,000, and usually less," reports the English architecture historian Mark Girouard.[3]

Most of these utopias proved impractical for one reason or another. But the "Garden Cities" Sir Ebenezer Howard has first proposed in his little book *Tomorrow: A Peaceful Path to Real Reform,* published in 1898, were actually built all over England and have a continuing influence on humane city planning all over the world.

More perhaps than any other, the meteoric moment of Wilde's London gave new impetus to the search for civilized living. As William Blake prophesied a century before:

> *I will not cease from Mental Fight,*
> *Nor shall my Sword sleep in my hand:*
> *Till we have built Jerusalem,*
> *In Englands green & pleasant Land.*[4]

NOTES

INTRODUCTION

1. Erwin A. Gutkind, *International History of City Development,* 8 vols. (New York: Free Press, 1964–72), vol. 6, *Urban Development in Western Europe: The Netherlands and Great Britain* (1971), p. 473.

1 ART AND LIFE

1. From David Hunter-Blair's reminiscences *In Victorian Days* (Freeport, NY: Books for Libraries Press, 1969), pp. 121–22.
2. Max Beerbohm, "1880," in *The Yellow Book,* 4 (1895): 277–78.
3. Ibid., pp. 278–79.
4. Vyvyan Holland, *Oscar Wilde: A Pictorial Biography* (London: Thames and Hudson, 1960), p. 29.
5. From "Phrases and Philosophies for the Use of the Young," in *The Chameleon* (November 1884): 1.
6. "The Decay of Lying" in *Intentions,* vol. 6 of *Complete Works of Oscar Wilde* (hereafter referred to as *Works),* 14 vols. (London: Methuen, 1908), p. 42.
7. From "Conclusion" in *The Renaissance: Studies in Art and Poetry* (London: Macmillan, 1888), pp. 250, 252.
8. "Impression du Matin" in *Poems, Works,* vol. 11, p. 101.
9. From "The Earthly Paradise" in *Collected Works of William Morris,* 24 vols. (London: Longmans, Green, 1910–15), vol. 3, p. 3.
10. "The English Renaissance" in *Miscellanies, Works,* vol. 9, p. 256.
11. Holland, op. cit., pp. 54–57.
12. *Letters of Oscar Wilde,* ed. Rupert Hart-Davis (London: Rupert Hart-Davis, 1962), p. 175.
13. "The Critic as Artist" in *Intentions, Works,* vol. 6, p. 179.
14. "Phrases and Philosophies for the Use of the Young" in *The Chameleon* (November 1884): 1.
15. W. R. Lethaby, "Of Beautiful Cities," in *Art and Life, and the Building and Decoration of Cities: A Series of Lectures by Members of the Arts and Crafts Exhibition, 1896* (London: Rivington, 1897), pp. 103–4.

16. From "The Beauty of Life," a lecture delivered to the Birmingham Society of Arts and School of Design, 1880, in *Collected Works of William Morris,* op. cit., vol. 22, pp. 53, 72, 54.

17. "The Soul of Man Under Socialism" in *Intentions, Works,* vol. 6, pp. 297, 300–1, 334–35.

18. "Style" in *Appreciations* (London: Macmillan, 1890), p. 36.

2 LILIES AND SUNFLOWERS

1. *Lord Arthur Savile's Crime* in *Works,* vol. 8, p. 23.

2. Quoted from the *Burlington Magazine,* in Elizabeth Aslin, *The Aesthetic Movement* (London: Elek Books, 1969), p. 180. For the description of the Liberty fabrics, see p. 157.

3. *Collected Works of William Morris,* 24 vols. (London: Longmans, Green, 1910–15) vol. 22, pp. 4–5. From Morris's first public lecture on "The Lesser Arts" delivered in 1877; published in pamphlet form in 1878 with the title "The Decorative Arts."

4. From Morris's own discussion of the principles of pattern and design in an essay written in 1888: "Textiles," in May Morris, *William Morris, Artist, Writer, Socialist,* 2 vols. (Oxford: Basil Blackwell, 1936), vol. 1, p. 250.

5. John Ruskin, *Fors Clavigera,* June 18, 1877, p. 201.

6. Recounted in Whistler's *The Gentle Art of Making Enemies* (London: William Heinemann, 1890), p. 5.

7. From an 1885 review in the *Pall Mall Gazette* of a famous Whistler lecture delivered at ten o'clock in the evening, in order not to disturb dinner: "Mr. Whistler's Ten O'Clock" in *Miscellanies, Works,* vol. 9, p. 67.

8. Whistler's letter to the *World* was published on November 17, 1886; Wilde's response (November 24, 1886) was also published there. The exchange, with Whistler's final comment, was reprinted in his *The Gentle Art of Making Enemies,* pp. 164–65.

9. *The Times,* February 15, 1877.

10. From a letter to his friend G. F. Scotson-Clark, written in February 1893; *Letters of Aubrey Beardsley,* eds. Henry Maas, J. L. Duncan, and W. G. Good (Cranbury, NJ: Fairleigh Dickinson University Press, 1970), p. 43.

11. From a letter to his friend Reginald Turner, August 1897. *Letters of Oscar Wilde,* ed. Rupert Hart-Davis (London: Rupert Hart-Davis, 1962), p. 631.

12. Julius Meier-Graefe, *Modern Art,* tr. F. Simmonds and G. W. Chrystal (London: William Heinemann, 1908), vol. 2, p. 253.

13. "The Critic as Artist" in *Intentions, Works,* vol. 6, p. 206.

14. Quoted in Aslin, op. cit., p. 15.

15. From Mary Eliza Haweis, *The Art of Beauty* (New York: Harper and Bros., 1878), pp. 273–74.

16. From his lecture "The English Renaissance of Art," first delivered in Chickering Hall, New York, in January 1882, and many times thereafter on his American tour, in *Miscellanies, Works,* vol. 9, p. 276.

3 THE CALL OF THE STAGE

1. From D'Oyly Carte's "Inaugural statement" of October 6, 1881. Quoted in Raymond Mander and Joe Mitchenson, *The Theatres of London* (London: Rupert Hart-Davis, 1963), p. 194.

2. "Literary and Other Notes" in *The Complete Writings of Oscar Wilde* (New York: Nottingham, 1909), vol. 4, p. 239.

3. From a letter written on October 10, 1896 from Terry to George Bernard Shaw. *Ellen Terry and Bernard Shaw: A Correspondence,* ed. Christopher St. John (New York: G. P. Putnam's Sons, 1932), p. 71.

4. John Oxenford in *The Times,* November 28, 1871.

5. George R. Sims in the *New York Evening News.* Quoted in David Mayer, ed., *Henry Irving and the Bells* (Manchester: Manchester University Press, 1980), p. 6.

6. *"Hamlet* at the Lyceum" in *Reviews, Works,* vol. 12, p. 16.

7. Quoted in Clement Scott, *Ellen Terry* (New York: Frederick A. Stokes, 1900), pp. 76–77.

8. Ibid., p. 110.
9. Quoted in Tom Prideaux, *Love or Nothing: The Life and Times of Ellen Terry* (New York: Charles Scribner's Sons, 1975), p. 141.
10. Quoted in George Rowell, *Queen Victoria Goes to the Theatre* (London: Paul Elek, 1978), p. 112.
11. Ibid.
12. From *Fun,* quoted in George Rowell, *Theatre in the Age of Irving* (Oxford: Basil Blackwell, 1981), p. 109.
13. Henry Arthur Jones, "The Theatre and the Mob," in *Nineteenth Century,* 14: 455–56.
14. *World,* May 31, 1893.
15. Arthur Wing Pinero, *The Second Mrs. Tanqueray* (London: William Heinemann, 1895), pp. 188–90.
16. Quoted in *The Complete Plays of Henry James,* ed. Leon Edel (New York: J. B. Lippincott, 1949), p. 475.
17. *The Saturday Review,* January 12, 1895.
18. Kate Terry Gielgud, *A Victorian Playgoer,* ed. Muriel St. Clare Byrne (London: Heinemann Educational Books, 1980), p. 19.
19. Quoted in *The Complete Plays of Henry James,* op. cit., p. 476.
20. Quoted in Hesketh Pearson, *The Life of Oscar Wilde* (London: Methuen, 1946), p. 257.
21. Quoted in Charles Archer, *William Archer: Life, Work and Friendships* (London: George Allen and Unwin, 1931), p. 215.
22. Quoted in Rowell, *Theatre in the Age of Irving,* loc. cit.
23. Clement Scott, "Why Do We Go to the Play?" in *The Theatre,* 11, 4th series (1888): 124.
24. Quoted in Raymond Mander and Joe Mitchenson, *British Music Hall* (London: Gentry Books, 1974), p. 44.
25. D. D. Arundell, *The Story of Sadler's Wells, 1683–1977* (London: David and Charles, 1978), p. 176.
26. *The Saturday Review,* January 23, 1897.
27. Quoted in Paul Sheridan, *Penny Theatres of Victorian London* (London: Dennis Dobson, 1981), pp. 85, 88.

4 READERS AND WRITERS

1. Walter Bagehot, quoted in Richard D. Altick, *Victorian People and Ideas* (W. W. Norton, 1973), p. 60.
2. "Literary and Other Notes" in *The Complete Writings of Oscar Wilde* (New York: Nottingham, 1909), vol. 4, p. 261.
3. Altick, op. cit., p. 61.
4. Ibid., p. 68.
5. *Academy,* 29 (March 28, 1886): 200.
6. Rudyard Kipling, "Recessional," in *The Five Nations* (New York: Doubleday Page, 1903), p. 214.
7. "The Critic as Artist" in *Intentions, Works,* vol. 6, p. 134.
8. Arthur Symons, *The Symbolist Movement in Literature* (London: William Heinemann, 1899), p. 8.
9. Holbrook Jackson, *The Eighteen Nineties: A Review of Art and Ideas at the Close of the Nineteenth Century* (London: Grant Richards, 1923), p. 127.
10. Recollected by Edmund Gosse in *The Life of Algernon Charles Swinburne* (London: Macmillan, 1917), p. 133.
11. *The Times,* February 9, 1886.
12. Jackson, op. cit., p. 105.
13. Richard Le Gallienne, "A Ballad of London," in *Robert Louis Stevenson: An Elegy, and Other Poems* (London: John Lane, 1895), p. 26.
14. James A. M. Whistler, from his 1885 lecture, reprinted in *Ten O'Clock* (Portland, ME: T. B. Mosher, 1925), p. 13.
15. Charles Whibley, *Scots (National) Observer,* July 5, 1890.
16. Henry James, "London," in *Century,* 37 (1878): 233.

17. From the "Introduction" to *The Oxford Book of Modern Verse, 1892–1935,* ed. W. B. Yeats (Oxford: Clarendon Press, 1936), p. xi.

5   LONDON'S GROWTH

1. *Lord Arthur Savile's Crime* in *Works,* vol. 8, p. 24.
2. *The Times,* March 25, 1868.
3. *Building News,* 27 (1874): 481.
4. Quoted in Gavin Weightman and Steve Humphries, *The Making of Modern London* (London: Sidgwick & Jackson, 1983), p. 99.
5. Henry James, "London," in *Century,* 37 (1888): 223.
6. H. G. Wells, *Love and Mr. Lewisham* (New York: G. H. Doran, 1899), pp. 129–30.
7. George Bernard Shaw, *Four Plays* (New York: Modern Library, 1953), p. 224.
8. *Journal of the RIBA,* vol. 1, 3d series (1894): 202.
9. Weightman and Humphries, op. cit., p. 52.
10. Ibid.
11. "The American Invasion" in *Miscellanies, Works,* vol. 9, p. 79.
12. Weightman and Humphries, op. cit., pp. 62–63.
13. George Gissing, quoted by Asa Briggs in *Victorian Cities* (London: Odhams Press, 1963), p. 364.
14. *Building News,* 28 (1875): 1.
15. Thomas Verity, "The Modern Restaurant," in *Architect,* 21 (1879): 31.
16. Charles Dickens, *Dickens's Dictionary of London* (London: C. Dickens, 1879), p. 127.
17. Karl Baedeker, *London and Its Environs* (Leipzig: Karl Baedeker, 1905), p. 19.
18. Dickens, op. cit., p. 116.
19. *Building News,* 48 (1885): 878.
20. Charles Eyre Pascoe, *London of To-day* (Boston: Roberts Bros., 1888), p. 27.

6   . . . AND LONDON'S SHAME

1. Gavin Weightman and Steve Humphries, *The Making of Modern London* (London: Sidgwick & Jackson, 1983), p. 95.
2. Henry Mayhew, *London Labour and the London Poor,* 4 vols. (1861, reprinted by London: Frank Cass, 1967), vol. 3, p. 301.
3. Karl Baedeker, *London and Its Environs* (Leipzig: Karl Baedeker, 1905), pp. 106, 172.
4. Weightman and Humphries, op. cit., p. 90.
5. Ibid., p. 89.
6. Suppressed testimony of the coroner concerning the mutilation was published only in the medical periodical *The Lancet.* See Tom Cullen, *Autumn of Terror: Jack the Ripper, His Crimes and Times* (London: The Bodley Head, 1965), p. 84.
7. Mark Girouard, *Victorian Pubs* (New Haven, CT: Yale University Press, 1984), p. 113.
8. *Building News,* 41 (1881): 1.
9. Ibid., 47 (1884): 159.
10. Ibid., 64 (1893): 760.
11. *Architect,* 45 (1891): 330.
12. Girouard, op. cit., p. 2.
13. *Licensed Victuallers' Gazette* (August 3, 1888): 75.
14. *The Trials of Oscar Wilde,* ed. H. Montgomery Hyde (London: William Hodge, 1948), pp. 192–93.

7   THE LOWER CLASSES

1. Benjamin Disraeli, *Sybil; or, The Two Nations,* 3 vols. (London: H. Colburn, 1845), vol. 1, pp. 149–50.
2. Quoted by Ebenezer Howard, *Garden Cities of Tomorrow* (London: Faber and Faber, 1902), p. 42.

3. Ernest Rhys, "A London Feast," in *A London Rose and Other Rhymes* (London: E. Mathews and J. Lane, 1894), pp. 4–6.

4. General William Booth, *In Darkest England and the Way Out* (London: International Headquarters of the Salvation Army, 1890), p. 42.

5. Ibid., pp. 26–27.

6. Beatrice Potter Webb, "The Jewish Community," in Charles Booth, *Labour and Life of the People,* 9 vols. (London: Macmillan, 1889), vol. 1, pp. 580–84.

7. "The Poet's Corner" in *Reviews, Works,* vol. 12, p. 342.

8. "Begging in the Streets of London" by "an amateur street-beggar" (January 10, 1884). Noble Collection, Guildhall Library, London.

9. *The Little Ballad of Little Alice Moss. Written and Printed for Her with the Kind Permission of the Authorities* (London: 1880). Broadside Collection, Guildhall Library, London.

10. James Greenwood, *Low–Life Deeps* (London: Chatto and Windus, 1876), pp. 144–48.

11. "A Cry from a Counter Slave" in *Truth* (March 17, 1881): 366.

12. Edward Salmon, "Domestic Service and Democracy," in *The Fortnightly Review,* 49 (1888): 408–9.

13. "The Soul of Man Under Socialism" in *Works,* vol. 6, pp. 279–80.

8   RELIGION, SPIRITS, AND HOSANNA

1. John Cale Miller, *The Church of the People* (1855) (London: College Pamphlets, vol. 1332), p. 11. Quoted in *The Victorian City,* eds. Harold J. Dyos and Michael Wolff, 2 vols. (London: Routledge and Kegan Paul, 1973), vol. 2, p. 829.

2. F. W. Head, "The Church and the People," in *The Heart of the Empire,* ed. Charles F. G. Masterman (London: T. Fisher Unwin, 1901), pp. 278–81.

3. *The Importance of Being Earnest, Works,* vol. 5, pp. 87–88.

4. Quoted in Bernard and Margaret Pawley, *Rome and Canterbury Through Four Centuries* (New York: The Seabury Press, 1975), p. 190.

5. *Mystic London: or Phases of Occult Life in the British Metropolis* (London: Lovell, Adam, Wessen, 1875), pp. 212–18.

6. *Proceedings of the Society for Psychical Research,* 3 (1885): 207.

7. *Annie Besant; an Autobiography* (Philadelphia: H. Altemus, 1893), p. 346.

8. David H. Tribe, *President Charles Bradlaugh, M.P.* (London: Elek Books, 1971), p. 178. See Appendix to *The Queen v. Charles Bradlaugh and Annie Besant* (1877), p. 322.

9. Mohandas K. Gandhi, *An Autobiography, or: The Story of My Experiments with Truth* (Ahmedabad: Navajivan Publishing House, 1927), p. 91.

10. Masterman, op. cit., pp. 263–64.

11. Charles Maurice Davies, *Unorthodox London, or Phases of Religious Life in the Metropolis* (London: Tinsley, 1876), pp. 33–34.

12. "The Siege of Whitechapel" in *The Saturday Review,* 48 (1879): 19.

9   THE SOUNDS OF LONDON

1. Comment recorded by Vincent O'Sullivan. Quoted in *Letters of Oscar Wilde,* ed. Rupert Hart-Davis (London: Rupert Hart-Davis, 1962), p. 65, n. 3.

2. Quoted in George Rowell, *Queen Victoria Goes to the Theatre,* (London: Paul Elek, 1978), pp. 99–100.

3. George Bernard Shaw, *Music in London, 1890–94,* 3 vols. (London: Constable, 1932), vol. 2, pp. 303–6.

4. Ibid., vol. 1, p. 21, and vol. 2, p. 302.

5. Wilde, *Letters,* op. cit., p. 177.

6. Quoted in D. D. Arundell, *Critic at the Opera* (London: Ernest Benn, 1957), p. 361.

7. Ibid., p. 363.

8. *The Times,* May 11, 1882.

9. *Punch,* May 27, 1882.

10. F. Anstey, "London Music Halls," in *Harper's New Monthly Magazine,* 82 (1891): 190, 192–93.

11. Ibid., pp. 190–92.
12. Quoted in H. C. (Chance) Newton, *Idols of the "Halls"* (London: Heath Cranton, 1928), pp. 59–60.
13. Ibid.
14. John Davidson, *In a Music Hall and Other Poems* (1891), in *The Poems of John Davidson,* ed. Andrew Turnbull, 2 vols. (Edinburgh: Scottish Academic Press, 1973), vol. 1, pp. 23–24.
15. T. S. Eliot, "London Letter," in *Dial,* 73 (1922): 659–60, 662.
16. Quoted in Hesketh Pearson, *Gilbert and Sullivan* (London: Hamish Hamilton, 1935), pp. 261–62.
17. From the *Journal of the Folk Song Society,* 1 (1899): 2–3.
18. "The Critic as Artist" in *Intentions, Works,* vol. 6, pp. 103–4.
19. *Chambers's Journal,* 18 (1881): 417.
20. W. E. Henley, *Poems* (London: David Nutt, 1898), pp. 35–36.

10 VIRTUES OF SPORT

1. From a speech to the annual music festival of Welsh nonconformist choirs at Cardiff in 1896. Quoted in Tony Mason, *Association Football and English Society, 1863–1915* (Brighton: Harvester Press, 1980), p. 1x.
2. *The Times,* April 17, 1899.
3. Lytton Strachey, *Eminent Victorians* (London: Chatto and Windus, 1918), p. 207.
4. Quoted in Brian Dobbs, *Edwardians at Play* (London: Pelham Books, 1973), p. 31.
5. F. E. Smith, *C. B. Fry's Magazine,* New Series, vol. 1, no. 1, April 1911.
6. From an account of the inaugural meetings of the Football Association, in Geoffrey Green, *History of the Football Association* (London: Naldrett Press for the Football Association, 1953), pp. 28–29.
7. Henry Newbolt, "Vitae Lampada," in *Collected Poems, 1897–1907* (London: Thomas Nelson and Sons, 1910), pp. 131–32.
8. Quoted in Christopher Brookes, *English Cricket* (London: Weidenfeld and Nicolson, 1978), pp. 141–42.
9. "Cricket and the Victorian Era" in *Blackwood's Edinburgh Magazine* 162 (1897): 8.
10. Neville Cardus, "William Gilbert Grace," in *The Great Victorians,* eds. H. J. and Hugh Mossingham (London: Ivor Nicholson and Watson, 1932), pp. 225–26, 231.
11. Quoted in H. S. Altham and E. W. Swanton, *A History of Cricket* (London: George Allen and Unwin, 1962), pp. 123–24.
12. Benjamin Disraeli, *Lothair,* 3 vols. (London: Longmans, Green, 1870), 1: 23–25.
13. From *Northern Wheeler* (1893), quoted in James Walvin, *Leisure and Society, 1830–1950* (London: Longman Group, 1978), p. 93.
14. Quoted in Frederick Alderson, *Bicycling: A History* (New York: Frederick A. Praeger, 1972), p. 94.
15. Ibid.
16. Mrs. Elizabeth R. Pennell, "Cycling," in *Ladies in the Field: Sketches of Sport,* ed. Lady Violet Grenville (New York: D. Appleton, 1894), pp. 252–54.
17. "Literary and Other Notes" in *Reviews, Works,* vol. 12, p. 206.
18. "More Radical Ideas upon Dress Reform" in *Miscellanies, Works,* vol. 9, p. 59.
19. Quoted in Alderson, op. cit., pp. 86–87.
20. Ibid., pp. 88, 91.
21. Hippolyte Taine, *Notes on England,* tr. W. Fraser Rae (London: Chapman and Hall, 1885), p. 42.

11 JUMBO AND SUNDRY DIVERSIONS

1. Quoted in Rupert Croft-Cooke and Peter Coates, *Circus* (London: Paul Elek, 1976), p. 91.
2. From the May 7, 1872, diary entry of the Reverend Francis Kilvert, *Kilvert's Diary,* ed. William Plomer, 3 vols. (London: Jonathan Cape, 1977), vol. 2, pp. 192–93.
3. *Punch,* 6 (1844): 157.

SELECTED READINGS

Abercrombie, Sir Patrick, *Town and County Planning* (Oxford, 1961).

Acton, William, *Prostitution* (London, 1870).

Aldous, Tony, *The Illustrated London News Book of London's Villages* (London, 1980).

Altholz, Josef L., *Victorian England, 1837–1901* (Cambridge, 1970).

Altick, Richard D., *Victorian People and Ideas* (New York, 1973).

———, *Victorian Studies in Scarlet* (New York, 1970).

Amor, Anne Clark, *Mrs. Oscar Wilde: A Woman of Some Importance* (London, 1983).

Archer, Thomas, *The Terrible Sights of London* (London, 1870).

Avery, Gillian, *Victorian People in Life and Literature* (London, 1970).

Baker, H. Barton, *History of the London Stage* (London, 1904).

———, *The London Stage: Its History and Traditions,* 2 vols. (London, 1889).

Banks, F. R., *The New Penguin Guide to London* (London, 1984).

Barker, Felix, *The House That Stoll Built: The Story of the Coliseum Theatre* (London, 1957).

——— and Peter Jackson, *London: 2,000 Years of a City and Its People* (New York, 1974).

Batho, Edith, and Bonamy Dobrée, *The Victorians and After, 1830–1914* (New York, 1938).

Beardsley, Aubrey, and Oscar Wilde, *Salome* (Mineola, NY, 1967).

Beer, Gillian, *Darwin's Plots: Evolutionary Narrative in Darwin, George Eliot, and Nineteenth-Century Fiction* (London, 1983).

Beerbohm, Max, *Around Theaters,* 2 vols. (New York, 1930).

———, *Herbert Beerbohm Tree: Some Memories of Him and His Art* (London, 1920).

Bell, Ernest, ed., *Handbook of Athletic Sports,* 8 vols. (London, 1890).

Bell, Walter G., *Unknown London* (London, 1922).

Bentley, Nicolas, *The Victorian Scene* (London, 1968).

Besant, Sir Walter, *London in the Nineteenth Century* (London, 1909).

Betjeman, John, *Victorian and Edwardian London from Old Photographs* (London, 1970).

——— and J. S. Gray, *Victorian and Edwardian Brighton from Old Photographs* (London, 1972).

Bobrick, Benson, *Labyrinths of Iron: A History of the World's Subways* (New York, 1982).

Booth, Charles, *On the City: Selected Writings,* ed. H. W. Pfautz (Chicago, 1967).

———, *Pauperism* (London, 1892).

Booth, General William, *In Darkest England and the Way Out* (New York, 1890).

Boucicault, Dion, *The Art of Acting* (New York, 1926).

4. *The Graphic,* 25 (1882): 179.

5. Letter to the Editor, *The Times,* February 21, 1882.

6. P. T. Barnum, *The Story of My Life: A Personal Narrative, Covering a Period of Seventy-five Years (1810 to 1885), Sixty of Which Were Devoted to a Variety of Colossal, Popular and Successful Enterprises* (Cincinnati: Forshee and McMakin, 1886), pp. 448–49.

7. George Gissing, *The Nether World* (London: Smith, Elder, 1890), pp. 110–11.

8. *Tempted London: Young Men* (London: Hodden Stoughton, 1888), pp. 61–62.

9. George R. Sims, *How the Poor Live* (London: Chatto and Windus, 1898), p. 138.

10. James Greenwood, *In Strange Company* (London: Vizetelly, 1883), pp. 217–23.

11. George Augustus Sala, *London Up to Date* (London: Adam and Charles Black, 1894), pp. 63–64.

12. Max Beerbohm, *Seven Men* (London: William Heinemann, 1920), pp. 5–6.

13. Quoted in Geoffrey Lamb, *Victorian Magic* (London: Routledge and Kegan Paul, 1976), pp. 107–8.

14. Ibid., p. 93.

12   JULIETS OF A NIGHT

1. "London Ballad," cited by Ronald Pearsall, *The Worm in the Bud: The World of Victorian Sexuality* (New York: Macmillan, 1969), p. 247.

2. Arthur Symons, "Stella Maris," in *London Nights* (London: Leonard Smithers, 1895), p. 40.

3. Excerpts from Dante Gabriel Rossetti, *Poems* (London: Ellis and White, 1881), pp. 115–18.

4. H. Montgomery Hyde, *Oscar Wilde* (London: Magnum Books, 1977), p. 329.

5. See Pearsall, op. cit., pp. 257–60.

6. *The Pearl, A Journal of Facetiae and Voluptuous Reading* (December 1879).

7. William Booth, op. cit., pp. 58 ff.

8. Pearsall, op. cit., p. 278.

9. *Annual Report for 1875 of Capt. Harris, Commissioner of Police of the Metropolis on the Operation of the Contagious Diseases Acts* (London: Her Majesty's Printing Office, June 12, 1876).

10. *The Pearl,* Christmas Number (1879), pp. 14 ff.

11. Quoted by Graham Ovenden and Peter Mendes, *Victorian Erotic Photography* (New York: St. Martin's Press, 1973), p. 87.

12. *Report on the Select Committee of the House of Lords on the Law Relating to the Protection of Young Girls* (Sessional Papers, August 25, 1881), pp. 76 ff.

13. Beatrice Potter Webb's observations on sex life in the slums were omitted as too shocking from her article "Pages from a Workgirl's Diary" (in *Nineteenth Century,* 24 [1888]: 301–14), but appeared in a footnote in her autobiography, *My Apprenticeship* (New York: Longmans, Green, 1926).

14. Pearsall, op. cit., p. 288.

15. *Pall Mall Gazette,* July 6, 1885.

16. Pearsall, op. cit., p. 302.

17. *Truth,* March 20, 1890.

18. Charles Whibley, *Scots (National) Observer,* July 5, 1890.

19. *Scots (National) Observer,* July 12, 1890.

EPILOGUE

1. *The Complete Works of Alfred Lord Tennyson* (New York: R. Worthington, 1878), p. 62.

2. " 'Locksley Hall' and the Jubilee," *Nineteenth Century,* 21 (1887): 7–10.

3. Mark Girouard, *Cities and People* (New Haven, CT: Yale University Press, 1985), p. 349.

4. From the Preface to *Milton* in *The Complete Poetry and Prose of William Blake,* ed. David V. Erdman, newly revised edition (Garden City, NY: Anchor Books, Anchor Press/Doubleday, 1982), p. 95.

Braddon, M. E., *London Pride* (Leipzig, 1897).

Brander, Michael, *The Victorian Gentleman* (London, 1975).

Breach, R. W., and R. M. Hartwell, eds., *British Economy and Society, 1870–1970* (Oxford, 1972).

Bridgwater, Patrick, *Nietzsche in Anglosaxony* (Leicester, 1972).

Briggs, Asa, *A Social History of England* (New York, 1984).

———, *Victorian Cities* (London, 1982).

Brookes, Christopher, *English Cricket* (London, 1978).

Buchanan, Robert, *London Poems* (London, 1883).

———, *Master-Spirits* (London, 1873).

Bullock, Rev. Charles, *The Queen's Resolve* (London, 1887).

Burdett, Osbert, *The Beardsley Period* (London, 1925).

Butt, J., and I. F. Clark, eds., *The Victorians and Social Protest* (Newton Abbot, 1973).

Caine, T. Hall, *Cobwebs of Criticism* (London, 1883).

Carr, J. Comyns, *Some Eminent Victorians* (London, 1908).

Cecil, David, *Max: A Biography* (London, 1964).

Chamberlin, J. E., *Ripe was the Drowsy Hour: The Age of Oscar Wilde* (New York, 1977).

Champlin, John D., and Arthur E. Bostwick, *The Young Folkes' Cyclopaedia of Games and Sports* (New York, 1899).

Chesney, Kellow, *The Victorian Underworld* (London, 1970).

Chesterton, G. K., *The Victorian Age in Literature* (New York, 1913).

Child, Ruth C., *The Aesthetic of Walter Pater* (New York, 1940).

Coleman, John, *Players and Playwrights I have Known,* 2 vols. (Philadelphia, 1890).

Cook, Dutton, *Nights at the Play,* 2 vols. (London, 1883).

Cook, Rev. Richard Briscoe, *The Wit and Wisdom of Rev. Charles H. Spurgeon* (London, 1892).

Cornwallis, Kinahan, *Royalty in the New World* (New York, 1860).

"Craven," *Walker's Manly Exercises* (London, 1878).

Croft-Cooke, Rupert, *The Unrecorded Life of Oscar Wilde* (New York, 1972).

——— and Peter Coates, *Circus* (London, 1976).

Cruse, Amy, *The Victorians and Their Books* (London, 1935).

Cullen, Tom, *Autumn of Terror: Jack the Ripper, His Crimes and Times* (London, 1965).

Daiches, David, *Some Late Victorian Attitudes* (London, 1979).

Daly, Frederic, *Henry Irving in England and America, 1838–84* (London, 1884).

Dangerfield, George, *Victoria's Heir: The Education of a Prince* (London, 1941).

Darbyshire, Alfred, *The Art of the Victorian Stage* (London, 1907).

Darracott, Joseph, *The World of Charles Ricketts* (London, 1980).

Davidson, John, *Fleet Street and Other Poems* (London, 1909).

———, *In a Music-Hall and Other Poems* (London, 1891).

Dawes, Edwin A., *The Great Illusionists* (Newton Abbot, 1979).

De Cordova, R. J., *The Prince's Visit: A Humorous Description* (New York, 1871).

Deghy, Guy, and Keith Waterhouse, *Café Royal: Ninety Years of Bohemia* (London, 1955).

Desmond, Shaw, *London Nights in the Gay Nineties* (New York, 1928).

Doré, Gustave, and Blanchard Jerrold, *London: A Pilgrimage* (London, 1872).

Douglas, Lord Alfred, *Oscar Wilde and Myself* (New York, 1914).

Douglas, Norman, *London Street Games* (London, 1931).

Dowling, Linda C., *Aestheticism and Decadence* (New York, 1978).

D'Oyly Carte Centenary, 1875–1975 (London, 1975).

Du Bois, William R., ed., *English and American Stage Productions* (Boston, 1973).

Dunning, Eric, and Kenneth Sheard, *Barbarians, Gentlemen and Players* (Oxford, 1979).

Dunning, Richard, *Victorian Life and Transport* (Surrey, 1981).

Dyos, Harold J., and Michael Wolff, eds., *The Victorian City,* 2 vols. (London, 1973).

Edwards, W. H., *The Tragedy of Edward VII: A Psychological Study* (London, 1928).

Elder, William, *A Burns Bouquet* (London, 1875).

Eldridge, H. Wentworth, ed., *World Capitals: Toward Guided Urbanization* (London, 1975).

Ellmann, Richard, ed., *Edwardians and Late Victorians* (New York, 1960).

Ellmann, Richard, et al., *Wilde and the Nineties* (Princeton, 1966).

Ensor, R. C. K., *England, 1870–1914* (Oxford, 1936).

Ervine, St. John G., *Some Impressions of My Elders* (New York, 1922).

Escott, T. H. S., *Social Transformations of the Victorian Age* (New York, 1897).

Evans, Hilary and Mary, *The Party That Lasted 100 Days: The Late Victorian Seasons* (London, 1976).

————, *The Victorians at Home and Work* (Newton Abbot, 1973).

Evans, Joan, ed., *The Victorians* (Cambridge, 1966).

———— and John Howard Whitehouse, eds., *The Diaries of John Ruskin,* 3 vols. (Oxford, 1956).

Everett, Edwin M., *The Party of Humanity* (Chapel Hill, 1939).

Ferriday, Peter, ed., *Victorian Architecture* (Philadelphia, 1964).

Feurtado, W. A., *The Jubilee Reign of Queen Victoria in Jamaica* (Kingston, 1890).

Ffrench, Yvonne, ed., *News from the Past, 1805–1887* (London, 1934).

Fitzgerald, Percy, *London City Suburbs as They are Today* (London, 1893).

————, *The World Behind the Scenes* (London, 1881).

Flora, Joseph M., *William Ernest Henley* (New York, 1970).

Forshaw, Charles F., *Tributes to the Memory of the Late Sir Henry Irving* (London, 1905).

Friswell, J. Hain, *Modern Men of Letters Honestly Criticized* (London, 1870).

Frith, David, *The Golden Age of Cricket, 1890–1914* (Guildford, 1978).

Funke, Peter, *Oscar Wilde* (Reinbek bei Hamburg, 1969).

Garforth, John, *A Day in the Life of a Victorian Policeman* (London, 1974).

Garrett, Edmund, ed., *Victorian Songs* (Boston, 1895).

Gilbert, Sir William S., *A Stage Play* (New York, 1916).

Gilman, Richard, *Decadence: The Strange Life of an Epithet* (London, 1979).

Gilman, Sander L., and J. E. Chamberlin, eds., *Degeneration: The Dark Side of Progress* (New York, 1985).

Girouard, Mark, *Victorian Pubs* (New Haven, CT, 1984).

Gissing, George, *The Nether World* (Brighton, 1974).

Gladstone, W. E., *Bulgarian Horrors and the Question of the East* (London, 1876).

Glosstone, Victor, *Victorian and Edwardian Theaters* (London, 1975).

Gomme, Alice B., ed., *Children's Singing Games* (London, 1894).

Graham, Beatrice Violet, Lady Grenville, ed., *Ladies in the Field: Sketches of Sport* (New York, 1894).

Granville-Barker, Harley, ed., *The Eighteen-Seventies* (Cambridge, 1929).

Grebanier, Bernard D., et al., *English Literature and Its Background* (New York, 1949).

Green, Benny, ed., *London* (New York, 1984).

Greenwood, James, *Low-Life Deeps* (London, 1876).

————, *The Seven Curses of London* (London, 1869).

————, *The True History of a Little Ragamuffin* (London, 1866).

Grigson, Geoffrey, ed., *The Victorians* (London, 1950).

Haining, Peter, ed., *The Penny Dreadful* (London, 1975).

Halliday, Andrew, ed., *Comical Fellows* (London, 1863).

Hammerton, J. A., ed., *The Passing of Victoria* (London, 1901).

Hammond, Peter C., *The Parson and the Victorian Parish* (London, 1977).

Hardwick, Michael, *The Drake Guide to Oscar Wilde* (New York, 1973).

Harrison, Brian, *Drink and the Victorians* (Pittsburgh, 1971).

Harrison, Fraser, *The Dark Angel: Aspects of Victorian Sexuality* (New York, 1977).

Harrison, Michael, *The London of Sherlock Holmes* (Newton Abbot, 1972).

Hatton, Joseph, *Club-Land* (London, 1890).

————, *The Lyceum "Faust"* (London, 1894).

Heckethorn, Charles W., *London Souvenirs* (London, 1899).

Henderson, W., ed., *Victorian Street Ballads* (London, 1937).

Henley, W. E., *London Voluntaries* (London, 1893).

Henry Irving: A Short Account of His Public Life (New York, 1883).

Hiatt, Charles, *Ellen Terry and Her Impersonations* (London, 1898).

Hibbert, Christopher, *Victoria* (London, 1979).

Hibbert, H. G., *Fifty Years of a Londoner's Life* (New York, 1916).

Hindley, Diana and Geoffrey, *Advertising in Victorian England, 1837–1901* (London, 1972).

Hobsbawm, Eric J., *Industry and Empire* (London, 1968).

Holland, Vyvyan, *Son of Oscar Wilde* (London, 1954).

———, *Oscar Wilde and His World* (New York, 1960).

Holledge, Julie, *Innocent Flowers: Women in the Edwardian Theater* (London, 1981).

Hughes, M. Vivian, *A London Family, 1870–1900* (London, 1946).

Hyde, H. Montgomery, *The Cleveland Street Scandal* (London, 1976).

———, *The Trials of Oscar Wilde* (London, 1948).

———, *Oscar Wilde: A Biography* (New York, 1975).

Irvine, William, *Apes, Angels, and Victorians* (New York, 1955).

Iser, Wolfgang, *Walter Pater* (Tübingen, 1960).

Jackson, Holbrook, *The Eighteen Nineties* (New York, 1922).

Jacobs, Joseph, *George Eliot, Matthew Arnold, Browning, and Newman: Essays and Reviews from the "Athenaeum"* (London, 1891).

———, *Literary Studies* (New York, 1896).

Jervis, Simon, *High Victorian Design* (Ottawa, 1974).

Johnson, E. D. H., ed., *The World of the Victorians: An Anthology of Poetry and Prose* (New York, 1964).

Kauvar, George B., and Gerald C. Sorensen, eds., *The Victorian Mind* (London, 1969).

Kennedy, J. M., *English Literature, 1880–1905* (London, 1912).

Kent, William, *An Encyclopaedia of London* (London, revised 1970).

Kumar, Shiv K., ed., *British Victorian Literature* (New York, 1969).

Lamb, Geoffrey, *Victorian Magic* (London, 1976).

Lancaster, Henry H., *Essays and Reviews* (Edinburgh, 1876).

Leech, William, *The Obliviad: A Satire* (New York, 1879).

Le Gallienne, Richard, *The Romantic 'Nineties* (London, 1951).

Legge, Edward, *King Edward in His True Colors* (London, 1912).

———, *More About King Edward* (London, 1913).

Le Roy, George, *Music Hall Stars of the Nineties* (London, 1952).

Levy, Amy, *A London Plane-Tree and Other Verse* (London, 1889).

Longford, Elizabeth, *Queen Victoria: Born to Succeed* (New York, 1964).

Mackerness, E. D., *A Social History of English Music* (London, 1964).

Mander, Raymond, and Joe Mitchenson, *Victorian and Edwardian Entertainment* (London, 1978).

Mare, Margaret, and Alicia C. Percival, *Victorian Bestsellers* (London, 1947).

Margetson, Stella, *Leisure and Pleasure in the Nineteenth Century* (London, 1969).

———, *Regency London* (New York, 1971).

———, *Victorian High Society* (London, 1980).

Massingham, H. J. and Hugh, eds., *The Great Victorians* (London, 1952).

Masterman, C. F. G., ed., *The Heart of the Empire* (London, 1901).

Maurois, André, *Points of View from Kipling to Graham Greene* (New York, 1968).

Mayhew, Henry, *London Street Life*, ed. Raymond O'Malley (London, 1966).

McCarthy, Justin, *Charing Cross to St. Paul's* (London, 1891).

McCrie, George, *The Religion of Our Literature* (London, 1875).

McLean, Ruari, *Victorian Book Design and Colour Printing* (New York, 1963).

Meade, Marion, *Madame Blavatsky* (New York, 1980).

Mearns, Andrew, *The Bitter Cry of Outcast London* (New York, reprint: 1970).

Metcalf, Priscilla, *Victorian London* (London, 1972).

Meyers, Robert C. V., *Victoria: Queen and Empress* (Philadelphia, 1901).

Middleton, Empson E., *Ah, Happy England!* (London, 1871).

Monsman, Gerald C., *Pater's Portraits* (Baltimore, 1967).

Morley, Henry, *Of Literature in the Reign of Victoria with a Glance at the Past* (Leipzig, 1881).

Morley, John, *Nineteenth-Century Essays* (Chicago, 1970).

Morris, Charles, *The Life of Queen Victoria* (London, 1901).

Morrison, Arthur, *A Child of the Jago* (Leipzig, 1897).

Moscheles, Felix, *In Bohemia with Du Maurier* (New York, 1897).

Moss-Eccardt, John, *Ebenezer Howard: An Illustrated Life of Sir Ebenezer Howard* (Buckinghamshire, Eng, 1973).

Munro, John M., *The Decadent Poetry of the Eighteen-Nineties* (Beirut, 1970).

Nagel, I. B., and F. S. Schwarzbach, eds., *Victorian Artists and the City* (New York, 1980).

Nelson, James G., *The Early Nineties: A View from the Bodley Head* (Cambridge, MA, 1971).

Nicholson, Watson, *The Struggle for a Free Stage* (Boston, 1906).

Nicoll, Allardyce, *A History of Late Nineteenth Century Drama, 1850–1900,* 2 vols. (Cambridge, 1949).

Nicoll, W. Robertson, and Thomas J. Wise, *Literary Anecdotes of the Nineteenth Century,* 2 vols. (London, 1896).

Oliphant, M., *The Victorian Age of English Literature,* 2 vols. (New York, 1892).

Olsen, Donald J., *The Growth of Victorian London* (London, 1979).

———, *Town Planning in London: The Eighteenth and Nineteenth Centuries* (New Haven, CT, 1982).

Orel, Harold, ed., *The World of Victorian Humor* (New York, 1961).

Orme, Michael, *J. T. Grien: The Story of a Pioneer, 1862–1935* (London, 1936).

Ovenden, Graham, and Peter Mendes, *Victorian Erotic Photography* (New York, 1973).

Parker, Joseph, *The Ark of God* (London, 1877).

Partington, Wilfred, *Echoes of the 'Eighties: Leaves from the Diary of a Victorian Lady* (London, 1921).

Pater, Walter, *Imaginary Portraits* (London, 1919).

———, *Selected Works,* ed., Richard Aldington (New York, 1948).

Pearsall, Ronald, *Victorian Popular Music* (Newton Abbot, 1973).

———, *Victorian Sheet Music Covers* (Newton Abbot, 1972).

———, *The Worm in the Bud: The World of Victorian Sexuality* (London, 1969).

Pearson, Michael, *The £5 Virgins* (New York, 1972).

Peters, Robert L., ed., *Victorians on Literature and Art* (New York, 1961).

Peterson, William S., *Interrogating the Oracle: A History of the London Browning Society* (Athens, OH, 1969).

Pevsner, Nikolaus, and J. M. Richards, *The Anti-Rationalists* (New York, 1976).

Pike, E. Royston, *"Golden Times": Human Documents of the Victorian Age* (New York, 1967).

Pollard, Arthur, ed., *The Victorians* (London, 1970).

Priddle, Robert, *Victoriana* (Wimbledon, 1959).

Prideaux, Tom, *Love or Nothing: The Life and Times of Ellen Terry* (New York, 1975).

Private Life of King Edward VII by a Member of the Royal Household, The (New York, 1901).

Proesler, Hans, *Walter Pater und Sein Verhältnis zur deutschen Literatur* (Freiburg, 1917).

"Q", *Dramatists of the Present Day* (London, 1871).

Quennell, Peter, ed., *London's Underworld* (London, 1950).

Rasmussen, Steen Eiler, *London: The Unique City* (Cambridge, MA, 1982).

Reade, Brian, *Aubrey Beardsley* (London, 1976).

———, ed., *Sexual Heretics: Male Homosexuality in English Literature from 1850 to 1900* (New York, 1970).

Redman, Alvin, ed., *The Wit and Humor of Oscar Wilde* (Mineola, NY, 1959).

Rhys, Ernest, *A London Rose and Other Rhymes* (London, 1894).

Richards, Kenneth, and Peter Thomson, eds., *Essays on Nineteenth Century British Theatre* (London, 1971).

Richardson, Leander, *The Dark City or Customs of the Cockneys* (Boston, 1886).

Robbins, Keith, *John Bright* (London, 1979).

Rogers, Robert Emmons, *The Voice of Science in Nineteenth-Century Literature* (Boston, 1921).

Rossetti, Dante Gabriel, *Poems* (London, 1881).

Rothenstein, John, ed., *Sixteen Letters from Oscar Wilde* (London, 1930).

Routly, Erik, *The Puritan Pleasures of the Detective Story* (London, 1972).

Rowell, George, *The Victorian Theater: A Survey, 1792–1914* (Cambridge, 1978).

———, ed., *Victorian Dramatic Criticism* (London, 1971).

Ruskin, John, *The Eagle's Nest* (New York, 1883).

———, *Fors Clavigera* (Kent, 1884).

———, *The Poetry of Architecture: Cottage, Villa, etc.* (New York, 1883).

Russell, William H., *The Prince of Wales' Tour: A Diary in India* (New York, 1878).

Saintsbury, George, *Corrected Impressions: Essays on Victorian Writers* (New York, 1899).

Sala, George A., *London Up to Date* (London, 1894).

Sansom, William (intro.), *Victorian Life in Photographs* (London, 1974).

Saunder, Ann, *The Art and Architecture of London: An Illustrated Guide* (Oxford, 1984).

Scott, Clement, *From "The Bells" to "King Arthur"* (London, 1896).

Scott, Constance M., *Old Days in Bohemian London* (London, 1919).

Seitz, Don C., ed., *Whistler Stories* (New York, 1913).

Shaw, George Bernard, *Dramatic Opinions and Essays,* 2 vols. (New York, 1906).

———, *Dramatic Opinions and Essays with an Apology by Bernard Shaw,* 2 vols. (New York, 1907).

Sherard, Robert Harborough, *The Life of Oscar Wilde* (London, 1906).

Shuster, George N., *The Catholic Spirit in Modern English Literature* (New York, 1922).

Sims, George R., *Without the Limelight: Theatrical Life as It Is* (London, 1900).

Small, Ian, ed., *The Aesthetes: A Sourcebook* (London, 1979).

Smith, Clive, *Flying at Hendon* (London, 1974).

———, *Golders' Green as It Was* (London, 1973).

———, *Hendon as It Was* (London, 1973).

———, *Mill Hill as It Was* (London, 1973).

Smith, Warren S., *The London Heretics, 1870–1914* (London, 1967).

Somerset, Henry, Duke of Beaufort, *Driving* (Boston, 1889).

Speaight, George, *A History of the Circus* (London, 1980).

Standen, John M. A., *The End of an Era* (London, 1968).

Stanford, Derek, ed., *Pre-Raphaelite Writing: An Anthology* (London, 1973).

Stead, W. T., ed., *Real Ghost Stories* (London, 1891).

Stebbins, Lucy Poate, *A Victorian Album* (New York, 1946).

Stedman, Edmund Clarence, ed., *A Victorian Anthology, 1837–1895* (Boston, 1895).

Steegman, John, *Victorian Taste: A Study of the Arts and Architecture from 1830 to 1870* (Cambridge, MA, 1971).

Stewart, John A., *Letters to Living Authors* (London, 1892).

Stoker, Bram, *Personal Reminiscences of Henry Irving,* 2 vols. (New York, 1906).

Strachey, Lytton, *Eminent Victorians* (London, 1918).

Summerson, John, *Georgian London: An Architecture Study* (New York, 1970).

Symons, Arthur, *London Nights* (London, 1896).

Taine, H. A., *Notes on England* (London, 1885).

Temperley, Nicholas, ed., *Music in Britain: The Romantic Age, 1800–1914* (London, 1981).

Tennyson, Alfred Lord, *The Poems and Plays* (New York, 1938).

Thomas, Donald, *Swinburne: The Poet in His World* (London, 1979).

Thompson, E. P., *William Morris: Romantic to Revolutionary* (New York, 1976).

Timbs, John, *Clubs and Club Life in London* (London, 1899).

Tobias, J. J., *Nineteenth-Century Crime in England* (New York, 1972).

Trevelyan, George M., *British History in the Nineteenth Century, 1782–1901* (London, 1922).

———, *Illustrated English Social History,* 4 vols. (London, 1949–52).

Trilling, Lionel, and Harold Bloom, eds., *Victorian Prose and Poetry* (New York, 1973).

Trollope, Anthony, *An Autobiography* (London, 1947).

Wakeman, Geoffrey, *Victorian Book Illustration: The Technical Revolution* (Newton Abbot, 1973).

Walvin, James, *Leisure and Society, 1830–1950* (London, 1978).

Watson, J. N. P., *Victorian and Edwardian Field Sports* (London, 1978).

Weightman, Gavin, and Steve Humphries, *The Making of Modern London: 1815 to 1914* (London, 1983).

Weintraub, Stanley, *Reggie: A Portrait of Reginald Turner* (New York, 1965).

———, *Whistler* (London, 1974).

———, ed., *The Yellow Book: Quintessence of the Nineties* (Garden City, NY, 1964).

Welland, D. S. R., *The Pre-Raphaelites in Literature and Art* (London, 1953).

Wheatley, Henry B., *London Past and Present,* 3 vols. (London, 1891).

White, E. W., *The Rise of English Opera* (London, 1951).

Whitney, Caspar W., *A Sporting Pilgrimage* (New York, 1895).

Wigley, John, *The Rise and Fall of the Victorian Sunday* (Manchester, 1980).

Wilde, Oscar, *Oscariana* (London, 1910).

———— and James Whistler, *Wilde vs. Whistler: Being an Acrimonious Correspondence on Art between Oscar Wilde and James A. McNeill Whistler* (London, 1906).

Winwar, Frances, *Oscar Wilde and the Yellow 'Nineties* (New York, 1940).

Woodham-Smith, Cecil, *Queen Victoria: From Her Birth to the Death of the Prince Consort* (New York, 1972).

Yonge, Charlotte M., *Womankind,* 2 vols. (Leipzig, 1878).

Young, G. M., *Victorian England: The Portrait of an Age* (London, 1936).

INDEX

A

Aestheticism, xi, xii, 8, 88; images of, 12, 18, 41, 202; reactions to, 256; theories, 19, 21–22, 32; Wilde and, xii, 1, 6, 28, 29, 38. *See also* Art Nouveau; Design and ornamentation

Albert Victor, Prince, 259

Altick, Richard D., 80–81

Anti-Semitism, 131–32, 137, 152–54

Archer, William, 67–68, 74, 78

Architecture, 19, 28, 32, 34, 47, 48, 83, 139–40; Georgian, 111, 113, 120, 139; monumental, 25, 48, 141; varying styles, 140–42. *See also* Residences

Art Nouveau, 6, 28–29, 32, 41. *See also* Design and ornamentation

Arts and Crafts movement, ix, xi, xii, 37–41, 47. *See also* Aestheticism; Art Nouveau; Design and ornamentation

Aynesworth, Allan, 72, 73

B

Baden-Powell, Lord, 200–1

Balfour, Arthur, 7

Bancroft, Marie Effie Wilton, 58, 63–64

Bancroft, Sir Squire, 58, 63–64

Barnardo, Dr. Thomas, 131, 154, 156, 157

Barnum, Phineas T., 221, 223, 224–25

Beardsley, Aubrey, 16, 29, 34, 37, 51, 82, 88; illustrations for *Salome,* 37, 52, 53, 73

Beauty. *See* Aestheticism

Bedford, Earl of, 111, 118

Beerbohm, Max, 1, 5–6, 88, 231

Belmont, George, 76

Bernhardt, Sarah, 73, 74, 180

Besant, Annie, 173

Blake, William, 264

Blavatsky, Helena, 173

Book(s), 96; publishing, 36, 37, 83; stores, 83; Wilde's, 16. *See also* Literature and reading

Booth, Charles, 148

Booth, General William, 147, 148, 177, 243; on prostitutes, 244–46, 258

Bradlaugh, Charles, 5, 173, 175

Breuer, Josef, 93

Browning, Robert, 86, 87

Bülow, Hans von, 185

Burnand, F. C., *The Colonel,* 69, 180

Burne-Jones, Sir Edward, xii, 43, 45, 89

Business and merchandizing, 28, 122-24, 198

C

Café Royal, 231
Cameron, Julia Margaret, 84
Campbell, Mrs. Patrick, 16, 67, 71
Cardus, Neville, 205, 207
Carroll, Lewis, 240, 242, 248
Carter, Lady Charlotte Bonham, 104, 116, 119
Catholicism, 167, 169–70
Children: homeless, 150; as laborers, 148, 149, 156–62, 248; home for, 131, 156; pornography of, 239; sexual abuse of, 246, 248, 250–54, 258–59, 271
Churchill, Lady Randolph, 9
Churchill, Randolph, 5, 7, 175
Cleveland Street scandal, 259
Clubs, 230–31
Collcutt, T. E., 140
Contagious Diseases Act, 246, 248
Corelli, Marie, 83
Covent Garden, 111, 118; Royal Opera House, 185, 186, 196

D

Darwin, Charles Robert, ix, 170, 171. *See also* Darwinism
Darwinism, xi, 17, 19, 170, 172
Davidson, John, 193–94
Davies, Charles Maurice, 172–73
Design and ornamentation: book, 37; fashion, 28–29; interior, 17, 34, 35, 38; Japanese, 34, 37; stained glass, 29, 38; theatrical, 56–57
Determinism, hereditary, 17, 19
Dickens, Charles, 127, 170
Disraeli, Benjamin, 3, 4, 6, 142, 146, 207–8
Douglas, Lord Alfred, 13, 27, 52, 73, 231, 254

Dowson, Ernest, 95
Doyle, Sir Arthur Conan, 93, 94, 154
D'Oyly Carte, Richard, 12, 54–55, 181
Dunlap, Joseph, 250–52

E

East End, x, 91, 99, 120, 126–32
Eastman, George, 22
Edward (Albert Edward), Prince of Wales, 1–4, 50, 73, 180, 198, 218, 235, 238, 259
Electric lighting: of London, ix, 93, 99; theatrical, 54, 56
Elgar, Sir Edward, 183
Eliot, T. S., 194–95
Ellis, Havelock, ix, xi
Environmental concerns, 17, 19, 21

F

Fabian Society, x–xi, 90, 92, 151
Fashion, 28–29, 211–12, 216
Fellowship of the New Life. *See* Fabian Society
"Firm, The," 32
Freud, Sigmund, 93

G

Galton, Francis, 17, 19
Garden City movement, 12, 264
Garrick Theatre, 65
Gaudí, Antonio, 28
George, Lloyd, 200
Gielgud, Kate Terry, 72
Gilbert, Alfred, 141
Gilbert, Sir William Schwenck, 12, 73, 179; comic operas by, 54, 55, 181; on musical comedy, 195–96. *See also Patience*
Gissing, George, 122–23
Gladstone, William, 5, 6, 10, 63, 169, 262–64
Godwin, Edward William, 13, 14, 34, 57

Gogh, Vincent van, 28
Grace, William Gilbert, 205–7

H

Hardy, Thomas, 37, 67, 85
Hare, John, 65
Harris, Augustus, 185
Haweis, Mary Eliza, 38, 41
Haymarket Theatre, 63, 73
Henley, William Ernest, 94, 199
Holland, Vyvyan, 15–16
Hollyer, Frederick, 30, 31, 43
Howard, Sir Ebenezer, 12, 264
Hughenden Manor, 4
Humphries, Steve, 116, 119, 128, 131

I

Ibsen, Henrik, 57, 67, 74, 78, 90; *A Doll's House,* 64–65, 74
Imperial Institute of Kensington, 140
Industrialization, 127–28; attacks on, 22, 32; growth, 97–99
Irving, Sir Henry, 57, 58–61, 62, 63, 65, 74

J

Jackson, Holbrook, 88, 93
Jack the Ripper murders, 131–39, 259
James, Henry, 73, 95, 96, 104
   Works: *The Americans,* 69; *Guy Domville,* 69, 72, 73
Jews, immigrant, 131, 137, 146, 151–54
Johnson, Lionel, 27
Jones, Henry Arthur, 65, 74
Jones, Inigo, 111, 118
Jones, Sidney, *The Geisha,* 195
Jumbo, affair of, 221–25

K

Kelmscott Press, 36, 83
Kendal, Madge, 65, 87
Kendal, William, 65
Kerr, Robert, 113
Kipling, Rudyard, 86, 89
Klimt, Gustav, 28

L

Labouchère, Henry, 162, 259, 261
Langtry, Lillie, 7, 11, 180, 198, 238
Lankester, E. Ray, 237
Law suits, 32–34, 49, 50, 73–74, 215, 237, 257, 259, 261
Le Gallienne, Richard, 93
Lethaby, William Richard, 19, 21
Lewis, Leopold, *The Bells,* 58, 61
Leyland, Frederick, 34
Liberty, Arthur Lasenby, store of, 28
Literature and reading, 80–88; new currents, 90, 93; newspapers, 81; novels, 80, 83, 247; poetry, 84, 86, 88, 93; pornographic, 243–44. *See also* Books; Magazines
Livingstone, David, 170
Lloyd, Marie, 194–95
London: artistic and literary climate, 5–6, 93, 94–96; early division of, 111; general views, x, 1–2, 25, 262–64; growth, x, 5, 97; plans for, 19, 99–100, 111; squares and parks, 111, 113, 117, 120; traffic problems, 99–100, 102–4. *See also* East End; West End
London Season, x, 116, 119, 120
Lower classes, ix, 80; housing for, 101, 113, 131, 141–42; living conditions, 17, 160, 175; recreation, 78–79, 80, 142–44, 225–26; religion for, 168; riots and strikes, 88, 90. *See also* Children; Servants; Slums; Social issues; Suburbs; Working conditions
Lyceum Theatre, 57, 61–65, 76

M

MacDermott, G. H. ("The Great"), 186, 193
Magazines, 38, 81, 82, 83, 88, 95
Malthus, Thomas Robert, 17
Martin, Paul, 19, 20
Marx, Karl, x, 167
Maskelyne, 237
Meier-Graefe, Julius, 37
Mesmer, Dr. Friedrich Anton, 170
Mies van der Rohe, Ludwig, 41
Miles, Frank, 6–7, 11, 13
Millais, Sir John Everett, 41, 44, 46
Morris & Company, 35, 36
Morris, Jane, 40
Morris, William, xi, xii, 8, 30, 83, 90; and interior decoration, 35, 36, 38, 39; as printer, 36, 37; theories, 21, 22, 32
Morse, Colonel F. W., 18
Moving pictures, 76, 218, 219, 229
Music: choral singing, 198–99; classical, 199; folk songs, 196, 198; musical comedy, 195–96; opera, 178, 180, 185, 196; oratorios, 182–83; promenade concerts, 183; religious, 178, 180, 182; street, 199. *See also* Music halls
Music halls, 57, 186–92; performers, 193–94; songs, 192–93

N

Nash, John, 100, 103
Newcombe, Bertha, 92
Nostalgia 83, 86

O

O'Connor, John, 2
Oliphant, Margaret, 81

P

Parke, Ernest, 261
Parker, Charles, 143, 158

Parry, Herbert, 182–83, 196
Pater, Walter Horatio, 1, 8, 14, 22
Patience (Gilbert and Sullivan), 12, 18, 28, 38, 54, 63, 178, 180
Patti, Adelina, 185, 196, 198
Paul, Robert, 218
Pawsey, May, 119–20
Photography, 19, 20, 22, 23
Pinero, Sir Arthur Wing, 65, 68; plays by, 65, 67; *The Second Mrs. Tanqueray,* 65–68, 71
Police, 112, 113, 114
Polish Jew, The. See Lewis, Leopold
Politics, 88, 142; changing, x–xi, 5. *See also* Fabian Society
Population, 126; growth, 146; middle-class, 81, 83, 95, 122. *See also* Jews; Lower classes; Upper classes
Pound, Ezra, 32
Pre-Raphaelite movement, xi–xii, 14, 43; images of, 40, 41, 46, 88
Prince Albert Memorial, 48
Prostitution, 10, 116, 238, 241, 243, 244–52; brothels, 252, 259; child, 248, 250–54, 258–59; male, 158, 241, 256, 259, 261
Public health problems, 24; bad air, 104, 113, 148; sexual diseases, 246, 248; water, 110. *See also* Working conditions
Pubs, 142–44, 225–26

Q

Queensberry, Marquess of, 73–74, 215, 256

R

Ranjitsinhji, Prince, 204–5
Reade, Charles, 62
Recreation and diversions, 219–37; beach, 232–33; circus, 220, 221; fairs, 219, 234, 236, 237; magic, 235, 237; law courts, 237; peep shows, 219; zoo, 221, 225. *See also*

Music; Music halls; Sports; Theater(s)

Regent Street, 100, 103

Religion, 167–77; and music, 178, 180, 182

Residences, 3, 4, 34, 39, 100, 141–42; Wilde's, 6–7, 13–17, 97, 256

Restaurants and hotels, 124–25; café restaurants, 231

Reszke, Jean de, 185

Rhymers' Club, 94–95

Ricketts, Charles, 37

Robertson, Thomas William, 63–65

Rosa, Carl, 185

Rossetti, Dante Gabriel, xi–xii, 40, 41, 42, 241

Rothenstein, William, 27

Royal Albert Hall, 183

Royal Porcelain Works, 34

Ruskin, John, xi, 17, 31, 32, 47, 139; libel suit, 32–34, 49, 50, 237; theories, 1, 22, 32

S

Sadler's Wells, 67, 74, 76

St. James's Theatre, 65, 67, 72, 73, 74

St. Pancras station, 2, 140

Sala, George Augustus, 230–31

Salvation Army, 147, 148, 176, 177, 243, 258

Sanger, George, 220–21

Sanger, James, 219, 220

Sargent, John Singer, 13

Savoy Theatre, 54–56, 63, 178, 181

Scott, Clement, 62–63, 74

Scott, Sir G. Gilbert, 2, 48, 140

Servants, 115–16, 119, 120, 149, 163–66, 248

Shakespeare, William, 62; *Hamlet,* 46, 61–62

Shaw, George Bernard, x, 57, 67, 76, 173; as critic, 58, 69–72, 77–78, 182–83, 185; plays of 74, 78; and politics, x, 90; *Pygmalion,* 108, 111, 118

Shaw, Norman, 140, 141

Sims, George, 58

Slade, Henry, 237

Slums, 127, 131, 177, 271n13

Smith, F. E., 201

Smith, Sydney, 168

Smithers, Leonard Charles, 239

Social Darwinism, 170

Social Democratic Federation, 31, 32, 90

Social issues, 17, 88, 131, 262–64; alcoholism, 226–27; begging, 154–58, 159, 165; crime, 132–39; drugs, 227–28; homelessness, 148, 151; homosexuality, 73, 74, 144; pornography, 238, 239; poverty, 144–45, 146, 148, 166; public health, 24, 246, 248; unemployment, 98, 146, 148

Socialism, x–xi, 88

Solomon, Simeon, 16, 40

Somerset, Lord, 259, 261

Spencer, Herbert, 170

Spiritualism, 167, 170–72, 173, 174, 176, 237

Sports: bicycling, 209–12, 216–17; boxing, 214–15; cricket, 202, 204–7; croquet, 207–8; football, 200, 201–5; horse racing, 215–18; hunting, 235; rowing, 212–14; rugby, 202; tennis, 208, 209; spectators, 200–201; for women, 208–12, 216

Spurgeon, Charles Haddon, 168

Stanford, Villiers, 182

Stead, William Thomas, 173, 248, 252–55, 258–59

Stevenson, Robert Louis, 93

Street(s): dirtiness, 104, 109; life, 24, 112–13; performers, 237; scenes, 103, 105–10. *See also* Regent Street; Tite Street

Suburbs, x, 101, 104, 113, 121, 122, 142

Sullivan, Sir Arthur, 12, 178, 179; comic operas by, 54, 55, 178, 180,

181; "The Lost Chord," 180. *See also Patience*
Swinburne, Algernon Charles, 86, 88
Symons, Arthur, 88, 238, 241

T

Tarkington, Booth, 56
Tennyson, Alfred, Lord, 84, 86, 140, 262, 263
Terry, Ellen, 57–59, 61–63
Thames River, 98, 99, 139; Embankment, 102–3
Theater(s), 56–57, 63, 65; actors and actresses, 57–63; lighting of, 54–56; for lower classes, 78–79; magic shows, 235; plays, 63–74; variety shows, 76, 78, 195. *See also* Music halls
Theosophical Society, 173
Thompson, J. W., 24
Tiffany, Louis Comfort, 28, 29, 38
Tite Street, 11, 13–17, 34, 97, 256
Trafalgar Square, 25, 99, 100
Transportation, 99–108, 110. *See also* Underground
Turner, J. M. W., 33, 139
Tuxen, L., 3

U

Underground, 5, 101, 102, 138, 139
Upper classes, 1, 115, 116, 230. *See also* London Season; Servants

V

Van Gogh, Vincent, 28
Victoria, Queen, 1, 2, 3, 63, 64, 83, 243–44; entertainment for, 69, 178, 180, 235; jubilees, ix, 25, 26, 86
Victorian Age, 1, 2, 25, 65; changes, 88; morality, 32, 65; and royal family, 2, 3; social problems, 144–45

W

Wagner, Richard, 90, 184, 185; Ring cycle, 185–86
Walters, Catherine (Skittles), 238, 249
Waterhouse, J. W., 46
Waugh, Thomas, 204
Webb, Beatrice Potter, x, 90, 92, 151–53, 252, 271n13
Webb, Philip, xi
Webb, Sidney, x, 90, 92
Weightman, Gavin, 116, 119, 128, 131
Wells, H. G., 93, 104
West End, x, 65, 91, 99, 116, 120, 122–25, 126
Whibley, Charles, 94
Whistler, James McNeill, 13, 14, 50, 94, 139; libel suit, 32–34, 49, 50, 237; and Wilde, 34; "Nocturne in Black and Gold," 32, 34, 49
Wilde, Constance Mary Lloyd, 13, 14, 167
Wilde, Oscar, 231, 239; arrest and trials, 74, 96, 143–44, 162, 196, 212, 237, 256; arrival and early days in London, ix, 1, 7, 32; and beauty, xi, xii, 1, 6; death, 27, 96; as dramatist, 58, 72–74; imprisonment, ix, 261; literary encounters, 94–95; portraits, 27, 50, 76, 255; satires and caricatures, 12, 16, 18, 52, 178, 180, 202; trip to America, 12–13, 18, 38, 256; visitors to, 17. *See also* Residences; Wilde's views
Works: *The Duchess of Padua*, 58; *An Ideal Husband*, 72–73; *The Importance of Being Earnest*, 21, 72–73, 168–69; "Lord Arthur Savile's Crime," 28, 97; *The Picture of Dorian Gray*, 37, 83, 94, 261; *Salome*, 37, 52, 53, 73, 74, 83; "The Soul of Man Under Socialism," 21, 86, 166; *The Sphinx*, 37; *Vera, or the Nihilists*, 58

Wilde's views: on Art, 12, 37, 221–22; on Art and Nature, 7–8, 41; on books, 261; on Ellen Terry, 61–62; on interior decoration, 17; on Irving, 61; on life, 21–22; on London, 8; the novel, 80; on the poor, 166; on preaching, 169; on sin, 86; on Whistler, 34; on work, 21
Wingfield, Clopton, 208, 209
Wood, Sir Henry, 183

Working class. *See* Children; Lower classes; Servants
Working conditions, 98, 118, 120, 121, 128, 131, 159, 162–64, 166
Wright, Frank Lloyd, 28

Y

Yeats, W. B., 95, 96
Yellow Book, The, 51, 82, 83
Yerkes, Charles Tyson, 138–39